Canada's Social Economy

Canada's Social Economy

Co-operatives, Non-profits, and
Other Community Enterprises

Jack Quarter

James Lorimer & Company, Publishers
Toronto, 1992

James Lorimer & Company Ltd. acknowledges with thanks the support of the Canada Council, the Ontario Arts Council and the Ontario Publishing Centre in the development of writing and publishing in Canada.

Cover photo: Gloria Aucoin, Gloria's One-Hour Photo

Canadian Cataloguing in Publication Data

Quarter, Jack, 1941-
    Canada's social economy

Includes index.

 ISBN 1-55028-387-1 (bound). ISBN 1-55028-386-3 (pbk.)

1. Corporations, Nonprofit — Canada. 2. Cooperative societies - Canada. I. Title.

HD62.6.Q37 1992   338.7'4   C92-093758-6 1992

James Lorimer & Company, Publishers
Egerton Ryerson Memorial Building
35 Britain Street
Toronto, Ontario
M5A 1R7

Printed and bound in Canada

To Willows

CONTENTS

Acknowledgements   viii
Introduction   ix

Part 1 - Conceptualizing the Social Economy
1   Defining the Social Economy   1

Part 2 - An Overview to the Social Economy
2   An Overview to Co-operatives   15
3   Non-profits in Public Service   41
4   Mutual Non-profits   63

Part 3 - Case Studies
5   Community Economic Development   89
6   Social Housing   112
7   Social Service   124
8   Social Capital   144

Part 4 - Overcoming the Obstacles
9   Building a Social Economy   167
     Notes   180
     Selected Bibliography   199
     Index   203

ACKNOWLEDGEMENTS

I am grateful to the people who helped me to bring this manuscript to completion. Diane Young, the senior editor at James Lorimer & Company, offered both encouragement and much constructive advice. Melinda Tate's copyediting was very helpful to me in establishing a consistent style and in presenting the ideas in a readable manner. Yvonne Girdwood was very patient in inputting the manuscript and in making the revisions.

I would like to express my appreciation to the people whose constructive comments on the first draft helped with the preparation of the final product: Jo-Ann Hannah, Brian Iler, John Jordan, David Livingstone, James Lorimer, Ian MacPherson, George Melnyk and Paul Wilkinson.

I was also helped greatly by people who provided feedback on particular sections: Gilles Emond, Martha Friendly, Judy Goldie, Maggie Keith, Sherman Kreiner, Greg MacLeod, Judith Martin, Skip McCarthy, Mary Lou Morgan, Bill Morris, Jean-Guy Poirier and Dale Reagan.

In preparing this manuscript, I spoke to dedicated people in organizations across Canada who work tirelessly at providing a service to the public and their members. I thank them for helping me to learn about their organizations, and I hope that this book creates some awareness of the unique contribution that they and their organizations are making to this wonderful country. Canada's social economy deserves a higher profile.

Jack Quarter
September, 1992

1

INTRODUCTION

Canada's economy is often described as a mix of private owner-ship with some government ownership for selected services and industries. Yet this simplified description obscures the fact that there is a surprisingly large portion of the economy which is neither in the private sector nor government-owned. Some ex-amples illustrate the point: social service agencies (such as Children's Aid, homes for the aged, Meals on Wheels, rape crisis centres, the John Howard Society); health services (hospitals, Canadian Cancer Society, Canadian Heart Foundation, Cana-dian Red Cross, St. John Ambulance, Victorian Order of Nurses); educational organizations (universities, Boy Scouts, Girl Guides); ethno-cultural organizations; religious organizations and related institutions such as convents, monasteries, and youth groups; the arts (theatre groups, opera, ballet, dance); sports and recreation (organized hockey, baseball); unions, professional and business associations; political parties; feminist and environmen-tal organizations; social housing; non-profit daycare; the many forms of co-operatives and credit unions; mutual insurers; social clubs; veterans' groups (the Royal Canadian Legion) ... we could go on and on.

Many institutions in society — not just peripheral but central to its well-being — are neither private-sector businesses run for a profit nor state corporations owned by federal, provincial or municipal governments. Rather, they are independent organiza-tions created to provide a service either to the public or to a defined membership. The assets of these institutions — in some cases quite large — exist for the sole purpose of providing the service of the organization.

The tradition in Canada has been to refer to such organizations as the "third sector" of the economy — a label signifying relative unimportance. In Western Europe, a more descriptive term — *économie sociale* or "social economy" — has been coined, and it shall be used throughout this book.

In contrast to "third sector," the label "social economy" can be criticized for being too grandiose and partially misleading. The social economy implies an integrated system of institutions working toward common social goals, rather than the current reality of relatively independent institutions, some financed through tax revenues and charitable donations, assisted by volunteers, and functioning within the shadow of an economy dominated by the private sector. Yet the term "social economy" is not simply descriptive but also prescriptive. It implies a vision of social transformation, a vision which will be articulated in this book.

Although there are many thousands of organizations in Canada's social economy, there is no systematic set of data describing its extensiveness. Statistics Canada, which keeps records of virtually every facet of Canadian society, lacks a profile of the social economy. There are statistics on various types of enterprises within the social economy, which will be cited in this book. For example, according to statistics released by the federal Co-operatives Secretariat, by the end of the 1980s, there were 6,916 co-operative corporations in Canada, with 12 million Canadians belonging to at least one such organization and with a total membership exceeding 21 million. Co-operatives are typically small, but some, particularly in the agribusiness, are among the largest corporations in the country. Overall, the revenues of non-financial co-operatives in Canada in 1989 were $15.3 billion; financial co-operatives (credit unions and caisses populaires) had savings at $59.4 billion. The cumulative assets of all co-operatives in 1989, including insurance companies, totalled $105.9 billion; total employment was 70,000.

A neat statistical profile is not available for non-profits, which are another component of the social economy, but a related study of the financing of Canada's "humanistic" organizations, *An Essential Grace*, by Samuel Martin, a professor at the University of Western Ontario, sheds some light on their extensiveness. By "humanistic organizations," Martin refers to those delivering healthcare, education, welfare, religious and cultural services — categories overlapping in part with the social economy. At the time of publication in 1985, Martin estimated that "Canada has close to 50,000 humanistic organizations; they handle nearly one-third of the country's national income," and their employment exceeds that of all levels of government.

The concept of non-profit used in this book goes beyond "humanistic services," as defined by Martin, and includes a broad array of mutual-interest associations (unions, professional and business associations, social organizations), both incorporated and unincorporated; that is, all the types of organizations which are neither in the private nor government sectors of the economy. Although it is not possible to give a precise figure of the number of non-profits in Canada, the most recent reports from government sources (see Chapter 3) indicate there are at least 175,000 such organizations, including 66,000 with charitable status.

Inevitably, if organizations are part of the economy, financial statistics are indicators of their importance. However, as the term "social economy" implies, the social value of an organization stands alongside and indeed precedes its economic import. Organizations of the social economy touch some of the most important aspects of our lives — higher education, recreation, religion, healthcare, culture.

This book, more than anything else, is a record of innovative experiments in Canada's social economy, and an analysis of how these innovations can be extended so that the social economy can play an even greater role in our society. The areas of the social economy that are highlighted are ones in which there has been innovation and ones that are central to society. Most of the experiments are Canadian, but given the obvious social interpenetration in the modern world, selected international examples are cited that have had an impact upon our country. Bearing in mind space constraints, the emphasis upon positive examples has resulted in some sacrifice of critical analysis. Nevertheless, the emergence of a social economy in particular areas of society is set within a context of conditions that have led to its development.

This book is divided into four parts: the first defines the social economy and presents some common dimensions shared by the variety of organizations associated with it; the second presents an overview of the key areas of the social economy, co-operatives and non-profits; the third part consists of case studies of recent innovations in the social economy — in regional development, housing, healthcare, childcare and finance; and the fourth part discusses the potential for further development of the social economy through overcoming some of the obstacles it faces.

The primary reason for writing this book is to create greater awareness of the social economy and the potential that it contains for Canada's future. The social economy in part represents a response to the modernization of capitalism that has led to economic decisions being made without concern for their impact upon a particular community. The social economy is based upon organizations meeting the needs of people within their communities. It is also based on the attempt by people to overcome the weakening of geographic communities by creating new communities of common interest. Many of the organizations within the social economy give voice and vote to their members, thereby extending democracy from the political to the broader social realm. Therefore, there are some important features of the social economy that compensate for limitations within the other sectors of the economy, features that could have an important impact upon our society.

1
Conceptualizing the Social Economy

1

Defining the Social Economy

In Canada, the term *social economy* is seldom used, and when it is applied, it lacks clear definition. Typically, the social or third sector is a catch-all for the area between the private and state sectors, rather than a qualitatively distinct approach to economic organization. But in Western Europe, and particularly in France, where the social economy has achieved a higher profile, it includes four categories of organizations:[1] co-operatives, mutual insurers, non-profit corporations, and unincorporated associations (both formally constituted and informal).[2]

All of these types of organizations exist in Canada. This book, however, will concentrate on co-operatives, including mutual insurers; non-profits in public service; and mutual non-profits serving a membership. Both types of non-profits include corporations, unincorporated but formal associations, and, to a lesser extent, informal associations, and both include organizations with charitable status.

Given the range of organizations that fall within these three broad categories, it is a formidable task to define the common dimensions which form the basis of a social economy and which differentiate it from the private and government sectors. These dimensions represent an ideal to which not all organizations in the social economy will conform completely. Nevertheless, by analysing common dimensions, the basis for a dialogue may be created through which organizations with differing functions and differing types of members might find common cause.

SOCIAL OBJECTIVES

What makes the social economy different from the private and government sectors? In the private sector, control is associated with property rights, usually in the form of shares. As American economist David Ellerman argues, a private-sector company is a form of property representing an investment by its owners.[3] The owners are entitled to the net income (profit or loss) and the market value of the company. In businesses with shares, they are also entitled to vote their shares to elect a board of directors or governance that is legally responsible for the company.

In the state or second sector, control is exerted by a level of government, either directly (as through the civil service) or through arm's length corporations. Crown corporations are established by government to provide a service to the public because the service is essential, because government wants some influence over policy, or because it is difficult for the private sector to earn a profit by providing the service. In Crown corporations, a level of government holds the shares and has the same rights as shareholders in a private-sector enterprise.

But a Crown corporation differs from a private-sector company in some important ways. Its primary purpose is to serve the public, not to meet the shareholders' needs for a return on investment, and the beneficiary of any profit or any increase in the value of the assets is the government representing the public-at-large, rather than a small group of shareholders. The public-at-large may not see itself as the beneficiary, however, because it has no direct involvement in the enterprise. The governance of a Crown corporation is appointed by the government and is beholden to the government.

Organizations in the social economy overlap with Crown corporations in that they also have objectives which are not strictly commercial. For organizations in the social economy, the primary purpose is to serve either a defined membership or the public in a manner which will permit the organization to develop. Development may involve accumulating capital, as is done by private-sector corporations, but such capital is used by the organization to provide its service, rather than for the benefit of private owners.

Organizations in the social economy vary from those that are very dependent upon external funding from government and private donors (such as universities, social service agencies), through those that are partly self-financed and partly financed externally (theatres, for example) to those relying almost exclusively on their own revenues, either from services to members (many forms of co-operatives) or from commerce in the market much like private-sector enterprises. Where they are financially self-reliant, these organizations can be described as "enterprises," in that they are at risk in a competitive market. In contrast to private enterprise, which risks capital in order to bring an appropriate financial return to investors, social enterprise's primary purpose is to meet the social objectives of the organization. Capital is put at risk in the service of the organization's social objectives. Instead of private entrepreneurship, these organizations engage in social entrepreneurship.

Arguably, this difference between private and social enterprise is more extreme in theory than in practice, for in order to turn a profit, private enterprise must also satisfy its customers' needs. However, capital invested in the private sector, and particularly in mature companies, has very weak social commitments. It remains loyal as long as it yields a satisfactory rate of return. When a greater return is possible from other investments, the owners will shift their loyalties. By comparison, social enterprises not only set the service first, but the organization also tends to have loyalties to either a defined community or a defined membership. In that respect, social enterprises may also be characterized as community enterprises, defined around such features as a geographic location, a common ethno-cultural or religious bond, or a particular workplace, features that stand in contrast to the rootless, impersonal structures of mature private-sector corporations.

In social enterprises, capital and other assets are for the purpose of supporting services, not primarily to satisfy investors. While this subservience of capital to the social objectives of the organization occurs throughout the social economy, not only in enterprises that are self-financed, in cases where an organization is self-financed and operates in a competitive market, the term "social enterprise" is very appropriate.

INDEPENDENCE FROM GOVERNMENT

In Western Europe, "independence from the state" is one of the defining criteria for inclusion in the social economy. That criterion is adopted to differentiate the social economy from the government sector — a sector which has also been referred to as "socially owned."[4] This need to accentuate the difference between the social economy and the government sector originates in an attempt to reverse a type of thinking prevalent in socialist movements in the period following the Russian Revolution. At that time, it was argued that government ownership ought to be the primary strategy for "socializing" the means of production.

In Canada, that point of view was emphasized when the CCF (the forerunner to the NDP) produced its seminal policy document, the Regina Manifesto, in the summer of 1933. The Manifesto stressed "a planned socialized economy" in which natural resources, chartered banks, transportation, communications, electrical power and all other industries essential to social planning would be government-owned.[5] Producer and consumer co-operatives were advocated to assist farmers, and consumer co-operatives were encouraged "in the retail distribution of staple commodities such as milk." But in the words of Ian MacPherson, the leading historian of Canada's co-operative movement, "the Manifesto did not dwell at great length on co-operatives. The sections devoted to them were brief and truncated."[6] Other organizations in the social economy received no mention at all. One of the delegates to the Regina convention, W.C. Good (also the president of the Co-operative Union of Canada), drew up an alternative manifesto advocating co-operativism.[7] It was largely ignored, and Good was believed to be one of the few delegates to vote against the Regina Manifesto.

Therefore, by the 1930s, there was already a split between democratic socialism and co-operativism. Democratic socialism defined social ownership largely as government ownership, while co-operativism defined it as voluntary and decentralized organizations based on the democratic principle of one-person/one-vote. Other organizations within the social economy also followed their own course of development, and by no means a unified one. That aside, it is noteworthy that the extensive development of Canada's social economy has proceeded independently from the political parties which were advocating "social ownership."

The CCF, and then the NDP, has retreated from its emphasis on government ownership because these policies proved unpopular and of questionable effectiveness. The retreat started after the Saskatchewan provincial election of 1934, in which the CCF did poorly because of its policy that farmers be given the option of shifting from private ownership to a "usehold" system, through which they would lease their land from the provincial government.[8] The retreat continued after the Saskatchewan CCF's first term of office (1944–48), which may be described as the only effort by a Canadian government to institute widespread government ownership.[9] From that point forward the CCF, and then the NDP, curtailed its emphasis upon government ownership and turned to the private sector as the vehicle for industrial development, and to provide tax revenues to finance social programs, which became the party's priority.

This change of policy was reflected in the Winnipeg Declaration of 1956, in policies adopted at the time of the formation of the NDP in 1961, and in the defeat of the Waffle Manifesto of 1969, which had advocated government ownership as a means of overcoming American domination of Canada's economy.[10] Moreover, where social ownership is mentioned in NDP policy documents, as in the major policy statement of 1983, it is still lumped together with government ownership:

> ...social ownership is an essential means for achieving our goals. This means not simply the transfer of title of large enterprises to the state. We believe in decentralized ownership and control, including co-operatives and credit unions, greater public accountability, and progressive democratization of the workplace.[11]

Therefore, the more restrictive definition of the social economy, emphasizing independence from government, may be seen as an attempt to overcome this tendency to lump government ownership and social ownership together.

Independence from government may be questioned considering the financial reliance that many social organizations have upon government. But even where this financial dependence exists, social organizations still have an autonomous board of directors which is responsible for the interests of the organization in much the same way as any other board.

Moreover, in modern societies government financing, tax expenditures and contracts affect the revenues of many companies, even in the private sector. It is naïve to view a modern economy as functioning independent of government when governmental policies have such an impact upon business. The Free Trade Agreement negotiated between Canada and the United States is a classic example of the interconnection between government policies and business. Therefore, including in the social economy organizations dependent upon government financing seems appropriate for both the Canadian experience and for modern economies in general.

VOLUNTEERISM

The emphasis upon social objectives within the social economy raises the question of whether informal, totally voluntary arrangements should be included. The formal economy is a cash economy based upon paid labour. However, within the social economy, most organizations, including those with paid staff, use volunteer or non-paid labour to some degree (typically for their boards of directors), and some rely upon it completely. For that reason, social organizations are often referred to as voluntary.

A recent Statistics Canada survey indicates that 27 per cent of Canadians (a 78 per cent increase between 1980 and 1987, when the survey was taken) are volunteers in formal organizations — mostly religious, recreational, educational, health and social service.[12] Ottawa consultant David Ross estimates that this volunteer labour represents the equivalent of 615,000 full-time jobs.[13]

Organizations in the social economy can be placed on a continuum from those operating within the cash economy with little or no volunteer contribution (business associations), through organizations using a mix of paid staff and volunteers, to associations relying exclusively upon volunteers (for example, ratepayers' groups). In addition, there are social arrangements not involving formal organizations (either incorporated or duly constituted) to which volunteers make a valuable contribution. Such arrangements are referred to as the "informal economy."[14]

In regions of Canada where the formal economy depends upon seasonal industries and people live off unemployment insurance for much of the year, the informal economy is a vital part of society. But difficulties arise when volunteer activity in the informal economy is included as part of the social economy, not so much in the question of its value, but because some of this work is self-maintenance activity related to the household economy, and, more important, because the arrangements are informal, and are therefore difficult to ascertain. Nevertheless, these informal volunteer arrangements can be seen as one aspect of volunteerism, which in turn is an important feature of the social economy.

Another aspect of volunteerism (to be discussed in detail in Chapter 3) is the charitable financial donations that support many types of organizations in the social economy. Although financial donations are usually characterized as distinct from volunteer service, this separation seems arbitrary since both are donations and both are given of free choice. Voluntary service touches a broader number of organizations within the social economy than financial donations. Whereas volunteer service pervades the social economy, financial donations are directed primarily toward non-profits with charitable status (about one-third of non-profits). Volunteer service may be seen as a purer form of donation since, unlike a financial contribution for which the provider derives a tax credit, volunteers derive only the satisfaction of their contribution. The similarities between voluntary service and financial donations, however, seem greater than the differences.[15]

The relationship of the donor to the organization within the social economy may be contrasted to that of the citizen and government agencies. While the former is based upon free choice (bearing in mind the social pressures affecting choice), the latter is based upon legally enshrined obligations such as tax payments. As such, volunteers, whether they are donating service or money, will often identify more strongly and feel more positively toward their organizations of choice than the public feels toward government. Ironically, government grants derived from tax payments are an important source of support for organizations within the social economy.

PROFIT AND LOSS

In the private sector and in Crown corporations, the shareholders are the recipients of the net income, usually receiving dividends when there is a profit and suffering a reduction of share values when the company loses money. By comparison, social organizations normally have no shares, as in non-profits, or they have shares with a relatively constant value, as in co-operatives. These shares are comparable to a membership fee, though they also represent an important type of financing for the enterprise.

Within the social economy a profit is referred to as a surplus and a loss as a deficit. When a social organization has a surplus, that income generally is applied to the service (its primary objective), often improving and broadening its availability. Within user-based co-operatives, surplus earnings often result in a patronage dividend, not based on shareholdings as in the private sector, but on use of the service. More use results in a higher dividend. When organizations in the social economy lose money, unless the loss can be absorbed through reserves the service is usually reduced or its cost to patrons is increased. A dividend for patronage would not be paid out, and if losses become too great, the company may have to close.

OWNERSHIP RIGHTS

Private-sector enterprises and Crown corporations are a type of property belonging to their owners. In the event of a sale, the owners receive the net proceeds. It is also possible for non-profit corporations without charitable status to divide their net proceeds among members, but this is not common for organizations in the social economy. When registered charities dissolve themselves, for example, they often donate any proceeds to other charities with a similar purpose. The same is true of many non-profits without charitable status (unions, for example). Co-operatives, except those that are non-profits, do have shares, but these are tantamount to a loan, repaid with interest when a member leaves, rather than a claim on the net worth of the company.

In each of these examples, the net assets are owned by no one. They belong to the organization as a whole for as long as it operates, and subsequently become a social dividend passed from generation to generation. These social dividends become the building blocks of a social economy — blocks which are the property of neither the individual nor government. Arguably, the view that no one owns the organizations of the social economy is based on a narrow definition of ownership — one which equates ownership with property rights. As Robert Dahl suggests, ownership can be conceived as a bundle of rights, an important one being corporate control.[16] In the social economy, members do have the right to control the organizations to which they belong. But unlike owners in the other sectors, they do not benefit financially from the sale of their assets. Members of social organizations, through their representatives on the board of directors, are analogous to trustees, with the responsibility to see that the assets are being utilized in a manner consistent with the organization's objectives.

THE GOVERNANCE

Since organizations in the social economy are not owned in the traditional sense, democratic control by members is a fundamental characteristic. An organization within the social economy can be described as a social democracy, not in the sectarian political sense, but quite literally democracy within a social institution. The vision associated with the social economy is to extend democratic control beyond the political domain to society at large.

Voting rights in the social economy are accorded to members of an organization on the basis of one-member/one-vote, rather than on property holdings as in other sectors of the economy. There are private-sector enterprises, for example an equal partnership, that also have equal voting rights among owners. However, these rights are still based upon property (rather than on membership as in the social economy), and as such are altered as property is bought and sold. Therefore, an equal partnership, or to use another example, an equal shareholding arrangement in a limited company, are anomalous arrangements within the private sector.

Similarly, some organizations within the government sector of the economy, such as boards of education, are based upon direct democratic control. Citizens living within a jurisdiction, each having one vote, elect trustees who have legal responsibility for the board. A board of education, albeit a government-created organization with the power to tax, is much the same as organizations in the social economy. It provides a service to a public that has the opportunity to democratically elect its governance.

But most government organizations and corporations lack the direct democratic control of boards of education. The exceptions in the private and government sectors of the economy are the rule in the social economy. Members, each with one vote, elect a board which in turn appoints management. This circumstance bears direct parallels to a political democracy, in which citizens, each bearing one vote, elect a government that in turn appoints deputy ministers to act as senior management.[17] The parliament or legislature in an organization in the social economy is the board of directors or board of governors, and the deputy ministers are senior managers appointed by the board. As in a political democracy, there is a tension between these two levels of governance, with senior management often assuming greater control because of its technical competence.

This same tension exists in the private sector as well. As a company matures and separation between ownership and labour increases, the owners are less likely to be involved in management. In large publicly traded corporations with widely held shareholdings, senior management can operate with great autonomy from the board, often dominating it. This dominance remains intact as long as management is able to meet the shareholders' needs for a satisfactory return on their investment. However, a company's board of directors, like a political government, still retains official authority, including the authority to hire and fire, and the authority to create policy guidelines within which management must function. The board approves major initiatives undertaken by management, and it may also reject them. Moreover, the board, like the members of a political government, must be responsive to the people who elect it. In the social economy those people are members with one vote, although within that general rule, there is a lot of variety. Many organizations define users of the organization's service as their members. That practice is followed in many forms of co-operatives and in some mutual non-profits. Others base membership upon volunteers.

A criterion emphasized among co-operatives is that of open and voluntary membership. That principle was initiated by the Rochdale Pioneers in Rochdale, England, in 1844, and has been maintained to this date. Open membership has always been tempered by pragmatic concerns about suitability and availability of space. For example, to join a dairy marketing co-operative, someone would have to be in that business, or similarly, a housing co-operative will restrict members if it has no vacant units. In practice, the bond of association that defines the common features of membership is open within limits. The same is true of mutual non-profits, be they business or labour associations or ethno-cultural or religious groups. However, there are also non-profits with a closed membership defined around its board. These can be family foundations, universities, hospitals and social service agencies. The board becomes a self-perpetuating group, beholden to government regulation and large external funding sources, that nominates new members as vacancies arise. There are also non-profit boards utilizing proxy voting when their members are widely dispersed and uninvolved in the organization.

Both of these examples reflect a lack of well-defined guidelines for membership in organizations in the social economy. Unlike a political democracy based upon one type of member — its citizens — a social democracy may have different constituent groups relating to the organization. In the chapters that follow, one of the major issues to be addressed is the problem of determining who the legitimate stakeholders are and how their rights are to be balanced.

CONCLUSIONS

Canada's social economy consists of co-operatives, including mutual insurers, non-profits in public service and mutual non-profits serving a membership. It is conceptualized around some basic criteria that form the boundaries for inclusion. First, it is based on a primacy of social objectives over strictly commercial ones. Within the social economy organizations are set up for a social purpose, and although they must generate enough revenues to meet their expenditures, commercial goals exist within the context of social objectives.

Second, within the social economy there is a range of organizations, from enterprises that are self-reliant and generate their revenues from commerce and membership fees, through to those that depend upon financing from external sources, usually government and private donors.

Third, organizations within the social economy depend upon donations of service and money. With the exception of some mutual associations financed by their members and enterprises earning their revenues from commerce, volunteerism is a salient characteristic.

Fourth, within the social economy, surplus earnings are used to strengthen the organization and to improve its services. Dividends, if paid, are based upon patronage, rather than on shareholdings as in other sectors of the economy.

Fifth, the net assets of organizations within the social economy are analogous to a social dividend passed from generation to generation. With the exception of some non-profits, business assets are not owned by anyone.

Sixth, democratic control based upon one-member/one-vote is a fundamental feature of the social economy. The social economy extends democracy from the political domain to the economy.

2
An Overview to the Social Economy

2

An Overview to Co-operatives

By the end of the 1980s there were 6,916 co-operative corporations in Canada with a total membership exceeding 21 million
people.[1] Twelve million Canadians belonged to at least one co-
operative corporation, and the assets of the movement were
$105.9 billion.

The stereotype of a co-operative is a small, informal, personal
association. In Britain, co-operatives were referred to as "friendly
societies." Against the backdrop of their image, the reference to
co-operatives as corporations seems odd. Yet, from a business
point of view, co-operatives are corporations which, like private-
sector corporations, rely largely upon their own revenues for
their operation. Many co-operatives are small and personal, but
some are among the largest corporations in Canada. Eighteen of
Canada's agri-food co-operatives were in the *Financial Post 500*
for 1988, and four of these (Saskatchewan Wheat Pool, Federated
Co-operatives, Coopérative fédérée de Québec, and Alberta
Wheat Pool) are among the one hundred largest corporations in
Canada.

Although co-operatives come in many sizes and are involved
in many aspects of our society, all are voluntary associations of
people providing a service to themselves. The people using the
co-operative are also members, each with a voice but only one
vote at general meetings and in electing a board of directors that
has legal responsibility for the corporation. In that respect, a
co-operative is referred to as "member-owned and -operated."

Yet like most slogans, this one is oversimplified. Co-operatives are owned in common by their members, but aside from membership share(s), which are purchased upon joining and are analogous to a membership fee, a member does not normally have a personal claim on the assets of the co-operative. In fact, the co-operative movement was founded largely as a reaction to the domination of capital. The purpose of financing is to permit a co-operative to provide its services, not for the members to make money from the increased value of their investment. Unlike a private-sector firm that accords dividends to shares, surplus earnings (profits) either are retained in the co-operative in order to strengthen the organization financially and to improve its services, or are returned to members as dividends, usually according to patronage or use of the services.

Similarly, the view that co-operatives are operated by their members can be misleading if the term suggests that members make the day-to-day decisions. Co-operatives generally hire management, though the members may provide important volunteer services on the board of directors and committees. It is to the board of directors representing the membership that management is beholden. The board hires management and establishes broad policy guidelines for it. In that respect, co-operatives are member-operated.

The limitation of voting rights to members, a fundamental aspect of democracy in co-operatives, can also make these organizations unattractive to outside investors because, unlike capitalist corporations, they cannot purchase voting shares or be represented on the board of directors. That factor, coupled with limited rates of return paid to member-investors, has led to an intense debate within the movement, both in Canada and internationally, about improving methods for raising capital so that co-operatives can compete effectively with large international firms unencumbered by such restrictions. It is expected that, at minimum, limitations on the rate of return paid to member-investors will be lifted.

Another noteworthy feature of co-operatives is that they are not simply individual organizations meeting the needs of their memberships; they also belong to a movement, both national and international in scope. One of the six basic principles of the International Co-operative Alliance, adopted in 1966, is co-operation between co-operatives.[2] To the extent that it is practical, co-operatives co-operate with each other and have some obligations to help other types of co-operatives get started and to develop.

The principle of co-operation between co-operatives dates back to England's Rochdale Pioneers, the founders of the first modern co-operative in 1844, and the grand vision of a co-operative commonwealth, very influential through to the early twentieth century.[3] But over time, the movement has weakened, and co-operatives now emphasize their practical objective of service to their members. Co-operation between co-operatives tends to occur primarily for practical reasons, as when co-operatives with similar types of functions form a second-tier organization (retail food co-operatives creating a common wholesaler, for example). Outreach for ideological purposes (selling the idea of co-operatives to the public) is still practised, but more quietly and without the ideological fervour that marked the pioneer era.

MODELS OF ORGANIZATION

Although co-operatives are organized around some common principles, they vary in their structure according to the membership group and its objectives. It is to these basic groupings, that this chapter now turns.

Marketing Co-operatives

The roots of Canada's co-operatives are in the rural traditions of mutual aid. The movement was established during the latter half of the nineteenth and early twentieth centuries when farmers began forming co-operatives that would permit them to control the marketing of their products and the basic purchases that they required.[4] The objective was for the farmers, who became members of the co-operative, to obtain a fair price for their products. Surplus earnings that were not invested in the co-operative were rebated to the farmers.

These early experiments in farm-marketing co-operatives were influenced by the efforts of an American organization, the Grange (Patrons of Husbandry), and started in Canada during the 1870s. Subsequently in the 1890s, a second American farm organization, the Patrons of Industry, started assisting Canadian farmers, particularly in the Brantford area. By the turn of the century there were about 1,200 co-operative creameries, most in Ontario and Quebec, and a well-established tradition for mutual insurance among farmers. These early experiments laid the ground for the Prairie grain-marketing co-operatives that formed in the early twentieth century and the large number of powerful agri-food co-operatives that formed subsequently. The first of these was the Grain Growers Grain Company, started by Manitoba farmers in 1907, and followed a few years later by the Saskatchewan Co-operative Elevator Company and the Alberta Co-operative Elevator Company. Today farm-marketing co-operatives have become powerful corporations that account for about 40 per cent of total farm cash receipts in Canada. Seven of the ten largest agri-food corporations in Canada are co-operatives.

Broken down by market sector, farm-marketing co-operatives have a 68 per cent market share for grain and oilseeds, 56 per cent for dairy products, 28 per cent for poultry and eggs, 26 per cent for honey and maple products, 18 per cent for livestock and 15 per cent for fruits and vegetables. In total, Canada's farm marketing co-operatives have 188,914 members, more than 23,000 employees, and transacted $8.7 billion of business in 1989.

The largest of these corporations are the Prairie wheat pools, and Coopérative fédérée and Agropur in Quebec. However, farm-marketing co-operatives have established a strong presence in all parts of the country and for virtually every type of product. On the West Coast, there are Fraser Valley Milk Producers and B.C. Fruit Packers; in the Atlantic are such co-ops as Scotsburn and West Kings Livestock; and even in Ontario, where the market penetration has been the weakest, there are Gay Lea and Norfolk Fruit Growers.

Subsequent to the creation of farm-marketing co-operatives, farmers formed other types of co-operatives which they joined as primary producers. Among these are seed cleaning co-operatives, to which more than 40,000 farmers in Alberta and Saskatchewan belong. There are also farmer co-operatives engaging in artificial breeding, grazing, forage production, feeder cattle and livestock feedlots. In 1989 there were 262 such co-operatives across Canada with more than 10,000 members.

Farmers' markets also are becoming popular, particularly in Saskatchewan, Manitoba and Prince Edward Island. In 1989, there were 39 such markets incorporated as co-operatives, with 2,900 vendors as members.

From the viewpoint of corporate sales, co-operatives based upon independent farmers are the most successful form of producer co-operative in Canada. Fishing co-operatives have not achieved the same success. There were 61 of these in 1989, situated in the Atlantic provinces and the West Coast, engaged in processing and marketing. Their sales were $184.9 million. The only major corporation is Prince Rupert Fishermen's Co-op, though some smaller ones, such as the Fogo Island Co-operative in Newfoundland, have helped to save their communities from extinction.

A variation of the marketing co-operative for primary producers is the artisan co-operative, like those set up by the Inuit in the Northwest Territories and the Cree and Inuit of northern Quebec. Frustrated by the low prices being paid through retail chains, native artisans established their own marketing outlets, organized co-operatively. There are now 34 artisans' co-operatives in the Northwest Territories affiliated with Arctic Co-operatives in Winnipeg, and 11 such co-operatives in northern Quebec, affiliated with the Fédération des coopératives du Nouveau-Québec in Ville St. Laurent.

Artisans, unlike farmers and fishers, are craftspersons rather than primary producers. But like primary producers, they may belong to a co-operative which markets their products. The common feature of this first model, then, is that the members are independently employed, most often self-employed, and establish a co-operative to provide themselves with a common service, usually marketing. Although the roots of the model are in primary production, there are also examples in transportation (such as taxi co-operatives with a common radio and dispatch service), and consultants who market a service in common.

Consumer or User Co-operatives

Although farm marketing co-operatives have achieved the greatest business success among Canadian co-operatives, the Canadian movement is based primarily upon consumers or users of a service. There are many types of user-based co-operatives providing a wide range of products and services, from farm supplies, food retailing and wholesaling, to daycare, healthcare, housing, financial services and even burial services. Although each of these services differs, the common denominator is that the people who use the co-operative for its services are also its members.

The roots of the user co-operative in Canada go back to the nineteenth century, to mutual insurance organizations formed by farmers, and co-operative stores in mining communities across the country (the first believed to be in Stellarton, Nova Scotia, in 1861).[5] Some of these early experiments in co-operative stores were supported by trade unions.[6] Although these early experiments formed the basis for the user co-operative in Canada, the real impetus to that movement came from two sources: first, from the British movement, which championed the user co-operative, through the many early immigrants and co-operative leaders who were from Britain; second, from farmers, as the producer co-operatives they formed for marketing also established stores where farmers as consumers purchased their supplies. The first of these farm-supply organizations developed in Ontario and the Prairies between 1906 and 1914, started either as buying clubs or as independent co-operatives. Since then they have burgeoned into major corporations supplying a full range of farm products, from animal feed, seeds and fertilizers through to petroleum, building materials and machinery. By 1989, 207 farm-supply co-operatives in Canada transacted $2.1 billion of business with their 305,000 members. Among the largest of these corporations were the United Co-operatives of Ontario, United Farmers of Alberta and Coopérative fédérée de Québec. Of the 10 largest farm-supply co-operatives, 5 are in Quebec. In that province, co-operatives either dominate or have a strong presence in virtually every type of farm supply.

Although the initial strength of retail co-operative stores was related to the farm-marketing co-operatives, by the mid-1920s the retail movement had developed its own strength — a strength that has carried to the present. In Canada today, retail co-operatives are concentrated in the West and in the Atlantic region. The 360 retail co-operatives in the West belong to Federated Co-operatives, a powerful Saskatoon-based corporation with $2.2 billion of sales in 1989. Federated acts as a wholesaler and oversees the system. Although the retail co-operatives in the Federated system tend to be situated in small communities, the largest ones are in such urban centres as Calgary, Saskatoon and Regina. The Calgary Co-op is the largest retail co-operative in North America and has 40 per cent of the Calgary market.

The other concentration of retail co-operatives are the 176 outlets in communities throughout the Atlantic region affiliated with Co-op Atlantic in Moncton. Like Federated, Co-op Atlantic acts as a wholesaler and is also an organizer of the system. In 1989, it had sales of $480 million, making it the seventh largest Canadian-owned corporation in the Atlantic provinces.

There are many other types of co-operatives in which the users of the service are the members. Most of these are more recent, and thus are labelled "emerging" co-operatives. Since the mid-1970s, co-operatives have taken hold as a form of social housing (see Chapter 6).[7] As of 1990, there were about 1,400 such co-ops with more than 200,000 residents, and with a book value of more than $2.2 billion. In a housing co-operative, the residents (or users of the service) are also members, each having one vote in electing the board and in policy committees.

Housing co-operatives are concentrated in Ontario, Quebec and British Columbia, primarily in large urban centres where the private housing market has become too expensive for the average income earner. They are organized into regional federations and a national organization, the Co-operative Housing Federation of Canada, which has lobbied the federal government for support. Unlike most other co-operatives which are financially self-reliant, housing co-operatives require government assistance in the form of mortgage subsidies so that their housing charge can be affordable to the average resident. There are also special subsidies for low-income residents. Until 1992, co-operative housing was financed through both federal and provincial governments. In 1992, the federal government dropped its program. The dependence of co-operative housing upon government assistance differentiates it from the other forms of co-operatives discussed to this point.

Like housing co-operatives, healthcare and childcare co-operatives also rely upon government financial assistance. The healthcare co-operatives in Canada evolved from the doctors' strike in Saskatchewan when medicare was introduced in 1962. There are now nine such co-operatives (five in Saskatchewan), with a total membership of 227,823. As with other user-based co-operatives, members elect a board from among their group. In structure, healthcare co-operatives are very similar to other forms of community health clinics and are part of a common association, the Canadian Association of Community Health Clinics.

Childcare co-operatives come in two forms: nursery schools and preschool daycares. They are also non-profits and are governed by the parents using the service. Childcare co-operatives are growing rapidly in Canada. In 1989, there were estimated to be about 800. Childcare co-operatives belong to regional groupings affiliated with Parents Preschool Co-operative International, and they are also affiliated with more broadly based organizations lobbying government for more funding for non-profit childcare centres.

In addition to the aforementioned examples, there are other co-operatives organized around groups of users. The services they provide to members include: burial, transportation, recreation, communication, electrical services and waterworks. In total, there are 850 co-operatives providing such services to about 250,000 members, and with total revenues of nearly $240 million.

Second- and Third-Tier Models

In the traditional co-operative structure, members are individuals. This shall be referred to as a first-tier co-operative. In second-tier co-operatives, like Federated and Co-op Atlantic, the members are other co-operatives, each with one vote. Second-tier retail co-operatives across Canada (the wholesalers for regional systems) have also formed a third-tier co-operative, Interprovincial Co-operatives, which acts as a broker for the regional organizations with respect to national and international markets. Interprovincial owns co-op trademarks and also manufactures chemical products for agriculture. The members of Interprovincial are the second-tier wholesale co-operatives, again each with one vote only.

This second- and third-tier structure is common among Canada's user co-operatives, and it has been applied by other types of co-operatives as well. For example, the apex organizations for all of Canada's co-operatives — the anglophone Canadian Co-operative Association and the francophone Conseil canadien de la coopération — have members that are either first-tier co-operatives or second-tier federations of first-tier co-operatives.

The second- and third-tier structures represent a type of functional integration in which either first-tier co-operatives or federations of first-tier co-operatives with common needs co-operate with each other to establish an apex organization that will help them to provide their services in a more effective manner and which will assist with problems shared in common. Although these apex organizations are creations of the lower tiers, they are not subsidiaries. Rather, the lower tiers transfer some control to the apex organization so that they may be provided with services. The relationship between the apex organization and the first-tier co-operatives is complex and varies among types of co-operatives. In some cases, the apex organizations have much influence over the first-tier organizations; in other cases the influence is minimal.

Financial Co-operatives (Credit Unions and Caisses Populaires)
These are examples of co-operatives in which the users of the service are the members and in which the first-tier co-operatives have formed second-tier organizations, which in turn have formed third-tier organizations.

The financial co-operative movement in Canada emerged at the turn of the century because the urban working class and farmers could not get loans they required. The Canadian movement was founded by Alphonse Désjardins, a Quebecer who was influenced by similar experiments in Italy and Germany.[8] In 1900 Désjardins organized the first caisse populaire at Lévis, near Quebec City. By 1909, there were over 100 caisses populaires, most associated with Catholic parishes in rural Quebec. To this day, Quebec has the strongest financial co-operatives in Canada. Among the francophone communities across Canada, the caisse populaire movement has represented an opposition to anglo-controlled banks, and in Quebec it has taken a leading role in the nationalist struggle.

In Quebec the Désjardins caisse populaire system has more than 1600 outlets involving 4.4 million members. It has more outlets in Quebec than do the chartered banks. In 1989 the Quebec Désjardins group had $34.7 billion of assets and more than one-third of the province's total savings on deposit. It transacted about one-third of all consumer loans, about one-quarter of commercial and industrial loans and more than one-half of agricultural loans. There are also strong francophone federations of caisses populaires in the Acadian communities of New Brunswick, and among the francophone populace of northern and eastern Ontario and of Manitoba. As in Quebec, the local caisse populaire plays an important role in providing basic financial services, in some cases to small isolated communities which are not of interest to chartered banks, and also in sponsoring social events for the communities in which they serve.

With the exception of Saskatchewan, where 57 per cent of the total population belong to credit unions, financial co-operatives have not established such a dominant presence in other parts of Canada. Nevertheless, credit unions do play an important role in many communities. By 1989, there were 1,301 credit unions (a total of 2,181 outlets including branches) with nearly 4.3 million members and $29.8 billion of assets.

Credit unions are formed around a common bond of association for their members. Many of the earlier financial co-operatives, particularly in Quebec and in the Atlantic, where the Antigonish movement led by Father Moses Coady took hold in the 1930s, drew their members from Catholic parishes. However, union locals, and ethnic, professional and political associations have also had a history of organizing financial co-operatives. More recently, financial co-operatives have tended to operate with a community bond of association, thereby making membership accessible to everyone desiring to participate. VanCity, with a bond of association for the Vancouver area, is the largest individual financial co-operative in Canada, with assets of more than $2 billion.

As with retail co-operatives, financial co-operatives have formed second- and third-tier organizations. With the exception of Newfoundland and Quebec, credit unions are organized into province-wide credit union centrals that accept deposits of surplus funds and, when required, issue loans to local credit unions to meet their financial obligations. Each local credit union is a member of the central.

In addition, the eight credit union centrals belong to a national organization, the Credit Union Central of Canada (formerly the Canadian Co-operative Credit Society), which co-ordinates investments and speaks on behalf of the Anglophone system at the national level. Among the financial co-operatives of Quebec, there is a similar arrangement, with regional federations forming the second tier (along with four separate federations for the caisses populaires in New Brunswick, northern and eastern Ontario, and Manitoba), the Confédération des caisses populaires et d'économie Désjardins du Québec, forming the third tier.

Mutual Insurance

Another type of user-based service using the tiering structure is insurance. As early as the 1830s, farmers, as part of a rural tradition of mutual aid, began organizing mutual insurance to protect themselves against fires and accidents. Technically speaking, mutual insurers are not part of the co-operative system since they are incorporated under a special section of the Insurance Act.[9] Yet in a mutual, as in a user-based co-operative, the policyholder is a member with only one vote, regardless of the size and number of policies she or he has purchased.

Mutuals can be clustered into two categories: life insurance and other forms of insurance. Canadian life insurance mutuals are among the largest corporations in the country, having over $100 billion of assets in 1990.[10] Most of these converted to mutuals from joint stock companies in order to protect themselves from takeovers.[11] However, some, like Mutual Life of Canada based in Waterloo, Ontario, evolved from the same mutual help tradition as the property and casualty companies.[12] Started in 1869, Mutual Life has become one of the largest insurers in Canada with more than $12 billion of assets.[13]

As a service with widely scattered policyholders, mutual life companies utilize proxy voting to elect their board of directors. This procedure tends to reduce the influence of members and can result in a company with a closed self-perpetuating board under the control of senior management.

The property and casualty mutuals tend to be smaller regionally based companies conforming more to the co-operative tradition of organizations providing a service to members drawn from a defined community. The property and casualty mutuals are clustered in Quebec and Ontario, though there are some in New Brunswick and a smattering throughout the rest of the country. The Quebec mutuals belong to a federation, Groupe Promutuel, which in 1989 had $193 million of assets among 300,000 policyholders.[14] The Ontario mutuals, belonging to the Ontario Mutual Insurance Association, had $421 million of assets among 162,561 policy holders.[15] There were also some larger federally incorporated mutuals with $2.3 billion of assets and 605,272 policyholders in 1989.[16]

In addition to mutual insurers, there are co-operative insurers. Since there is no legislation to incorporate insurance companies as co-operatives, the co-operative insurers are usually incorporated as joint stock companies which operate as subsidiaries to a holding company with members that are co-operatives. Co-operators Insurance is an example of such an arrangement.[17] It belongs to The Co-operators Group, a federally incorporated co-operative, whose 35 members are second-tier co-operative federations (for example, credit union centrals), some large first-tier co-operatives and two labour organizations. The Co-operators is among the largest general insurance companies in Canada with $2.1 billion in assets and 2.7 million policyholders. Unlike a mutual insurer, policyholders at The Co-operators are not members. Therefore, Co-operators Insurance is an example of a fourth model for co-operatives, co-operatively held subsidiaries, to which we now turn.

Co-operatively Held Subsidiaries

This fourth model consists of a company (not usually a co-operative) owned by a group of co-operatives. Usually the owners are well-established co-operatives of primary producers or of users of a service (or in some cases co-operative federations) that either have a need which they want served through a subsidiary or have identified an opportunity for investment.

For example, the francophone co-operatives affiliated with Groupe Désjardins have a general insurance company (Assurances générales), an investment company (Société d'investissement Désjardins) and a trust company (Fiducie Désjardins). The trust company in particular has achieved a good size for Canadian trust companies, administering $16.6 billion of assets in 1989. Co-op Trust serves a similar purpose in English Canada, administering $5.1 billion of assets in 1989. It is owned by anglophone co-operatives and credit unions. The CUMIS Group and Société d'assurance des caisses populaires acadiennes are other examples of subsidiary financial corporations owned by co-operatives.

There are also examples of co-operative subsidiaries in market sectors other than financial services. Co-enerco is an intermediate oil and gas exploration company, incorporated in 1982, that is controlled through its parent, Co-operative Energy Corporation. Co-operative Energy Corporation, in turn, is a 50-50 partnership between the federal government and 20 co-operatives. Twenty-three per cent of Co-enerco's shares are publicly traded on the Alberta and Toronto Stock Exchanges. Another example is Consumers' Co-operative Refineries Ltd. (CCRL), a wholly owned subsidiary of Federated Co-operatives, the wholesaler for retail co-op stores in the West. This refinery delivered 12.7 million barrels of oil in 1989. CCRL has just completed a $700 million heavy-oil upgrading plant, a joint venture between CCRL's parent, Federated Co-operatives, and the Saskatchewan government. This plant was designed to help to put to use Saskatchewan's huge reserves of heavy oil. It is expected that the upgrader will produce 50,000 barrels of oil daily.

Worker Co-operatives
The total exclusion of employees as a distinct membership group in co-operatives is a questionable basis for a democratic governance. Since employees are governed by management, it would be expected that employees would have a voice and vote in electing the board that selects management. There is one type of co-operative — a worker co-operative — in which workers do elect a board from among their ranks. Like most other types of co-operatives, it too has only one type of membership group, in this case the workers. Therefore, the worker co-operative represents a fifth model, quite distinct from the other four discussed to this point. In statistical terms, the worker co-operative is much less prominent than any of the other models, whether in business scale or membership. However, the worker co-operative presents a challenge to the other co-operative models that goes beyond its numbers.

In Canada, in 1989, there were about 300 worker co-operatives with 6,140 members and $233 million of revenues. These are very small, independent enterprises, often started by idealistic groups who value control over their workplace. About 60 per cent of Canada's worker co-operatives are located in Quebec, where in 1984 the Parti Québécois government put in place a system of development groups (*groupes conseils*) and a government corporation (the Société de développement des coopératives) to assist with financing.[18] Quebec's 41 forestry co-operatives account for 60 per cent of the business and about 50 per cent of the membership of all worker co-operatives in Canada.[19] The Quebec forestry co-operatives are organized into a provincial federation, the Coopératives forestières du Québec, that operates independently from the other worker co-operatives.

A second cluster of worker co-operatives in Quebec have been organized through the Confédération des syndicats nationaux (CSN), a confederation of 2,075 public and private-sector union locals with 250,000 workers. Since 1988, when the CSN set up its own consulting group (*groupe de consultation*) near its head office in Montreal, it has organized a series of buyouts structured primarily as worker co-operatives that now control about half of Quebec's ambulance services.[20]

Both Quebec's forestry co-operatives and the ambulance service co-operatives are of a scale that is much larger than most worker co-operatives in Canada. The only other significant cluster is in the natural foods business, where such worker co-operatives as CRS, Wild West and PSC dominate the wholesale trade on the West Coast, and the Big Carrot of Toronto is a leading retailer.

Most other worker co-operatives in Canada are micro businesses; the largest ones were established when an existing business was bought out. Aside from Quebec, there are significant regional clusters in eastern Nova Scotia and on the West Coast. The Quebec co-operatives belong to the Fédération québecoise des coopératives de travail. The worker co-operatives in the rest of Canada are organized into the Canadian Worker Co-operative Federation. [21]

In spite of the high level of growth at present, the worker co-operative has proven to be the most difficult of all forms of co-operatives to sustain, not just in Canada but internationally. This current spurt of development is the third wave. The first worker co-operatives were organized in the latter part of the nineteenth century while the second wave occurred during the 1930s.[22] The oldest worker co-operative currently functioning in Canada, Harpell Printing of Montreal, was formed at the end of the Second World War when James-John Harpell, a benevolent entrepreneur, transferred to his employees control of his business and an adjoining garden city where many of the workers lived and where adult education courses were conducted.[23]

Although the worker co-operatives formed in the nineteenth century did not endure, their experience is instructive for the present.[24] As early as the 1860s, worker co-operatives were started in Saint John, New Brunswick (the Saint John Trades Co-operative Association), and 20 worker-owned foundries were organized by the Iron Moulders International Union in Ontario. Many of the worker co-operatives formed during the nineteenth century were encouraged, both during prolonged strikes and in start-up situations, by the Knights of Labour, a very influential union group. The Knights' members started printing enterprises (*The Star*, the forerunner to Canada's largest daily newspaper in Toronto), a biscuit and confectionery works in Chatham, a shoe company in Montreal and a knitting factory in Norwich, Ontario. Its most celebrated projects were a cigar-making factory in Woodstock, Ontario, which produced "the Little Knight," and an attempted transportation co-operative in Toronto after a strike in 1886. According to historians Greg Kealey and Bryan Palmer, the Knights' "commitment to the co-operative commonwealth was well known and reported in the pages of local newspapers."[25]

The Canadian experience with worker co-operatives in the nineteenth century parallelled that of Britain, where analysts were already drawing the conclusion that worker co-operatives could not succeed — a viewpoint which, in the best of the colonial tradition, became influential in Canada. The critique was first developed by the Fabian theoreticians Beatrice Potter (Webb) and her husband Sidney Webb writing at the turn of the century.[26] Drawing on the data which indicated that worker co-operatives formed in the last half of the nineteenth century were not enduring, the Webbs formulated a broad critique. Although their concerns touched all aspects of the worker co-operative, they focused on inadequate finanacing, a problem that many analysts agreed was a central concern for this mode of organization.

Beatrice Potter observed that worker co-operatives took hold in market sectors with low capital needs ("in those trades untransformed by the industrial revolution"[27]), but even so, the workers lacked the resources to capitalize the business properly. To overcome this problem, workers turned to outside investors, with the consequence that they had to pay high rates of interest, thereby reducing the amount the members could pay themselves for their labour. In some cases they had to give outside investors voting rights, which sometimes resulted in a loss of control. One consequence of the financial problems described by Potter is that the members of the co-operative came to exploit hired labour (paying these employees less than worker-members received for the same task), in an effort to keep the business afloat.

Financing remains a problem in worker co-operatives to the present day. As in Potter's time, these enterprises tend to be concentrated in labour-intensive, low-capital economic ghettos and the nub of the problem is that workers lack sufficient capital for their business. This difficulty is exacerbated by the worker co-operative structure, which restricts voting rights to workers, each having only one vote. To maintain this arrangement, outside financing is limited to either loans or non-voting shares, not an attractive prospect for most investors. Neither is the worker co-operative an attractive arrangement to entrepreneurs, since they may not be able to receive the same level of financial benefit or the same degree of control as they would in a private-sector business. The democratic governance of the worker co-operative accords all workers equal voting rights, a circumstance which is intolerable to most entrepreneurs. The Webbs' critique of worker co-operatives was very influential, and it turned both the British co-operative movement and the International Co-operative Alliance away from co-operatives based upon workers as members to a structure based upon consumers or users of a service. Canada, as noted, followed the international trend, making user-based co-operatives the predominant model.

The Webbs' argument was not simply directed toward the limitations of worker co-operatives. Rather, they argued that consumers or service users were the appropriate group upon which to base an economic democracy because they were more representative of a community's interest than a group of workers:

> The association of producers, necessarily sectional in principle and working for its own gain, is being rapidly superseded by the contrary ideal of an association of consumers, carrying on industry, not for the profit of the worker but with the direct object of supplying the wants of the community in the best way.[28]

The Webbs' assumption that the users of a service were less self-interested than the workers seems naïve. The same could be said of their assumption that users of a service were the best group upon which to create an economic democracy. In general, users have been more committed to partaking of a co-operative's services than to fulfilling the responsibilities of membership, such as participation in the governance. Given the relatively small time allotment that people make to any given service, the desire to participate in the governance of a corporation providing the service generally is not great. The minimal time involvement of users may be contrasted to employees, who usually do devote a large portion of their time to their work.

Furthermore, the loyalties of service users can be fickle and "exit" (voting with their feet) is the usual solution when greater satisfaction is available elsewhere.[29] Although members may make a commitment to user-based co-operatives that transcends simple market forces (price, convenience, quality), this is more likely to occur in smaller organizations providing a vital service such as food retailing, daycare or housing.

Ironically, perhaps, the reason for the predominance of the user-based over the worker model may lie in its weakness as a co-operative. The worker model tends to require a large time commitment to decision-making and a substantial financial investment from members, while users tend to make only a small investment in money and time over and above their payment for service. The user model pools very small investments (membership fees) from a large number of people and can rely on the small subset of users who are interested in volunteering for the board of directors and committees.

It is unclear whether this third wave of worker co-operative development in Canada will sustain itself or, as in the past, will dwindle. The worker co-operative does appear to be a practical arrangement for micro businesses, and in that respect it has parallels to an equal partnership in the private sector. The worker co-operative also has demonstrated that it can be applicable to somewhat larger businesses, particularly when the types of jobs done by members are of similar skills (forestry, for example). There are also examples of successful worker co-operatives in industries with a broader range of skills. The Mondragon group in the Basque region of Spain includes Spain's largest manufacturer of household appliances, as well as other sophisticated industries.[30] Worker co-operatives are also involved in large sophisticated industries in northern Italy.[31]

However, in both of these examples worker co-operatives have evolved as part of a community-based system with a supportive infrastructure for both finance and entrepreneurship (see Chapter 5). In Canada, these supports have tended to be lacking.

Mondragon and northern Italy are the exceptions to the worker co-operative tradition. In general, worker co-operatives are micro businesses in labour-intensive services. What was true in the latter half of the nineteenth century appears to be the case near the end of the twentieth century. The wheel of history has turned a full circle.

Yet the worker co-operative model may have another type of significance that is of greater importance than its own success. The worker co-operative also poses a challenge to other models of co-operatives: Is it possible to create a democratic organization which ignores the workers as a distinct membership group?

The Canadian co-operative movement, like other modern co-operative movements, is based upon organizations with one type of member — users, primary producers, other co-operatives. However, does a community — and a corporation as one form of community — have but one interest? Recently, an experiment has been undertaken within some Canadian co-operatives that is challenging the tradition of basing the organization upon one membership group.

The Multi-Stakeholder Co-operative

In the mid-1980s, The Co-operators Group — the holding company for Co-operator Insurance — initiated a bold restructuring process. It challenged the most fundamental premise of co-operatives, that of basing the organization on one type of member.[32] This restructuring has implications for the role of employees within both social enterprises and the private sector. The Co-operators Group is a federally incorporated co-operative whose 35 member-owners are mainly provincial, regional and national co-operatives, involved in grain handling, dairies, food wholesaling, housing, financial services, and so on. Many of the member-organizations are themselves federations of first-tier co-operative organizations (for example, provincial credit union centrals), so the link between The Co-operators Group and people who belong to its member-organizations is at best peripheral. This link becomes even weaker with respect to The Group's subsidiaries. In theory these are social enterprises housed within an umbrella corporation with co-operatives as members, but in practice they are similar to subsidiaries of a private-sector corporation.

The Co-operators' restructuring is based upon stakeholder theory, a school of thought that suggests there are distinct interests in a corporate structure. Prior to its application by The Co-operators, the concept of the stakeholder already had some currency in private-sector corporations.[33] But according to John Jordan, one of the architect's of the Co-operators' initiative, "Generally, 'stakeholder' is taken as a metaphor rather than a legitimate interest with entailed rights. More cynically, some use it to identify those interests that a corporation should be wary of because they could interfere with the corporation's plans and strategies."[34]

Co-operators' initiative was unique in that it actually specified the stakeholders' rights and obligations with respect to such issues as governance, financing and profit-sharing, and then put the ideas into practice within a functioning corporation. A stakeholder was defined as "those organized interests who co-produce the results of the organization."[35] In the case of The Co-operators, they were The Group (or holding company), the employees and the users of the service (or clients). In providing a rationale for the classification of a stakeholder, Jordan argued:

> We sought to answer a simple question: who creates the value in an enterprise, and should therefore be entitled to it?
>
> This is hardly a new question, and if one surveys how it has been addressed in various ideologies, one finds a common thread in the positions taken: a single exclusive interest should take all. Thus, for example, the conventional consumer and producer co-operative tradition relies fundamentally on the logic of the primacy of use. The logic has a tradition in law extending back to the Roman concept of the *jus fructi*. Under it, the users are entitled to the benefit. Worker co-operative advocates, on the other hand, often justify their claims by reference to a Marxist-derived labour theory of value: Surplus is created exclusively by the efforts of the workers, and they alone are entitled to the surplus generated in the firm. Capitalists (and some co-operators apparently) believe it is capital

which is the generative force in enterprises and should thus be solely credited with the resulting rewards.

In considering these opposed claims, one might well ask why each must be exclusive. ... The Co-operators concluded that each of these groups can be creators of value, and should have the right to participate in the organization.[36]

The Group supplied much of the capital, and its senior management undertook much of the entrepreneurial initiative for the system. The Group also took a co-ordinating role with respect to both the operating companies and in explaining the reorganization to other co-operatives.

The employees fit the criterion for a stakeholder insofar as they had a key role in producing the results of these companies. Some of the younger, more mobile employees preferred not to join the co-operative. Membership implied a commitment that some were unprepared to make. The users of the services were also a mixed group, ranging from long-time committed clients to more transient ones. Like the employees, only some were interested in membership. Management was not included as a distinct stakeholder, even though it fit the operational definition to "co-produce the results of the organization," because it was perceived as already having sufficient power. Management could participate in the staff stakeholder group, but it could not be elected to the board. According to Jordan, "the intent was to enfranchise staff generally, not to give additional voice to management."[37]

The multi-stakeholder model has been applied to Co-operators Data, a company with 750 employees providing computer services to credit unions, insurance companies and other financial institutions. The governance is structured on the principle of relative balance between stakeholders' interests, so that no one stakeholder has sufficient power to make board decisions without some support from the others. The Group and clients each elect four representatives to the board, whereas employees have two representatives. As a reflection of their commitment, stakeholders make a financial investment in the organization. Clients purchase shares equivalent to 15 per cent of their annual billings, and staff shares are pegged to 15 per cent of the average annual salary at the time of joining. In both cases share purchases can be made over time, either as additions to monthly billings or as payroll deductions, and participation is strictly voluntary.

Each stakeholder has a capital account into which their original investment, the interest paid on their investment and a member's share of any annual profit (or surplus) are allocated. The board of directors has discretion in dividing annual surpluses or deficits between stakeholders; in 1988, for example, 51 per cent of the year-end surplus was allocated to employees, 44 per cent went to clients, and The Group received 5 per cent. The capital account becomes both savings for the individual member and investment capital for the enterprise.

Through the multi-stakeholder model, The Co-operators has introduced worker ownership into a larger-scale and better-financed social enterprise than is usual in Canada, albeit with a reduced level of corporate control for employees than would be found in a worker co-operative. The Co-operators' experiment has also created social enterprises which have the business advantages of being part of an integrated corporate system.

The experiment at The Co-operators Group may be the most interesting example of the multi-stakeholder co-operative in Canada, but it is not the only one. In the Atlantic fisheries there are now examples of dual stakeholder arrangements involving fishers and fish-processing plant workers.[38] In daycare, there are also dual stakeholder arrangements involving parents and workers.[39]

The multi-stakeholder co-operative is also being discussed at the international level. At the 1990 meetings in Madrid of the International Co-operative Alliance (the umbrella organization for the world's co-operatives), Sven Ake Böök, a Swedish delegate and the Chair of the Research Committee, issued a challenge:

> Why not radically rethink the concept of, and basis for, membership? Why not try a more mixed membership — at least in some parts of the co-operative organization, so that it is possible to be a member ... as a user [of service], an owner, a financier and as an employee.[40]

Instead of promoting organizations based on one particular type of member, the issue would become determining what interest groups should be accorded membership rights, and creating an appropriate balance of interests in the corporate governance. Ultimately, the inclusion of employees as a distinct membership group within a broader co-operative arrangement may be the most important outcome of the current spurt of worker co-operatives.

Multi-Stakeholder Co-operatives in Crown Corporations

The application of stakeholder theory to corporate governance could also be extended to the government sector. At present, there is a fierce debate regarding Crown corporations, with conservative governments desiring to privatize them and doing so in some cases. The public, which in theory owns these enterprises, has not shown much loyalty to maintaining them under government control, because the public's only direct involvement with them is as a consumer of the service. There was not a strong public outcry to the privatizations of either Air Canada or Petro Canada, for example, an indication that the majority of Canadians did not feel that these sell-offs would adversely affect them. An alternative to a straight private sector sale might be a restructuring based upon stakeholders, with board positions for the government, employees and consumers.

The NDP government in Ontario was presented with such a proposal for auto insurance.[41] The Co-operators, which holds the largest market share in the province's auto-insurance industry, had proposed to the province that it would create a non-profit auto insurer with three stakeholders: drivers, employees and the provincial government through the ministries of transportation and safety. The service would not be a monopoly of one company, but would be open to other non-profit sponsors. For this approach to be effective, The Co-operators argued that participants "must be a limited number of large, stable co-operative insurers."[42]

The Ontario NDP had campaigned to bring auto insurance under a government-controlled monopoly, as has been done in Saskatchewan, British Columbia and Manitoba, but it decided after about a year in office not to proceed with this plan. Given the government's decision, it is not clear whether The Co-operators will proceed with its proposal. Nevertheless, its initiative opened the door to an alternative that an innovative government could consider.

The Worker-Shareholder Co-operative

The experiments in the multi-stakeholder co-operative also have some parallels in the private sector of the economy. In Quebec there has been a move toward enfranchising workers within private-sector corporations through an arrangement called a worker-shareholder co-operative. In that arrangement, a worker co-operative holds only a portion of the stock in a private company, with proportional representation on the board. Between 1985 and 1990, the provincial Société de développement des coopératives had assisted the financing of 28 such enterprises, including 18 in 1991.[43] Many of these arrangements are in industrial corporations, a type of business that has led to relatively few worker co-operatives.

For example, a worker co-operative holds a 14.5 per cent interest in the $60 million Normick Chambord sign-production factory on Lac St. Jean.[44] This guarantees it one board seat with the right of first refusal in sales of shares. Through this arrangement, the worker co-operative can also increase its stake in the company over time. In that respect, the worker-shareholder co-operative bears some similarity to the popular Employee Stock Ownership Plans (ESOP) in the United States, which are structured as trust funds to which companies contribute stock and gain a tax deduction as benefit for their employees, and are also used for a gradual transfer of ownership.[45] However, unlike most ESOPs, in a worker-shareholder co-operative the workers have complete voting rights.

In most worker-shareholder co-operatives, which are often established to prevent plant closings, the workers' stake is larger than at Normick Chambord. At the Sacre Coeur saw mill the workers own one-third, and at ACG Jeans in Granby, the worker co-operative holds about 30 per cent of the stock.[46] Through this approach, co-operatives of workers can participate in larger, better-financed enterprises, albeit with workers having less representation on the corporate governance than in a worker co-operative.

Although Quebec is the only province with a program to encourage the formation of worker-shareholder co-operatives, there are indications that this same structure may catch on in other parts of the country. The recently completed employee buyout of Algoma Steel in Sault Ste. Marie involves 60 per cent ownership of the company by the employees — the employees' holdings structured as two worker co-operatives (one for hourly employees and the other for salaried workers).[47] This buyout, the largest ever undertaken in Canada, was organized by the Ontario District of the United Steelworkers of America. Like the worker-shareholder co-operatives in Quebec, it could become a trendsetter for employee investment. Moreover, there is already legislation in place in British Columbia and Saskatchewan and legislation being enacted in Ontario that should encourage this trend.[48]

As in Quebec, these three provinces are permitting employees to become stakeholders in their places of work by forming companies within their employers' companies. The company holding the employees' shares is referred to as a Labour Sponsored Venture Capital Corporation (LSVCC), thereby making employees' investments eligible for a 20 per cent federal tax credit — a credit which is matched by the provinces.

Only in Quebec can the employee stake be incorporated as a co-operative. Nevertheless, in the other three provinces the employee stake can be organized with equal voting rights for each employee — the functional requirement for a co-operative arrangement. Under those circumstances, the LSVCC would be very similar to a worker-shareholder co-operative.

CONCLUSIONS

This chapter presents an overview to the eight basic models around which co-operatives are organized. The first four models are: 1) Marketing co-operatives in which the members are either primary producers (farmers, fishers) or producers of a product (artisans). The members also can be providers of a service (for example, taxis). In this model, the co-operative is formed for a common need, usually marketing, and the members, for other purposes, operate independently from each other. 2) Co-operatives in which the members are consumers or users of a service. The service can be food retailing, farm supplies, financial services, housing, childcare, healthcare, insurance (mutual), burial, and so on. Except for the service they share in common, the members may have no relationship to each other. 3) Second- and third-tier co-operatives in which the members are other co-operatives. In general these are second- and third-tier organizations for user-based co-operatives (wholesalers for retail food co-ops, credit union centrals). However, they can also be an amalgamation of different types of co-operatives as in the Canadian Co-operative Association or the Conseil canadien de la coopération. 4) Co-operatively held subsidiaries. In contrast to second- and third-tier co-operatives, which are co-operatives with other co-operatives as members, subsidiaries are not usually co-operatives.[49] Rather, they are companies owned by a parent corporation which is a co-operative.

There are two other noteworthy features of these four models. First, they involve only a very specific aspect of their members' lives, whether the member is an individual or an organization. The exceptions are housing co-operatives and select individuals who devote a lot of their time as board members and through other activities. However, in general these co-operatives provide a very specific service that impinges on their members in a limited manner. In the words of co-operative analyst George Melnyk, they are "unifunctional" organizations, as contrasted to the more comprehensive structures of the past.[50] Like modern organizations in general, co-operatives have shifted from a comprehensive arrangement involving many aspects of people's lives (communes, for example) to highly specialized organizations with specific services for a membership interested in those services. It is quite possible for members to use the services of the co-operative, as consumers, without any other involvement in the organization. That degree of involvement is quite common for financial co-operatives and for other co-operatives involving services upon which the average person spends only a small amount of time in a week. If the membership is widely dispersed, these organizations may turn to proxy voting in electing a board of directors. Mutual life insurers follow this practice.

The second feature that these four models have in common is that the people working in them are employees of the co-operative rather than a distinct membership group. Whether the members are primary producers, users of a service, or other co-operatives, the board they elect hires senior management which in turn hires other employees. Therefore, the relationship between employees and management is similar to the private and government sectors of the economy.

In the last four models discussed, the workers have a more direct role in the governance of the organization. These models are: 5) The worker co-operative, in which the workers are the members. This has been the most difficult of all co-operative models to develop, largely because of problems of finance. 6) The multi-stakeholder co-operative, a leading-edge model, in which there is more than one membership group, including the employees. 7) The application of the multi-stakeholder co-operative to Crown corporations, and 8) The worker-shareholder co-operative, which involves the application of multi-stakeholder principles to the private sector.

3

Non-profits in Public Service

Non-profits and co-operatives partially overlap, in that some types of co-operatives — particularly for housing, daycare and healthcare — are also non-profit corporations. Non-profits can be divided into two broad categories: those that serve the public by providing humanitarian and social services, and those that serve a defined membership by satisfying a mutual interest. Non-profits serving a defined membership, each member having one vote at general meetings ("mutual non-profits"), are similar in structure to co-operatives.[1]

Unlike co-operatives, however, non-profits lack a tradition of perceiving themselves as part of a unified social movement. Rather, they are organized to meet particular needs not being satisfied through the private or government sectors. Their identity tends to be tied to their service, and sometimes to other organizations providing the same service (religious organizations, for example), rather than to a common movement with other non-profits or to a broader social economy.

The two general categories of non-profits — public service and mutual-interest organizations — are indeed very broad. In 1992, there were about 175,000 non-profit corporations registered in Canada involved in a wide array of endeavours.[2] (These figures do not include the many unincorporated non-profit associations.) Although these categories of non-profits in public service and mutual non-profits overlap in part, they serve as a useful organizing mechanism for dealing with this vast topic. This chapter will deal with non-profits in public service, while Chapter 4 turns to member-based non-profits or mutual-interest societies.

NON-PROFITS: FORM AND PHILOSOPHY

As a corporate form, a non-profit is simply a corporation without shares.[3] This feature is important because it means that all of its revenues or donations go to costs associated with the service. Any net earnings — that is, surplus after all of the expenses needed to render the service are paid — are retained and used for the purposes for which the corporation was set up. Similarly, any deficits, unless they are made up in the future or from reserves, lead to a reduction of service. In these respects, non-profits are similar to co-operatives.

Thus, the fundamental difference between a non-profit and a private-sector corporation is the absence of stock and other reflections of proprietorship. In a private-sector or for-profit corporation, profits may be distributed to shareholders as dividends, and shares reflect the net value of the corporation. A non-profit is an association created solely to provide a service for as long as there is financing and a need for the service.

The non-profit may be seen as both a corporate form and as a philosophy. Non-profit corporations are formally incorporated, much like any other corporations. However, there are other organizations which are not incorporated and are based upon the non-profit philosophy in that their purpose is to provide a beneficial service either to the public or to a defined membership. These include formally constituted associations (unions, some tenant and ratepayers' groups, some home and school associations) and informal associations. Therefore, non-profits may be placed upon a continuum based upon degree of formality and ranging from actual non-profit corporations, through formal associations, to informal associations. The term *non-profit*, as used in this chapter, applies to all three types.

Non-profits and Charities

Some non-profits (both corporations and formal associations) are charities, while others are not. Charities are required to spend at least 80 per cent of their donations upon their objectives, and in the event of dissolution, their net assets would be passed on to another charity.[4] If a non-profit applies and receives charitable status from Revenue Canada, donors gain tax benefit, thereby creating a useful fundraising opportunity.

The concept of charity originated in the religious traditions of the Middle Ages in England. Members of religious organizations believed that they were furthering the purpose of their religion by assisting those in need. Today, some of the areas with the strongest social economies (France, Italy, Spain, Quebec and eastern Nova Scotia), also have a strong Catholic influence, the Church taking a leading role in helping its needy parishioners.

While charity has religious roots, the concept has been broadened to include motivations which are largely secular; that is, the responsibility the members of a community have to support the services which people require. The development of the profession of social work may be seen as an outcome of this secularization of services with charitable purposes.

The secularization of charitable activities is not a recent phenomenon, but could be found in Canada's colonial period as well. For example, in 1781 the citizens of Halifax raised 750 pounds in order to build a public school. The funds were raised through a lottery which had received the approval of the House of Assembly.[5] In 1824, Montreal women began forming charitable organizations to care for infants who were being abandoned by mothers too destitute to care for them. Previously, such infants had been cared for by nuns at the General Hospital. However, the nuns were overwhelmed, and the government did not provide any assistance.[6] Twelve years later, Torontonians concerned about the growing number of poor people raised funds for a residence called a "House of Industry."[7] The government of Upper Canada refused to be influenced by England's Poor Laws through which the state provided residences for the destitute. The attitude in Toronto was that this need should be met by private citizens.

Not only has charity been broadened from its religious traditions, but the scope of the activities and of organizations claiming charitable status has also widened. The 66,000 organizations with charitable status in Canada[8] (all non-profits which are either incorporated or simply unincorporated registered charities) include services that, in addition to relief of poverty and international aid, involve education, youth programs, health, family services, culture and the arts, heritage and environmental protection. Like social programs in general, the thrust of organizations with charitable objectives has become universal, serving the well-to-do as well as the needy. Therefore, a distinction can be made between charity as a community's response to those in dire need, and organizations with charitable objectives (objectives meeting the criteria required for charitable status under existing taxation laws) serving a broader public. Although modern charities are of both types, the latter — organizations available to all those wanting to partake of the services — are more typical.

This change can be called the universalization of charity. In the modern world, charity has been both secularized and universalized, though the more traditional arrangements provided for by religious communities and directed towards those in dire need are still quite prominent.

NON-PROFITS, CHARITIES AND VOLUNTEERS

Most non-profits are small, labour-intensive setups with paid staff and volunteers that are devoted to the social purposes of the organization. Since volunteers frequently outnumber paid staff, non-profits are also referred to as voluntary organizations. Although a high level of volunteer participation is the general case for non-profits, there is some variation. Some non-profits, particularly business associations, are operated largely by paid staff, whereas at the opposite extreme informal associations are strictly voluntary. Non-profits with charitable status — either corporations or formal associations — usually have a high ratio of volunteers to paid staff.

Volunteering was the subject of a major national survey by Statistics Canada covering a 12-month period starting in November 1986.[9] (This survey had been urged by the Coalition of National Voluntary Organizations.) The survey indicated that 5.3 million Canadians, or nearly 27 per cent of those over the age of 15, were volunteers in formal organizations. In addition, there were another 3.2 million people who had been active volunteers in the past, but not during the 12 months surveyed by Statistics Canada.

On average, the volunteers in the survey contributed 191 hours of work per year, and about one-quarter were contributing more than 500 hours annually. In total, volunteers contributed more than one billion hours or the equivalent of 615,000 person-years of work. Ottawa social policy analysts David Ross and Richard Shillington estimate that if the volunteer labour contribution was costed at $12 per hour, it would be worth $12 billion in 1987 (or approximately $13.2 billion in 1990).[10] In addition, volunteers contributed another $841 million in out-of-pocket expenses ($925 million in 1990 dollars) that were not reimbursed. The economics of the volunteer contribution should not be trivialized, for it is worth almost triple the total of private financial charitable donations, and even more than that if the calculation takes into account that charitable financial donations also involve a tax expenditure by the government (a tax credit for the donation), whereas volunteer service lacks any financial benefit to the provider and may even involve an outlay for expenses. The 615,000 person-years of volunteer work in Canada are equivalent to the combined labour forces of Saskatchewan and New Brunswick.

There is no stereotype to describe volunteers in Canada. They are found in all parts of the country, though proportionately more so in the Prairie provinces, and come from all cultural groups, age groups, social classes and genders. Women are more likely to volunteer than men (30 per cent versus 24 per cent); English-language speakers more than francophones (33 per cent versus 22 per cent); married more than singles (31 per cent versus 19 per cent); those with a university degree more than those with high school (46 per cent versus 24 per cent); and the middle age groups more than youth and seniors. However, the differences are relatively small, and the similarities are greater than the differences.

Just as volunteers come from all parts of the Canadian mosaic, they participate in a broad array of organizations and perform many different functions. The largest number (17 per cent) helped religious organizations, and 16 per cent assisted organizations involved in leisure, recreation and sports. The figures for other types of activities were: education and youth development (14 per cent), health (10 per cent), social service agencies (9 per cent) and other community activities (8 per cent). The range of volunteer activities is staggering: fundraising (13 per cent), organizing (10 per cent), board of directors (8 per cent), teaching and education (6 per cent), office work (6 per cent), coaching (5 per cent), serving food (4 per cent), counselling (4 per cent), and so on.

Clearly, volunteerism is an important social and economic force in Canada. Its significance increases even more if informal volunteer activity is included. About two-thirds of Canada's adult population (over 13 million people) were involved in "informal" volunteer activity during 1986–87. The most common form was helping specific individuals outside of one's own household (for example, visiting the sick or elderly, helping someone in need with shopping or driving them to appointments). Over 3 million volunteers assisted with informal environmental and wildlife activities and another 1.85 million participated in other community activities. If one allows that volunteers in formal organizations are of economic value, it seems arbitrary to ignore informal initiatives, particularly if they go beyond the household.

Informal volunteerism is part of an informal economy, an arrangement discussed by David Ross and Peter Usher, in which people provide services to each other without payment.[11] Sometimes, the services can be part of an exchange or a barter system. Barter has also been drawn into formal non-profits referred to as Local Employment and Trading Systems (LETS), an idea originated by Michael Linton in Courtenay, British Columbia, in 1983.[12] Since then, LETS arrangements have spread throughout Canada, and to the United States, Australia, New Zealand and Britain.

However, more often than not, barter is arranged either informally or as part of the social networks forming the backbone of communities. In parts of Canada with below-average participation rates and substandard earnings in the formal economy, informal arrangements take on added importance, particularly when people in seasonal industries such as forestry and fishing are on unemployment insurance.

Although much of this is self-maintenance and maintenance of one's household, an important aspect involves contribution to one's community. It is difficult to define the organizational arrangements for informal volunteerism in the same way as volunteer activity in formal non-profits. However, it is an important part of society and the social economy.

FINANCING NON-PROFITS

Although volunteer labour is vital to non-profits, financing is essential as well. An important facet of non-profits — excepting business, professional, labour and some social organizations financed by members' fees — is fundraising. Financing comes from a wide variety of sources, including individual and corporate donations, benefits, fees from service, but in general, it is government that has become the primary source, although there are also some non-profits that receive no government funding at all.

The importance of government funding is documented by Samuel Martin, a professor at the University of Western Ontario, in his compelling text, *An Essential Grace*.[13] Martin argues that Canada has gone from a society in which non-profits providing "humanistic services" were financed largely by private charity to one in which government underwrites most of the costs. The involvement of government has been spurred by a broad array of universal programs in education, health and welfare, financed through various forms of taxation. As taxes have increased, they have become the predominant form of payment for these services, dwarfing private contributions.

Martin notes that in 1937, in the midst of the Great Depression which had already increased government involvement in the economy, the costs associated with public services were divided evenly between government and private donors. The ratio in favour of government has gradually increased so that by 1980 it was 4:1. In other words, about 80 per cent of the expenditure upon public services is coming from governments through taxes. Martin shows that this pattern of increased payment through taxes pertains to every type of service. For such services as education and welfare, in which there is a lengthy tradition of government involvement, the ratio of government to private expenditure is 13:1. For healthcare, the ratio is 4:1, and for culture, defined broadly to include recreation and religion as well as the arts, government spent slightly more than private donors.

The shift from private to government financing has corresponded to a reduction in private expenditure, both through direct payment for services and charitable donations. At the height of the Great Depression, according to Martin, about seven-eighths of private expenditure on public service was direct and the remainder was through charitable donations. By the end of the 1970s, direct personal expenditure represented only 3.1 per cent of the total and charitable donations amounted to only 0.7 per cent.

Of charitable donations, individual contributions, representing 0.6 of the national income, were much larger than corporate donations, which amounted to 0.09 per cent. In comparative terms, charitable donations from Canadians as a percentage of national income were the same at the end of the 1970s as at the height of the Great Depression. When compared to the post–World War II period, individual donations as a percentage of the national income dropped nearly in half, and corporate donations fell by about one-tenth.

Although charitable financial donations have declined, they remain a very important source of finance for Canada's public services. Figures for 1990 published by the Canadian Centre for Philanthropy indicate that individuals contribute $4.72 billion and corporations another $406 million, for a total contribution of nearly $5.2 billion.[14] Although the average or median individual donation is small ($62 in 1990), about three-quarters of adults filing a tax return were contributing something.

Of the 66,000 eligible charities in Canada, the most commonly supported were providing the following services: medical/health (29 per cent), religious (29 per cent), social and welfare service (11 per cent), civic/social/community/human rights (11 per cent), youth (10 per cent). Many donors to charities make individual decisions with respect to their gifts, often choosing causes with which they are personally involved. To assist donors, there are a multitude of campaigns conducted by large non-profits such as universities, hospitals, the Canadian Cancer Society, Easter Seals, and the Salvation Army. About 10 per cent of the private financial donations in Canada are organized through two primary mechanisms — the United Way and charitable foundations. These two mechanisms form a financial infrastructure for the non-profits they support.

The United Way

The concept of the United Way originated in Denver, Colorado, in 1887, when some religious leaders organized a co-ordinated fund-raising effort to assist fortune seekers who lost their livelihood during that community's ill-fated "gold rush."[15] Subsequently, it has taken hold in 23 other countries, including Canada, though sometimes under other names (Community Chest, Red Feather, Fondo Unido, United Fund).

Forerunners to the United Way in Canada were the Federation of Jewish Philanthropies founded in Montreal and Toronto in 1917, and the Toronto Federation of Community Service founded in 1918.[16] The federated fundraising organization underwent many permutations and name changes, until the United Way (Centraide in francophone regions) was adopted in 1974. The national office, United Way/Centraide Canada, was formed two years later, and is affiliated with United Way International in Virginia. There are other federated fund-raising campaigns besides the United Way; these include Sharelife, a campaign for Catholic charities, and the United Jewish Appeal. But United Way is the largest of these organizations, with 123 branches in Canada in 1991 blanketing all parts of the country with the exception of Newfoundland and the Northwest Territories. In total, these campaigns raised $215.9 million in 1991.

The United Way is a mutual benefit arrangement for member agencies that agree to limit their individual fundraising and to support a co-ordinated drive. For large, well known charities or charities with an identifiable constituency (a religious organization, for example), the United Way may not be the best arrangement.

The United Way, however, is a practical fund-raising mechanism for many types of non-profits. It is well known and has a credible reputation to a broad spectrum of donors. The United Way is well organized for its annual fund-raising drive. It is much easier for most agencies with charitable needs to operate through the co-ordinated effort of the United Way than to mount individual campaigns.

But the United Way generally satisfies only a minority of member-agencies' financial needs, and both its allocation and admission processes have been the subject of some controversy. A study of United Ways in the United States suggests that the rules for admission of new agencies "appear to be quite restrictive and leave considerable room for existing members to oppose new admissions."[17] The same study indicates that there is a tendency to exclude agencies fraught with controversy because this may bring unfavourable publicity and hinder the fund-raising capacity of the movement as a whole. In an effort to deal with these problems, the United Way of Greater Toronto, the largest United Way in Canada, permits its donors to designate to which of its member agencies they wish to donate.

Charitable Foundations

Unlike the United Way, which is a collective fund-raising mechanism with processes that are open to public scrutiny, foundations tend to be private preserves of the wealthy, and as such are shrouded in secrecy. A foundation is a non-profit organization that makes grants to other organizations (usually in financial need) that it wishes to support.[18]

In 1988, there were 848 active foundations in Canada with assets of $2.7 billion that made grants of $269 million. These donations were distributed as follows: social service (23 per cent), education (18 per cent), health (18 per cent), religion (15 per cent), arts and culture (12 per cent), science and technology (10 per cent) and sports and recreation (2 per cent). Although the first Canadian foundation, the Winnipeg Foundation, dates back to 1921, about 85 per cent of foundations in this country were formed since World War II, and more than 60 per cent in the last two decades.

About 90 per cent of Canada's foundations have been established by wealthy individuals and families to support their favourite causes. Family foundations have been the subject of criticism for being used as tax dodges to shelter family fortunes.[19] Nevertheless, they are also among the largest foundations in the country, comprising 43 of the 50 wealthiest ones. The largest and also the oldest family foundation in Canada is the J.W. McConnell Family Foundation, founded in 1937. It made $26.9 million in grants in 1988 from an asset base of $308.9 million. Other large family foundations are CRB (Bronfman), Kahanoff, Donner, Macdonald Stewart and McLaughlin.

Community foundations are set up by cities to support a range of local projects. Unlike family foundations that receive their contributions from one source, community foundations tend to have a large number of donors. The Vancouver Foundation is the second largest foundation in Canada with $220.8 million of assets. With the exception of the Winnipeg Foundation, all the others have less than $5 million of assets.

There are also 21 corporate foundations, operating at arm's length from their sponsoring organizations and through which they funnel charitable grants. The largest is Bombardier with $9.3 million of assets. In general, corporate foundations are small. The same is true of most special interest foundations patronizing health, medicine and legal issues. The Hospital for Sick Children

Foundation, however, is the third largest foundation in Canada. It differs from most other hospital and university foundations set up to support the sponsoring organization in that it also allocates 20 per cent of its annual grants to other organizations in the field of child health.

Very recently, the provincial governments of Alberta and Ontario have created foundations from surplus lottery revenues. Ontario's Trillium Foundation, for example, made $14.9 million of grants to social service agencies in 1988. It does not maintain an asset base.

Although foundations and United Ways are important sources of funds for non-profits unable to be self-supporting, it must be reiterated that most private financial donations are done on an individual basis, and that the primary source of unearned revenues is governments. Moreover, volunteer labour is a major factor in the ability of non-profits to deliver services to the public. Much of the charitable financial contributions and volunteer labour is directed towards non-profits providing services, often humanitarian services, to the public. This group is differentiated from mutual non-profits that provide services to their members (to be discussed in Chapter 4).

Non-profits serving the public can be divided into three primary groups: non-profits in which people using the service pay a fee that covers a substantial portion of the costs; non-profits supporteded largely by volunteers and private donors, sometimes in combination with government; non-profits funded largely by government, in combination with donors and users' fees.[20] Some non-profits do not fall neatly into one category. Nevertheless, the categories are used because they make it possible to raise some interesting issues.

Non-profits in Public Service with User Payments

Non-profits in which users pay for the service cover a range of activities. Although the portion of the cost borne by users varies from the total amount to less than half, the common denominator for all of these associations is that the people partaking of the service enter into a type of commercial arrangement with the provider. Unlike private-sector commerce, however, there is no profit paid to shareholders, and more often than not, the cost of the service is subsidized through financial donations, volunteer labour and some government assistance.

Commercial Non-profits
There are some non-profits in which fees paid by consumers cover the total costs of the service and in which employees of the business are the providers. Blue Cross, a large non-profit franchise of an American-based corporation, is one such example.[21] There are eight Blue Cross non-profits in Canada covering about one-third of the population for prepaid health services not included in provincial plans. (In Alberta, Blue Cross administers the provincial plan as well.) Travel CUTS, a system of 40 travel agencies across Canada, set up by the Canadian Federation of Students to help students and others to obtain discount air tickets, is another example of this type of enterprise.[22]

The Canadian Automobile Association is also a commercial non-profit organized to fill a defined consumer need.[23] In its case, the people using the service are members with defined voting rights as in a mutual insurance company (see Chapter 2) or other forms of member-based non-profits (see Chapter 4). However, member participation is not actively promoted, and actual attendance at annual general meetings tends to be very low. Therefore, membership may be viewed as a marketing tool to gain consumer commitment to the CAA and its services. The CAA has been very effective in organizing automobile users, currently with 3.4 million members in seventeen provincial and regional auto clubs across Canada, and affiliated with automobile clubs in other countries as well.

Whether commercial non-profits have defined membership rights as in the case of the CAA or whether they simply enlist people for their service, there are a growing number of enterprises of this sort for business travellers, people requiring home services, purchasers of home fuels, private schools, and so on. Like businesses in general, these organizations cover their costs with money paid by the users of their services. They remain, however, non-profit corporations.

Youth Programs
The roots of this type of organization are found in the "worker improvement movement" in mid-nineteenth century England, and similar movements somewhat later in the United States and Canada. As people shifted from the countryside to the city, there was concern about the breakdown of moral values. With a view toward "building character" in the younger generation, religious

groups and do-gooders among the middle class started sponsoring formal organizations. In the words of historian David Macleod, these organizations were "intended to counter urban disorder and restore the moral order of the small community."[24] Many organizations of this sort have operated within a religious and ethno-cultural tradition (Sunday schools, the Jewish community centres), and others, although emanating from religious and quasi-religious values, have become secular. The Young Men's Christian Associations (YMCA) were the first of these youth organizations, followed by the Scouts. Subsequently, programs were introduced for girls: the YWCA and Girl Guides. The Boys Clubs, later to become the Boys and Girls Clubs, were also started at this time, but these organizations were directed primarily at the urban poor, and therefore are part of our next category because the participants do not contribute in any significant manner to the program costs. A rural program directed toward youth is the 4-H club. The Junior Achievement programs of the business community are another variant of this theme.

In all of these non-profits, adult volunteers work together with a small staff to make programs available to youth. (The Ys also have adult programs.) Either the parents of the participants pay fees or the young participants support the program through services, as in Junior Achievement. These organizations have an impressive record of reaching young people.[25] The 115 Ys across Canada have 650,000 members, and about 1.5 million other participants who partake of specific activities such as summer camps. The Scouts involve about 194,000 boys in their programs, and the Guides involve 268,000 girls. The 4-H and Junior Achievement are smaller, each with about 40,000–50,000 participants.

Even more impressive than the numbers of people participating in these organizations' services is their ability to harness volunteers. The Scouts and Guides have more than 100,000 adult volunteers organizing their programs. In addition to their service, the volunteers participate in the governance as the voting members for each Scout group. As such, an analogy can be drawn to a worker co-operative, the difference being that the members of a worker co-operative earn an income for their labour, whereas the members of the Scouts are volunteer workers. As with other large non-profits, the Scouts have a tiering arrangement, consisting of provincial councils, a national council and a world organization based in Geneva.

Competitive Sports

In addition to youth organizations desiring to build character, there are many based on organized competitive sports. The Sports Federation of Canada, an Ottawa-based organization to which the national federations of 56 specific competitive sports are affiliated, estimates that 3.5–4 million Canadians, primarily in the younger generation, participate in the programs of the member organizations.[26] Competitive sport, it would seem, has become the religion of the modern world.

The sports federations in Canada are not only for the well-known sports such as hockey, baseball and basketball, but also for activities that capture less attention, such as table tennis, horseshoes and shooting. In general, the cost of these activities at the club level are covered by fees from participants and their families, as well as private donations and a lot of volunteer labour. There is also some government funding for administration of apex organizations, program development and particularly programs for high performance athletes.

For sports the volunteer contribution is very important. According to the national volunteer survey, 1.47 million Canadians are volunteers in leisure, recreation and competitive sports.[27] Five per cent of all volunteers in Canada serve as coaches, many for competitive sports teams.

Although competitive sports organizations affiliate with the Sports Federation of Canada, each has its own elaborate structure. Taking competitive hockey as an example, there are 26,000 teams and over 400,000 players.[28] The organizations in each local area form central associations that arrange the leagues for each age group and ability level. In addition, there is an association for each province, a national association, the Canadian Amateur Hockey Association, and the International Hockey Federation.

The type of structure created for hockey is similar to that for other types of sports. Each, in effect, is a type of volunteer society set up for the purpose of providing a service at cost.

The Performing Arts

In general, performing arts groups in Canada are non-profit organizations earning about half of their revenues from ticket sales and a variety of paid services.[29] Governments account for about one-third of their revenues and private donations cover the rest. There is also an important volunteer component assisting with board activities, fundraising and ticket-taking. Overall in Canada, there are 235 theatre groups, 92 music organizations, 57 dance associations and 17 opera companies.[30] Most of these organizations are small with annual revenues of less than $1 million. However, in total the performing arts earned $317 million in 1988–89.

In addition to performing arts associations, there are other non-profits that create an outlet for young performers to utilize their talents. Organizations such as the Canadian Music Competitions, Canadian Association of Youth Orchestras and Music for Young Children serve a role analogous to the Scouts, Girl Guides and competitive sports team, in that they arrange activities that encourage young people to develop their talents.[31]

Other Services

There are many other non-profit services for which the users pay a substantial portion of the costs. Within this category are about half of the homes for the aged,[32] non-profit housing (about 300,000 units by 1990 or about 10 per cent of the total housing built during the 1980s),[33] and non-profit daycare (about 185,000 units in 1990).[34] For these services, some users receive a subsidy geared to income through the Canada Assistance Plan, and there may be subsidies available to the project itself.

The non-profits that earn a large portion of their revenues from consumers or users vary, from those that are commercial outfits (such as the Canadian Automobile Association), to competitive sports teams that rely upon volunteers but cover their financial costs from fees, to non-profits requiring both financial subsidies and volunteers. The common denominator for all of these non-profits is that the users of the service pay a substantial portion of the cost. There are other non-profits in which the beneficiaries of the service pay either nothing or a token amount. These organizations rely upon volunteers, private donors, and in some cases government funding.

Volunteer-based Non-profits in Public Service

These are organizations depending primarily upon volunteers and financial donations for their operation; some also receive government support, while others manage without any government funding at all. The prototypical organization of this sort is the Red Cross (or Red Crescent in some countries), a vast international volunteer organization operating in 150 countries.[35] The Red Cross was the brainchild of Henry Dunant, a young Swiss, who was appalled by the neglect of the wounded during the war in northern Italy in 1859. Together with four citizens of Geneva, Dunant organized in 1863 the forerunner of the International Committee of the Red Cross, officially declared in 1867.

The Canadian Red Cross Society was founded in 1896, and officially incorporated in 1909. Its broad range of humanitarian services include disaster relief, international aid, blood services (clinics, donor registries), emergency services in Canada, water safety programs, first-aid services (training and public presentations), and community-based services (particularly homemakers). The Canadian Red Cross is able to provide these services by assembling a small army of volunteers, 2.5 million Canadians (including about 1.3 million blood donors). It has 741 branches across Canada, organized through provincial and territorial divisions, and a national office in Ottawa. Its paid staff is 5,950, about half of whom are homemakers. Its annual budget in 1990–91 was $346 million.

To many, the Red Cross symbolizes the humanitarian service organization. It is among the oldest, best known, and claims to be the largest volunteer organization in the world, involving 250 million people in its projects. However, the Red Cross is by no means an exception. It has taken a path followed by thousands of other non-profits that organize volunteers to serve people in need.

The Red Cross is atypical in one respect because it straddles the line between national and international service. Although there are many social organizations with international affiliations, most channel their energies into either domestic or international goals. Agencies in Canada involved in international aid affiliate themselves with the Canadian Council on International Co-operation. Among the better known organizations are OXFAM, CARE Canada, CUSO and Foster Parents Plan.

An organization that functions without any government support at all is Amnesty International, which focuses its energies on human rights abuses throughout the world.[36] Amnesty burst onto the international scene in 1961 when British lawyer Peter

Benenson wrote a newspaper article highlighting the plight of prisoners who were being unjustly detained. Today Amnesty has 1.1 million members and regular supporters in over 150 countries. To draw attention to the plight of people being unjustly imprisoned or receiving cruel treatment such as the death penalty, Amnesty has mobilized 50,000 volunteers working in 6,000 groups in 71 countries, including Canada, to write letters of support on their behalf. This 'Urgent Action' network has acted on behalf of 43,500 persons.

In addition to taking up the cases of victims on an individual basis, Amnesty publishes critical reviews of government policies and works with groups in affiliated countries to gain more humane laws and judicial procedures. Amnesty's independence from government is reflected in its decision not to accept any government funding. It relies upon its members, donors and dedicated volunteers to maintain its activities.

Domestic Organizations
Although the need for humanitarian services may differ in Canada than in some other countries, the needs are nevertheless very real. There is a broad array of organizations attempting to help people living in poverty and suffering from other handicaps such as racism and crippling health problems.

One type of organization addressing these needs is the club whose members join for charitable purposes. Members raise funding and also serve as volunteers. The clubs can be based upon a religious or ethnic bond of association, but most often their bond is simply an interest in the charitable objectives of the organization. Many of the better known organizations originated in the United States, with chapters being created in other parts of the world, including Canada. Among these are the Shriners, an organization that assists victims of burns and crippling injuries; the Kiwanis, the sponsors of a music festival and programs for expectant mothers and seniors; and the Lions Clubs, set up to help the poor.[37]

Other non-profits, like the John Howard and Elizabeth Fry Societies (organizations named after nineteenth century British reformers), are devoted to working with and advocating for men and women who come into conflict with the law.[38] They help former prisoners to become reintegrated into society through sponsorship of halfway houses and an impressive set of public education and mutual self-help initiatives. John Howard and Elizabeth Fry work closely with groups such as the Salvation Army, the Church Council for Justice and Corrections, the St. Leonard Society and the Association des services de rehabilitation sociale de Québec.

Big Brothers and Big Sisters are other major programs, the volunteer members entering into a supportive arrangement with boys and girls in need. The Children's Aid societies also target this group, as do the many adoption, counselling and family service agencies (Catholic Family Services, Jewish Family Services, Chinese Family Services, and so on). Family service agencies deal with the bewildering array of problems of modern societies, some precipitated by poverty and marital breakups. In Canada in 1990, there were nearly 45,000 cases of runaway children reported to the police — 1,200 on average at any given point in time.[39] (Children go missing for other reasons as well, such as abductions.) These problems have spawned a new set of specialized non-profit organizations such as Child Find and the Missing Children's Network/Le Reseau enfants retour.

Food and Shelter
Many charitable services are directed toward the basic need of food. Meals-on-Wheels organizes hordes of volunteers to bring lunches to shut-ins. Organizations such as the Salvation Army have soup kitchens for indigents. However, during the 1980s, the food programs provided through social agencies proved insufficient, and a new organization, the food bank, was created to funnel food to people in need. These non-profit charitable agencies pool supplies of food that loses its retail value because of mislabelling, overproduction and approaching expiry dates. They also have food drives to which the residents of a community contribute. In 1991 (10 years after the first one was founded in Edmonton), there were 292 food banks affiliated with the Canadian Association of Food Banks, operating in 300 communities across Canada, meeting the needs of two million people (7.5 per cent of the population), including 700,000 people under the age of 18.[40] Of these people, 590,000 — an underclass in a wealthy society — use the food banks on a regular basis.

In a similar manner to agencies specializing in food, there are others dealing with emergency shelter. There are 175 hostels for transients across Canada, 41 homes for single teenage mothers with children, and more than 1,500 childcare facilities for children who have either been removed from their families for reasons of abuse or whom the families feel would be better served in a special facility. There are also more than 2,000 homes for other kinds of needs — native friendship centres, shelters for women who are being abused by their husbands, homes for the psychiatrically and mentally handicapped, drop-in centres for seniors, and so on.[41]

Health Advocacy
There are hundreds of non-profits advocating for and offering services to people suffering from particular handicaps and diseases. The Association for Community Living, an organization serving the mentally handicapped, is one of the best organized.[42] Formerly the Canadian Association for the Mentally Retarded, it changed its name to reflect its primary objective of integrating the mentally handicapped into the community. This organization has 400 branches in communities across Canada providing a combination of day programs for the mentally handicapped and their parents, and organizing group homes. There are also provincial branches which, along with the national association, lobby governments on behalf of the mentally handicapped.

The Canadian Association for Community Living is a cross between a service organization and an advocacy group, a mix that is common for non-profit associations organized for a particular health need. There are hundreds of such associations specializing in every affliction that affects human beings. A better known one is the Canadian Cancer Society, which is able to raise more than $80 million annually, much of it through the efforts of armies of volunteers during its daffodil campaign every April. The Cancer Society finances research, public education and provides support to people suffering from the disease.[43] The Easter Seals campaign and the Muscular Dystrophy telethon are other high-profile campaigns. However, associations with a lower profile also follow this strategy of fund-raising to support research, provide service to the afflicted and advocacy on their behalf. The Canadian Diabetes Association, for example, amasses more than 50,000 volunteers to raise funds for its diabetes-month campaign each November.[44] There are 160 Diabetes Association chapters across Canada offering service to those in need and, like other health associations, provincial and national tiers doing advocacy with governments.

Other Community Organizations

In a similar manner to health organizations, arts councils have been formed across the country, offering service to artists, giving information to the public and lobbying government on behalf of artists. There are more than 500 local arts councils across Canada, with provincial tiers (the Ontario Arts Council), and with the Canadian Conference of the Arts and the Canada Council serving as apex organizations in Ottawa.[45]

The arts council may be seen as a community infrastructure for the arts. The 100 social planning and community councils across Canada serve a similar purpose in assessing community needs and advocating solutions.[46] Community information centres that publish listings (blue books in metropolitan areas) of the many services in their jurisdiction are also an important part of the infrastructure for non-profits in public service.[47] There are 73 such centres in Ontario alone. In addition, there are another 197 non-profit organizations across Canada affiliated with the Canadian Association of Volunteer Bureaus and Centres that recruit and refer volunteers to organizations in need, where they are trained and put into service.[48]

Arts councils, social planning and community councils, community information centres and volunteer centres form an infrastructure for non-profits. Like the organizations they assist, these are non-profits attempting to meet a social need with the assistance of charitable donations, government funding and volunteers.

Government-Sector Non-profits

All of the types of organizations discussed so far in this section operate independently of government, and depend upon volunteers, though some may receive a large share of their funding from government. In addition, there are other non-profits that either are working in areas served to a large extent by government or depend heavily upon government funding. For that reason, there is a tendency to view them as government-sector institutions. Yet they are incorporated independently of government and supplement their funding from government by their own fund-raising, fees from service, and volunteer labour.

Heritage institutions — museums, art galleries, historic sites, planetariums, zoos, botanical gardens — are examples of this type of organization.[49] Although a level of government directly administers many, more than 60 per cent operate under the administration of such non-profits as religious organizations, historical societies, co-operatives or institutions of higher education. These organizations earn much of their own revenues from memberships and admission fees, and like other non-profits have the assistance of volunteers.

Hospitals are another example of non-profits very dependent upon government. About 60 per cent of all beds are in hospitals administered by "lay" non-profit organizations, and another 11 per cent are in organizations sponsored by religious societies.[50] Public hospitals obtain more than 90 per cent of their operating revenues from provincial ministries of health as part of the provincial hospital insurance program.[51] Yet they undertake fundraising through their own foundations to help finance building costs, and utilize volunteers to supplement services.

Other extended care settings such as nursing homes, alcohol and drug abuse treatment centres, as well as centres for the emotionally disturbed, are also primarily non-profits that rely on similar sources as hospitals for their funding and labour support.[52] Institutions of higher education and research institutes follow this same pattern. Provincial and federal governments provide about 70 per cent of the income (1988–89).[53] Another ten per cent comes from fees, and the remainder is from gifts, donations and non-government grants.

CONCLUSIONS

The non-profits reviewed in this chapter provide a wide variety of services, including some of the most widely used and vital services in Canada. Not only is the range of services vast but the methods of organizing them also vary. There are services for which consumers or users enter into a commercial arrangement with the enterprise, much as with a private-sector service. For these entrepreneurial non-profits or social enterprises (Canadian Automobile Association, Blue Cross) the fees paid by the consumer or user of the service cover the costs.

There are other services (many youth programs, for example) in which users or their families pay for much of the cost, but there is also a large contribution from volunteers. Within this category, the portion borne by users can vary from a high percentage, as in competitive sports organizations, to a lower proportion, as in social housing.

The stereotypical non-profit in public service is for people in need (due to poverty, disability, disease) who either are unable or are not expected to pay for the service. There are thousands of these organizations across Canada ranging from the large well-known ones like the Red Cross to rape crisis centres, food banks, and family service agencies.

There are also a group of non-profits (hospitals, universities, heritage institutions) perceived as an extension of government because much of their funding comes from different levels of government. Yet these organizations operate independently of government, with their own boards of directors, separate fund-raising campaigns and volunteer support.

4

Mutual Non-profits

The non-profits discussed in Chapter 3 serve the general public. There are also non-profits that serve a defined membership, the members having a mutual interest that they seek to satisfy through the organization. These mutual non-profits[1] or mutual interest associations have the common feature of a membership who, according to the democratic principle of one-member/one-vote, elect a board of directors (in the case of a corporation) or an executive (for unincorporated associations) that is responsible for representing their interests. Therefore, mutual non-profits are similar to co-operatives in their membership structure, voting arrangements and their general orientation of attempting to serve the interests of members.

Unlike co-operatives, however, mutual non-profits are not part of a common movement. While all co-operative corporations have the word "co-operative" in their legal name as a symbol of their common affiliation, however weak, mutual non-profits taken as a whole lack a common identifier, even a symbolic one.

Some non-profits use the term "mutual" in describing themselves. Mutual benefit societies, for example, are associations of people, often of common religious or ethno-cultural heritage, that arrange services like insurance and burials for members. These societies date back to an earlier era when newcomers to Canada formed organizations based upon a common cultural bond to satisfy their social needs. As society has become modern-ized, and people have become involved in a multiplicity of specialized functions, mutual non-profits (a variation of the mutual benefit society) have been formed by people with common bonds such as a place of work, profession, business, religion or ethnic identity.

Mutual non-profits have a paradoxical social role: they draw people together in organizations based upon their common interests, but they also draw people apart, in that self-interest builds walls between organizations with unrelated interests. In that respect mutual non-profits transfer the individualization of modern societies to an organizational level, thereby creating a type of organizational individualization that causes them to focus upon their members' often very specialized interests. The individual organization transcends itself by forming relationships with other organizations with similar objectives. Through these bridging or tiering arrangements, local organizations with similar purposes create provincial levels, which in turn produce national structures with international affiliations.

Modern society therefore can be construed as a vast mosaic of mutual-interest organizations and related networks through which people find a type of social interconnectedness that overcomes in part the anomie of the modern world caused by the weakening of geographically specific communities. Whereas "community" in the traditional sense involves a comprehensive set of social relationships in which the same people relate to each other around many different activities, the communities of common interest of modern societies typically involve a group coming together for a very specific purpose. As a result, people usually find themselves in many different organizations (work, social, religious, political, recreational) and often with different individuals in each. Indeed, these involvements are so commonplace that people may not be able to note all of their own affiliations without a conscious effort.

Therefore a social map of Canada would involve tens of thousands of mutual-interest associations interconnected with organizations of overlapping interest spiralling across the country and indeed around the world. Not all mutual associations are equal in social influence; some represent the powerful and wealthy, while others represent the oppressed. Nor do all mutual associations work in harmony with each other. Even though all represent the interests of a defined membership, these interests can be in opposition to each other. Nevertheless, neither the social nor the economic impact of this phenomenon should be downplayed in importance. As shall be noted in this chapter, mutual-interest associations touch some of the most important aspects of our lives. Even though these organizations reproduce in part the individualization of the modern world, they are also a response to it, a response structured around a defined membership that pays fees in order to finance the organization and who control the organization through their votes. Therefore, mutual non-profits are neither private-sector nor government organizations, but rather fit within the social economy.

In the discussion that follows, mutual non-profits are divided into two broad categories: economic (unions, professional, managerial, business and consumer groups) and social (religious, ethno-cultural, recreational and political).[2] The economic organizations are normally financed by membership fees or dues, whereas social mutuals are more of a mixed bag in their financial arrangements, ranging from those that are covered by membership fees only to those that supplement contributions from members with private donations, government grants and volunteers (much like the non-profits in public service discussed in Chapter 3).

MUTUAL NON-PROFITS IN THE ECONOMY

Non-profits in the economy reflect distinct interest groups — labour, business, and consumer. Arguably, these non-profits are not involved in an economic function per se, but rather are seeking to promote and to regulate the interests of people who are. In doing so, however, they employ people, involve volunteers, and transact services with other businesses. Like other organizations of the social economy, they are both social and economic.

Labour Organizations

Associations of workers are among the oldest forms of non-profits, dating back to the mid-nineteenth century. They are also a classic example of a mutual-interest association in which members sharing a common employer finance their organization (normally unincorporated) through dues and also democratically elect an executive that represents their interests in establishing contracts dealing with such issues as pay and conditions of work.

The basic unit for unions is the local. About 80 per cent of Canadian workers are in locals affiliated with central unions, second-tier organizations that assist the locals with research, contract negotiating and in strikes should that need arise. By 1988, 3.8 million Canadians, more than one-third of the labour force, belonged to 15,176 union locals ranging in size from the United Food and Commercial Workers in Toronto with 39,308 members, and the Canadian Auto Workers in St. John's with 22,460 members, to some locals with only one or two members.[3]

Since the mid-1960s, the rate of unionization in Canada has remained relatively constant, though the composition of unions has altered. The most striking change has been in the numbers of members who are women — a four-fold increase in absolute numbers and nearly a two-fold increase as a percentage of women in the labour force. By 1988, women represented about 37 per cent, or three out of eight, of the members of Canadian unions. This change reflected both the increased participation of women in the labour force and the increased ability of unions, particularly white-collar unions, to organize women. The Canadian Union of Public Employees, one of the unions that has organized the white collar sector, has become the largest union in Canada with 1 of every 11 union members.

Unions also affiliate with each other in apex organizations (the Canadian Labour Congress, for example) that develop social policies on issues such as taxation, pensions, and childcare, and lobby government around labour's concerns. These apex organizations, the basis for "the labour movement," have undergone a major change in the growth of national affiliations at the expense of international affiliations, primarily with the AFL-CIO (American Federation of Labour/Congress of Industrial Organizations). Since the mid-1960s, representation by internationals has declined from 67 per cent to 33 per cent of all Canadian union members. National unions now represent 53 per cent of Canadian workers and government unions another 14 per cent. Nearly 6 out of 10 Canadian union members are in locals affiliated with the Canadian Labour Congress in Ottawa. The CLC also has affiliates in each province. About one-third of CLC union members are in locals also affiliated with the American apex organization, the AFL-CIO, and another 6 per cent of Canadian union members are in locals affiliated exclusively with the AFL-CIO.

There are also a number of smaller affiliations outside of the CLC and AFL-CIO networks. In English Canada there are the Canadian Federation of Labour (construction unions), the Confederation of Canadian Unions, and the Canadian National Federation of Independent Unions. In French Canada the affiliations are the Confédération des syndicats nationaux, the Centrale de l'enseignement du Québec and the Centrale des syndicats democratiques.

In addition to national and provincial affiliations, 112 municipalities in Canada have labour councils. This not only involves cities like Winnipeg, Edmonton and Moncton, but smaller communities such as Smiths Falls, Medicine Hat and Corner Brook. These organizations represent the unions within a particular municipality in their dealings with local government. Their role is analogous to the CLC in its relationship to the federal government. Much of the service provided through unions is from volunteers elected to the executive of their locals. However, the large unions and the apex organizations are also businesses with paid staff and offices. These expenses are covered from dues paid by members, which in 1988 amounted to nearly $746 million.

Professional Associations

With the movement toward a service-based economy, it has become not uncommon for professionals such as teachers and nurses to either belong to major unions or to have their own unions, and for others, such as university professors, to form independent locals. In addition, there is a vast array of professional associations representing the interests of members much like unions do. Although professional associations and unions serve somewhat different purposes, both are examples of mutual non-profits representing the interests of their members. It is possible —indeed not unusual — for people to belong to both a union and a professional association.

Unlike a union local that represents the employees of one employer, a professional association brings together members who share a profession in common but usually with differing workplaces. Professional associations represent the interests of their members to outside organizations such as government. They also encourage educational opportunities for their members through conferences and periodicals, and regulate the profession by certifying new entrants.

For professions such as medical doctors with fee schedules determined through negotiation between their provincial association and the provincial government, the difference between a professional association and a union is quite subtle. But since doctors are primarily self-employed, and their association is not negotiating a salary, there is still an arguable and important difference.

Associations Canada 1991 lists about 2,000 professional organizations, generally the larger ones. At least one major or umbrella association exists for each profession, along with a myriad of more specialized organizations, also with their own subspecialties, that affiliate with the umbrella association.

Let's take medical doctors again as an example. The apex organization, the Canadian Medical Association, has 46,000 members who may also belong to provincial associations. Then, there are numerous affiliates as well, some with their own sub-associations. For example, 16 faculties of medicine are affiliated with the Association of Canadian Medical Colleges, which is affiliated in turn with both the Canadian Association of University Teachers, and the Canadian Medical Association. Other specialized organizations affiliated with the CMA include the Association of Canadian Pharmaceutical Physicians, Canadian Academy of Sports Medicine, Canadian Association of Medical Microbiologists, and the Canadian Life Insurance Medical Officers' Association.

In addition, there are medical associations not directly affiliated with the CMA, and a myriad of associations for medical staff other than doctors (nurses, physiotherapists, medical secretaries, and so on). Many of these other healthcare professions have their own maze of subspecialties and affiliates. Then there are associations of professionals involved in different types or aspects of healthcare (the Canadian Public Health Association, for example).

Similar complex networks of associations, with provincial, national and international affiliations, exist for other occupations as well. In some cases these associations are highly specialized and do not involve a large number of members — for example, legal translators, nordic ski instructors, provincial court judges, chefs de cuisine, billiard and snooker referees, and seaplane pilots.

Professional associations may also be formed according to other factors such as ethnicity (for example, the Association of Polish Engineers of Canada), language (Alliance ontarienne des professeurs de français), religion (Federation of English-speaking Catholic Teachers), or gender (Association of Canadian Women Composers).

Given this interweaving of professional associations, the average member may have several affiliations; that is, a central association with an affiliation according to location and sub-specialization, as well as a sub-association based upon gender, ethnicity, or religion.

Managerial Associations

Managers, a group that is at times unsympathetic to labour unions, have nevertheless formed their own mutual-interest organizations. The organizational pattern is similar to other professional groups. There are central umbrella organizations (for example, the Canadian Institute of Management, with 22 local branches). There is also a myriad of more specialized associations for groups as diverse as principals, police chiefs, chamber of commerce executives, art museum directors, and golf superintendents.

The groupings are not only national, but also regional (Administrators of Medium-Sized Libraries of Ontario; Association of Registrars of Nurses of Newfoundland). And as in other professions, there are associations based on culture (B.C. Union of Indian Chiefs), language (International Association of French-Speaking Directors of Educational Institutions), religion (Canadian Catholic School Trustees Association), and gender (Canadian Association of Women Executives and Entrepreneurs). These sub-associations also tie their members into broader social networks based upon ethnicity and religion, to be discussed subsequently in this chapter.

Business Organizations

There are thousands of associations formed by businesses with a mutual interest.[4] These non-profits are member-based organizations financed through dues or membership fees much like a union or professional association. Since the purpose of these associations is to promote the interests of the private-sector businesses which form them, it may seem inappropriate to suggest that business associations are a part of the social economy. However, the business community is in fact supporting an alternative to the primary structure for which it advocates. Like other forms of non-profits, business associations are corporations without shares set up to promote a social objective, without direct pecuniary gain to its members.

The most basic business association in Canada is the local chamber of commerce or board of trade. It is a member-based organization that can be found in every city and town throughout Canada. Local business people join these organizations, which in turn communicate with members and advocate for their members to government on issues such as taxation and pollution standards. According to the Canadian Chamber of Commerce, the federal organization, there are 942 such associations across Canada.[5] As with other member-based organizations, there are provincial tiers, though the four Atlantic provinces have one chamber of commerce representing their region. Five hundred local chambers of commerce and boards of trade have decided to become members of the Canadian Chamber of Commerce, the federal tier. The provincial and federal tiers represent business concerns to the appropriate level of government.

In addition to chambers of commerce, there are some other broadly based general business associations. The Canadian Federation of Independent Business lobbies government on behalf of 88,000 member-businesses (of up to 100 employees) across Canada,[6]often promoting its agenda of reduced government spending. In addition to its head office in Toronto, there are nine regional branches from which members are served. The Business Council on National Issues is the voice of 150 large corporations in Canada (some of the members are General Motors, Royal Bank, Inco, Stelco) with 1.5 million employees and assets in excess of $1 trillion.[7] The Business Council endeavours to ensure that "Canadian chief executives play an influential role in international economic trade and foreign affairs domains."[8] During the Conservative governments of the 1980s and early '90s, the Business Council has been very effective in promoting free trade and advocating reduced corporate taxation.

Along with these general business associations, there are others that are specialized by market sector. Like unions and professional associations, there is usually an umbrella organization within a particular market, with provincial tiers and local branches, which in turn are subdivided into more specialized associations also with tiers and their own affiliates. Agriculture will serve as an example. Some associations in the agricultural industry are co-operatives (see Chapter 2). However, there are hundreds of others that are simply non-profit associations, with varying degrees of specificity.

The Canadian Federation of Agriculture is the umbrella organization for agricultural producers. Founded in 1935, its members are nine provincial federations of local producers, and product-specific associations (such as the Canadian Chicken Marketing Agency, Canadian Egg Producers Council, the Canadian Broiler Hatching Egg Marketing Agency), each of which brings together producers of a particular product.[9] There are other associations of agricultural producers, some of which maintain affiliations to the Canadian Federation of Agriculture but also tie into their own networks, for such products as sugar beets, honey, roses, different breeds of livestock, as well as for somewhat unusual animals like greyhounds, bison and snails.

Associations also exist for products related to agriculture, such as seeds, fertilizers, and water wells, and for related services such as soil science, pest management, and plowing. Associations have formed among those adhering to different philosophies of growing (organic, for example). The processing and marketing of foods is closely allied to agriculture, and does not take a back seat to it in spawning representative associations. The Food Institute of Canada represents 250 corporations involved in food processing. The Canadian Food Brokers Association has 241 corporate members organized through 10 provincial associations. Then there are product-specific associations for wine, soft drinks, potato chips, snack foods, specialty foods, and dairy products.

The pattern for agricultural associations is repeated for every type of business.[10] For manufacturing, the Canadian Manufacturers' Association, with divisions in each province, is the central association, with manufacturers for specific products forming their own associations. Some of these (steel producers, tobacco, pharmaceuticals, automotive parts, chemical products, nuclear energy) are major associations themselves. For construction, the Canadian Home Builders' Association, with 10 provincial councils represents 12,000 corporations involved in residential construction. This association has 70 affiliates, all related to residential construction, and some large associations (plumbing and heating) in their own right. Every mutual business association spawns its own sub-associations. The imagination, it seems, is the only limit upon the degree of specialization.

There are also business associations to facilitate trade and business exchanges with countries throughout the world (the Canada-Egypt Business Council, for example) and others for members of various ethno-cultural groups, both national (Canadian Council for Native Business) and local (Chinese Businessmen's Association of Edmonton). These associations help businesspeople with a common ethno-cultural heritage to form a social connection, and they also tie into the spiral of cultural networks. And like other interest groups in the economy, businesswomen have formed separate associations (Canadian Association of Women Business Owners).

The grouping pattern for business associations — as for other types of associations — helps businesspeople to connect with each other, if only superficially, around their common interests, and also divides people from each other by type of business location, ethnicity, gender, and so on. In the tendency to associate, both connection and division occur.

Consumer Organizations

In much the same way that labour and businesses have their associations, there are associations to represent consumer interests. There are some factors which would make it seem unnecessary for consumers to form their own associations. First, governments, through their departments of consumer and corporate affairs and other departments set standards by which businesses must abide. The Standards Council of Canada, the federal agency responsible for establishing standards, is assisted by non-profit organizations that recommend standards for particular products and services. Among these organizations is the Canadian Standards Association, representing about 7,000 members (corporations, government agencies, consumers) with five regional offices across Canada.[11] It recommends standards for a wide range of products, from medical equipment to hockey helmets.

Second, there is some self-regulation by businesses through the Better Business Bureaus in each province, which attempt to provide some ethical standards and also deal with consumer complaints.[12] Some industries create associations to police themselves (advertising, cable television, manufacturers and retailers), though the best examples of self-regulation are among professionals (lawyers, doctors and so on).

Third, consumer or user-based co-operatives (see Chapter 2) also represent consumer interests. Generally, these are community-based associations for specific services, though as noted, the local associations also form provincial and national federations. Although co-operatives and buying clubs are the predominant structures for consumers desiring to control commerce, some associations of this sort are simply non-profits; the Canadian Automobile Association (discussed in Chapter 3) fits this category, as do the hundreds of memorial societies across Canada which help people to arrange moderately priced funerals.

But although the mechanisms mentioned above help to protect the consumer interest, many consumers feel that a stronger consumer voice is needed. Therefore they have organized their own associations to bring additional concerns to the attention of government and industry and to lobby for stronger forms of consumer protection than business and professional groups might provide. Consumer associations also help to educate their members about choices available to them through their publications that members receive.

The Consumers' Association of Canada, founded in 1947, represents a broad range of consumer interests. It has 150,000 members and 10 provincial offices. It is also affiliated with the International Organization of Consumers Unions, as well as the Consumers Union-U.K. and the Consumers Union-U.S.[13] Although the Consumers' Association of Canada has a Quebec office, there is another Quebec association, the Association des consommateurs du Québec, with six offices in the province. A more focused consumer-awareness group is the Automobile Protection Association, publisher of its annual car-buying guide, *Lemon Aid*. There are also consumer awareness associations dealing with a variety of health issues (for example, the Canadian Council on Smoking and Health).

Associations of consumers, like those for business and labour and professional groups, support their objectives primarily through fees from members. As we turn to member-based associations established primarily for social purposes, financial dependence upon external sources is more prevalent. Nevertheless, these organizations also employ people, involve volunteers, and transact services for which they pay. In other words, they are social organizations with economic import.

MUTUAL SOCIAL ORGANIZATIONS

Ethno-Cultural Organizations

Traditionally, first-generation Canadians settled in communities of common origin. The prototype was the native community (the aboriginal peoples) based upon a tightly knit tribal culture. As people from countries throughout the world came to Canada, they were attracted to communities where the residents shared their culture, language and religion. With time, however, and with the birth of second and subsequent generations, this configuration of homogeneous ethno-cultural communities has changed to one of heterogeneity. In cosmopolitan cities like Toronto and Montreal, people whose ancestors originated from more than 100 different countries often live and work side by side. Although homogenous neighborhoods for first-generation Canadians still exist, and to a lesser extent for subsequent generations, they lack the uniformity of more traditional ghetto or tribal cultures. Members of an ethno-cultural group are not situated in just one location, but in many locations, both within one city and throughout the country.

In order to maintain traditions and to help each other, ethnocultural groups have formed a multitude of associations. These associations not only help members of a group to assist and relate to each other, but also represent the concerns of their group to various levels of government and to other communities. *The Ethnic Directory of Canada* lists about 6,000 ethno-cultural associations which are neither private-sector businesses nor government organizations.[14] These are voluntary social organizations established by the members of an ethnic group to serve their community. Among the larger ethnic groups, there are typically hundreds of voluntary associations.

Let us illustrate the point by selecting the Ukrainian community of Toronto, a large well-organized group with deep roots, though until recently not based upon an internationally recognized nation.[15] At the time the *Ethnic Directory of Canada* was published (1983), this community had about 130 mutual associations, in addition to a range of commercial enterprises such as restaurants, publishers and book stores. Among its social organizations in Toronto were 23 churches, 17 credit unions, 4 seniors' homes, 6 fraternal societies (including veterans), 9 music groups (including opera, choirs and ensembles), 6 youth groups, 3 student groups, 4 social centres, numerous educational, cultural, historical, scientific and research societies, 7 professional and business groups (including writers and engineers), 8 women's associations, and a range of other organizations for refugees, social welfare, daycare, art, dance, radio, recreation, and, not least, political organizations. In other words, the Ukrainians of Toronto are like a society within a society, connected to Ukrainians in other parts of Canada through the Ukrainian-Canadian Congress, appropriately headquartered in Winnipeg, with provincial councils in Alberta, Saskatchewan, British Columbia and Ontario, provinces where there are large Ukrainian populations. The Ukrainian-Canadian Congress represents 32 other Ukrainian organizations which form its members. It in turn belongs to the Ukrainian World Congress.

Similar networks are found in every ethno-cultural group in Canada. Associations are formed to meet needs which are not satisfied either through the private sector or through government. Local associations with a common purpose link up with each other and with related associations within their ethno-cultural network. For example, the Native Women's Association of Canada draws together native women's groups from across Canada to represent their concerns within both local native communities and other national native associations (Assembly of First Nations) as well as directly to Canada's governments. Other ethno-cultural groups, both large (the Canadian Polish Congress, the National Congress of Italian-Canadians, the Chinese-Canadian National Council, the German-Canadian Congress) and small (the National Council of Ghanaian Canadians, the Armenian National Federation, the Estonian Central Council in Canada, Federation des associations Lao du Canada) have formed national associations, bridging more specific associations within their communities, that speak on behalf of that group at the national level. Many of the apex organizations for Canada's ethno-cultural groups have international affiliations, and 38 of these organizations belong to another apex association in Canada, the Canadian Ethnocultural Council, which deals with the federal government on such common concerns as race relations, encouraging multiculturalism, employment equity and the accreditation of foreign degrees.[16] This association represents a positive commentary upon the Canadian experience in multiculturalism in that groups with a history of violent and seemingly intractable conflict in their countries of origin, such as Jews and Arabs, can participate together, as the Canadian Jewish-Congress and the Canadian Arab Federation have done as founding members of the Canadian Ethnocultural Council, in solving problems of common concern.

Religious Organizations

Religious organizations operate from the same principle as ethno-cultural organizations, the primary difference being that instead of a common culture, the bond of association is religious faith. Although the rules governing religions differ, in general these are voluntary non-profit associations organized through the basic unit of the congregation. Membership is both a theological concept as well as a social one, the latter, as in other types of mutual non-profit associations, involving the right to participate in the affairs and the obligation to help meet the expenses of the congregation.

The *Yearbook of Canadian and American Churches* lists 86 distinct religious bodies in Canada, most of which are Christian.[17] There are also Buddhist, Hindu, Jewish and Muslim congregations. In 1991, there were 20,582 congregations with about 2.5 million confirmed members.[18] The number of those just adhering to a religion (the inclusive membership), but without confirmed membership is much larger, 15.6 million Canadians. In general, religious observance is on the decline in Canada.[19] At the end of the Second World War about two-thirds of Canadians attended their congregation weekly. The most recent figures estimate that weekly religious observance involves about one-quarter of the population. The decline in religious observance is particularly marked in metropolitan areas, among the younger generation, and for the "mainline" Protestant churches. Evangelical churches have been increasing in both their membership and attendance throughout the 1980s.

The social and financial arrangements for religious organizations vary, but generally they are similar to those of other member-based mutual associations. The United Church of Canada, for example, is Canada's second largest religious organization, formed in 1925 out of a union between the Congregational, Methodist and Presbyterian denominations.[20] Like other member-based mutual associations, the United Church is organized by tiers, the most basic unit or form of association being the congregation, of which there are about 4,000, with more than 800,000 confirmed members. The members of a congregation, each with one vote, elect a board of trustees that is legally responsible for the congregation. The United Church is a denominational religion, meaning that the congregations are not just autonomous organizations but also participate in formulating church policies, which in turn guide the congregations. The congregations send delegates to presbyteries, 99 regional groupings of about 30–35 churches each. Members of the presbyteries in turn can participate in one of 13 conferences (the next highest policy body), which in turn select delegates to a bi-annual National General Council, the supreme policy body. Like other types of associations, this tiering arrangement extends into the international domain. The United Church of Canada is affiliated with the World Council of Churches, in Geneva, Switzerland, which in turn is affiliated with the International Council of World Religions and Cultures.

In the United Church, as in other religions, the congregation is responsible for meeting its expenses. The contribution by members to meet the organization's expenses is not a fee, in the usual sense applied by mutual non-profits, but a donation or a tithe. Church congregations are charitable organizations (the United Church being a charitable trust), and therefore donations are tax-deductible. On average in Canada, confirmed members of religious congregations contribute $370 per year, and other types of adherents donate $199.[21] Religious organizations also rely upon volunteers who assist in ceremonies and also with related activities. More than 1.5 million Canadians are volunteers in religious organizations.[22] Although religious congregations are established to meet social objectives, they also serve an economic purpose, for example, as employers of 28,000 clergy. In total, religious congregations in Canada expend more than $700 million. The assets of the United Church alone are more than $2.5 billion. Religions invest their liquid assets and also donate money to other charitable organizations (on average, 20 per cent of total revenues) that they want to support.[23]

Religious organizations serve other purposes as well. They sponsor a broad range of services both within the congregation and also more generally. The most basic service is the sabbath school which congregations organize for the younger generation. Some religions also sponsor their own schools and colleges, as well as summer camps, international relief agencies, counselling services, children's aid societies, hospitals, memorial societies, refugee societies, women's, student, youth and seniors' groups, social issue organizations dealing with peace, environmental concerns, temperance and justice. They also sponsor recreation groups and cultural organizations involved in Biblical studies, history, radio, television and book publishing. All religious groups are involved in sponsoring related associations, though among Canada's religions, the Catholic church, the largest denomination in the country, takes a particularly active role in this regard. These related associations are a method of serving the practical needs of members and also serve an evangelical purpose.

It should also be noted that associations started by religious orders in some cases shed their heritage and evolve into secular organizations. St. John Ambulance, founded by the Catholic Church during the Crusades of the eleventh century as the Most Venerable Order of the Hospital of St. John of Jerusalem, and touting itself as the oldest charitable organization in the world, is but one example of such an organization.[24] Its 11,000 brigades in communities across Canada offer instruction in first aid, its name the only remaining vestige of its religious past.

Social Clubs

There is throughout Canada a vast number of non-profit clubs or associations which people join to meet mutual social needs.[25] These can be both formal organizations and informal associations. Some are tied together by ethnic and religious bonds of association (Loyal Orange Association; Imperial Order of Daughters of the Empire). The main purposes of clubs with ethnic and religious bonds of association are to maintain and promote, at least among the members, their common heritage.

The bond of association in social clubs can also be university attendance, as in a fraternity or sorority, or other types of common experience, for example, having fought in a war. There are many war veterans' associations in Canada, with common bonds to a branch of the service (air force, navy), a particular war, or ethno-cultural background. However, the most extensive is the Royal Canadian Legion, embracing nearly 600,000 veterans of wars and their families in 1,750 branches across Canada.[26] Formed after the First World War, the Legion is both a social club for its members, who pay a modest fee, and a social service club that raises money (through its poppy campaign, for example) for both its members' needs and for those of the community at large. In 1990 the Legion contributed more than $43 million and nearly one million hours of volunteer time to charitable causes such as support for needy veterans, seniors' housing and home-support programs (like Meals on Wheels), geriatric medicine, and youth programs. It employs about 8,000 people, both full- and part-time. Like most major associations, the Legion is a society within a society, with 10 provincial councils and a national committee elected at a bi-annual convention. Although it is larger than most social clubs in Canada, both in its membership and service to the community, it is by no means an exception to the pattern of people with a common bond coming together for their mutual benefit and for the benefit of society.

In addition to ethnicity, religion, and a shared experience such as war, the bond on which associations are based can be gender, success in business (the Canadian Club, the Empire Club) or simply a common intellectual interest. The hundreds of learned societies across Canada are examples of such associations. These range from large mainstream organizations (Canadian Society for the Study of Education) with provincial and international affiliations, to others that are quite refined, even esoteric (Association for Psychophysical and Psychospiritual Studies, Association of Concern for Ultimate Reality and Meaning, B.C. Society for Skeptical Inquiry). Many learned societies are for academics. Others are broader and involve people with a common hobby, for example, the Canadian Railroad Historical Association, with 15 chapters across Canada.[27] This organization draws together individuals with an interest in the fascinating history of Canada's railways, by utilizing newsletters and public speakers to disseminate information and by maintaining libraries and museums for the public. It also takes on practical projects such as remodelling railroad cars and stations.

Genealogical associations are another type of organization based upon a common social interest.[28] There are dozens of such societies in Canada, by region, by ethnicity, and also bound together in provincial associations, the Canadian Federation of Genealogical and Family History Societies. Genealogical associations help their members to trace their family trees. They also disseminate information through their publications and seminars and undertake genealogical projects such as the indexing by region of Canada's first census in 1871 and ensuring that there is proper legislative protection for cemeteries.

Recreational groups, as distinct from organizations providing training and participation in competitive sports, are another important type of mutual association. There are so many such associations — both formal and informal — that even the thousands listed in directories do not do justice to the phenomenon. These include such pastimes as camping, fishing, hunting, gliding, boating, bridge, checkers, keeping particular types of pets (the Canadian Cat Association), roller skating, DX radios, skipping, snowshoeing, therapeutic riding, and the many associations for specific cars (Dodge Brothers Club Incorporated, Mustang, Citroën). The same pattern is found in the arts as a form of recreation. There are many musical societies, both general and for specific types of music (chamber, jazz, military, folk, blues), choral groups, dance (tap, folk), societies for people with an interest in a particular musical instrument (classical guitar, ukulele, drum), craft groups, literary societies, film societies, and even societies of ice carvers. These clubs, although primarily social, also offer marketing opportunities for businesses and may promote products specific to their interest among their members, thereby serving an economic purpose as well.

The tendency for people to form associations based upon a mutual social interest, however refined that may be, is strong in a modern society in which there are relatively weak bonds between people in a geographic location, and in which communication across vast distances is easy and inexpensive. Under those circumstances, a vast array of communities of common social interest have been formed by individuals who may associate for that reason only. Symbolic of how highly specialized these mutual interest associations can become are the Doctor Who Clubs, involving about 500 Canadians in associations across Canada. They share an interest in the BBC science fiction series, "Doctor Who," a television program that has been out of production since 1989.[29]

How do people with such a specialized interest find each other, particularly when the group lacks financing to do much promotion? With respect to Doctor Who, the clubs are often initiated by a core group of friends, and others become involved through knowing someone in the group or through hearing about it. The members of the clubs meet and share videos of the program, and the community of interest inevitably takes on a social meaning that goes beyond the original purpose of the group. The decision by the BBC to end the Doctor Who series has reduced the number of clubs in Canada. However, members still share reruns of the program. Some members of the Doctor Who clubs in Britain have taken their social groups in a somewhat different direction by launching legal action against the BBC to get the program back into production.

Mutual Self-Help

There are mutual associations set up to meet the interests of their members in other more serious fields of endeavour. In healthcare, for example, there is an array of mutual self-help groups for people with various forms of addictions or other afflictions. Alcoholics Anonymous, a self-help group for alcoholics, is the prototype.[30] There are about 4,000 AA groups across Canada, each self-supporting through the volunteer labour and donations of the participants. Although there are many components contributing to the success of AA programs, a primary aspect is the social support that members of a group give to each other. In the AA approach, people sharing a common problem come together to help each other overcome their affliction. Like mutual associations in general the members connect with each other around their shared experience. The AA approach to mutual self-help (12-step groups) has been used for other addictions (Overeaters Anonymous, Neurotics Anonymous, Cocaine Anonymous, Narcotics Anonymous, Sex and Love Addicts Anonymous).

Families also have formed mutual self-help groups to help cope with a member who has schizophrenia or Alzheimer's disease. A growing family self-help network is the Parents and Friends of Gays and Lesbians, to help parents deal with feelings of guilt and shame. Other parents' mutual self-help groups are Parents Without Partners, involving 145,000 people in 145 chapters and such widows' groups as Widows Helping Widows and Widows in Self-Help.

Mutual self-help groups often emerge in areas where there is a level of service already provided by government, church and social service agencies; for example, the Seventh Step Societies, which help people in trouble with the law to become reintegrated into society.[31] In general, the established self-help groups have an organizational structure that helps new groups to get started. However, the emergence of these mutual self-help groups also reflects a deficiency in the level of service available from government and social service agencies. They also reflect a pattern that is found throughout mutual associations whereby people relate best to others who share their interest, no matter how specific that may be. In the case of mutual self-help groups, the shared interest is either an affliction or a source of discomfort and even distress, which members of the group help each other to overcome.

The national volunteer study of 1986–87 indicated that more than one million Canadians participated in at least one mutual self-help organization of this type.[32] Moreover, the involvement in such groups is intensive and can be very time consuming.

Neighborhood Groups

Mutual aid is also found when the residents of a neighborhood organize around a common need. The prototypes are residents' and ratepayers' associations and tenants' associations. Ratepayers' and tenants' groups also form their own coalitions (Confederation of Resident and Ratepayer Associations) to lobby on one particular issue — reducing property taxes being a common one for ratepayers, and limiting rent increases being typical for tenants.

Heightened concern about crime has also caused the residents of neighborhoods to form mutual associations to protect their children. Through the Block Parents programs found across Canada, certain houses within a neighborhood are designated as safe havens for school children who feel threatened.[33] Block Parents, which originated in the United States, is usually organized through the Home and School or Parent-Teacher Associations at schools, another type of neighborhood mutual association. The local police provide support in promoting the Block Parents programs, assisting them to get started by screening the safe houses and instructing both school children and parents on how to use the programs.

This community-police liaison also can be found in programs such as Neigborhood Watch, designed to improve security in communities, and its spin-offs such as Vertical Watch for apartment buildings, Business Watch for shopkeepers and Caring Communities for Ontario Housing projects. As communities have become more impersonal, these organizations, assisted in their formation by the crime prevention units of the local police, help people to become more vigilant.

Mutual Socio-Political Organizations

All of the organizations discussed to this point are based upon a defined membership who come together to meet a mutual interest. In most mutual associations, the members bear the financial costs (through fees or dues), supply volunteer labour as needed and also reap the benefits. There are some mutual associations, however, that receive funding from government (both direct grants and tax deductions for charitable donations) and from private donors.

Although mutual associations are set up to meet the common needs of their members, they may also benefit a community extending beyond the membership. In some cases, the participating members are a subset of a broader group whom they may also seek to represent. Religious organizations differentiate between "confirmed" and "inclusive" members, the latter having a more nominal affiliation. Ethno-cultural, home and school associations, seniors' and feminist groups are also of this type. In feminist organizations, for example, the participating members feel, with justification, that they speak on behalf of a larger group of women. There are thousands of organizations with a defined membership and a broader public who has lesser ties to the group. Canada's political parties fall into this category. They have members who pay a fee and in some cases may volunteer for other tasks such as the executive of the local riding association or helping in an election, and then there is a broader group who have weaker allegiances, whose participation may only be to keep a sign on their lawn or to vote on a regular basis for the local candidate of a particular party.

Environmental groups are another example of mutual associations with a socio-political agenda that also enlist support from a broader public. *The Green List*, an annual publication, includes about 1,800 environmental organizations, some very specific and

others more broadly based.[34] Among the larger groups are
Greenpeace, with about 400,000 members in Canada and 3 mil-
lion worldwide;[35] Friends of the Earth, with 25,000 members in
Canada and also part of an international network operating in 43
countries with nearly one million members;[36] The Canadian
Wildlife Federation with more than a half a million members;
Pollution Probe; Energy Probe; the Canadian Arctic Resources
Committee; the Federation of Ontario Naturalists. There are dozens of associations dealing with a particular form of wildlife
(wolves, cage birds, wildflowers) or a particular location (the
Great Lakes, Carrot River) or a very specific issue (metro gar-
bage). The large national associations also have their provincial
tiers. The Canadian Environmental Network, based in Ottawa,
serves as an umbrella association for the movement, and it affiliates with the Environment Liaison Centre International.[37] About
180,000 Canadians are formal volunteers in environmental organizations.[38] Many others, who are not active volunteers, contribute money either as members or through additional donations.
These organizations also have corporate donors and receive
some government grants.

Concern about the exploitation of women has also led to a
large number of feminist organizations. The National Action
Committee on the Status of Women (NAC) serves as an apex
organization for about 500 feminist groups representing 3 million individuals.[39] NAC maintains offices in each province and
in the territories, which attempt to deal with feminist concerns in
those jurisdictions. The types of organizations affiliated with
NAC include other national women's organizations, women's
centres, service delivery groups, native women's groups,
women's committees of churches, labour organizations and political parties. It is difficult to estimate the total number of feminist organizations in Canada. However, the Canada Women's
Movement Archives had a mailing list of 4,000 groups in 1991 —
a list that did not include groups opposed to the feminist movement (Real Women of Canada or "Pro-Life" groups opposing
abortions) and did not include women's social clubs and
women's auxiliaries for hospitals.[40]

The peace movement is another example of a mutual organization relating to a broader public. The Canadian Peace Alliance
is an umbrella group that serves the same function as the National Action Committee does for feminists.[41] The CPA repre-

sents 300 member organizations, some coalitions themselves (the Coalition for Nuclear Disarmament). There are peace councils in communities throughout Canada, as well as associations in which the bond is a profession, an ethno-cultural identity or gender. There are also counter groups such as the Canadian Coalition for Peace Through Strength, a national group that was created in the mid-1980s in response to the peace movement.[42] As its name implies, it argued that the road to peace was through military power. When peace groups organized a rally, it would organize a counter rally, thereby getting publicity for itself and for its cause. The collapse of the Soviet Bloc in Eastern Europe has weakened both the main peace movement and its opponents.

The environmental, feminist and peace movements have spawned the largest number of mutual associations devoted to socio-political issues, but there are thousands of others devoted to a broad range of issues. These include civil liberties and human rights organizations such as the Canadian Civil Liberties Association and its provincial affiliates, and the grey power movement (One Voice — The Canadian Seniors Network; Canadian Coalition of Senior Citizens). Then there are organizations both for the increased use of French in English Canada (Canadian Parents for French) and against (Alliance for the Preservation of English). Other issues that include many advocacy groups are free trade, rights of people with various forms of physical and psychological handicaps, injured workers, prisoner's rights, capital punishment, victims of violence and drunk drivers, smoking (for and against) and advocates of daycare. Mutual associations formed for a set of socio-political concerns may also branch out through coalitions with other organizations. The Action Canada Network, a broad coalition that originally formed in opposition to free trade, is one example of such a coalition, as is the Ecumenical Coalition for Economic Justice, an association of churches focusing on social issues.

In a country such as Canada, there are many associations devoted to socio-political issues. Although these organizations are based on a membership, they also straddle the line between mutual non-profits, a primary purpose of which is to serve a defined membership, and non-profits in public service (as discussed in Chapter 3). It is stretching the point to suggest that the Canadian Civil Liberties Association, to use but one example, is primarily servicing a membership. Member-based socio-political associations are both mutuals and public-service groups.

CONCLUSIONS

Mutual non-profits can be placed in two broad categories: economic and social. Economic mutual non-profits are unions, professional and managerial associations, as well as business and consumer organizations. In general, these organizations have a clearly defined membership that pays a due or fee in order to support their objectives. The members, each with one vote, elect the organization's board, or executive (if there isn't an incorporation, as for unions), and the members are the beneficiaries of the organization's services. Although the organization might also view itself as undertaking a public service (for instance, trade unions are active in a broader range of social issues), serving members' interests is their primary objective. If the members see no tangible benefit for themselves, they would be unlikely to pay fees and to remain committed to the organization.

Benefit to members is also a primary force in many types of social organizations, for example, ethno-cultural associations, religious congregations, social and recreational clubs and mutual self-help groups. However, the base of funding is broader than for economic associations, often involving government and donors, and the participating members may also be linked to a broader group (for example, the confirmed and inclusive members of a religion). As mutual organizations with a social bond of association become political, they tend to straddle the line between benefit to members and public benefit. In that respect, feminist, environmental and peace associations, for examples, are a cross between mutual associations and those in public service, discussed in Chapter 3.

Although mutual associations have been classified as either economic or social, both types of organizations have social dimensions in that they draw together a group of people sharing a common interest, and both types have an economic impact in that they engage in commerce, and often have employees. Through providing a service to their members, who each have one vote in the governance, they have some similarity to co-operatives. Indeed, co-operatives were formed from the same tradition of mutual self-help as many of the organizations discussed in this chapter.

3
Case Studies

Community Economic Development

The mutual non-profit is a type of community in which individuals associate with each other around shared interests. The proliferation of associations based upon mutual interest is a modern phenomenon reflecting in part the weakening of geographic communities. However, geographic communities still play an important role in modern Canada, and an important aspect of activities within the social economy has been to strengthen geographic communities, particularly in the underdeveloped regions of the country.

Since its beginnings, Canada has had an uneven mosaic of development. In response to this problem, governments have attempted to provide financial incentives to private-sector businesses to invest more heavily in the poorer regions of the country. This conventional strategy has not overcome the problem. In recent years an alternative within the social economy — the community economic development (CED) strategy — has achieved some popularity. This approach involves local geographically defined communities taking control of their own development. After reviewing the conventional strategy, this chapter discusses various CED approaches.

REGIONAL INEQUALITY

Canada is made up of regions with varying degrees of prosperity. This problem has its roots in the foundations of the country, and it has continued to the present, albeit with some shifts between the haves and have-nots. The mosaic of regional inequality in Canada has been well documented by Paul Phillips in his book, *Regional Disparities*.[1] The problem can be illustrated through some general regional comparisons, such as the lower personal income and higher unemployment in the Atlantic region relative to the rest of Canada. However, as Phillips notes, this type of description is partly misleading. Ontario, on average, has had the highest per capita income and lowest unemployment rates among the provinces since World War II; but this prosperity has been concentrated in the southern industrial belt, which has had a disproportionate share of Canada's heavy industry and which has been the favoured location of subsidiaries of multi-nationals, most headquartered in the United States.[2] Since the Free Trade Agreement between Canada and the United States, there are doubts whether the privileged status of southwestern Ontario will endure. There has been a shrinking of the manufacturing sector, as industries shift their production to the United States. Nevertheless, southwestern Ontario still contains a disproportionate share of the province's industry. Other parts of the province — the resource-based north with many single-industry communities, and the east, relying on agriculture and light industry — have lacked the prosperity of the industrial belt.

This type of imbalance exists throughout the country. In Newfoundland, for example, there is much greater prosperity on the Avalon peninsula than in the rest of the province because St. John's is the main commercial centre and the focus of government activity. The Northern Peninsula, with its reliance upon the depressed fishing industry, has been described as "one of the least privileged areas of Newfoundland, which is itself disadvantaged in Canada as a whole."[3] Its official unemployment rate is between 20 and 25 per cent, and its residents are heavily dependent upon welfare and other forms of government support to maintain a minimum level of income.[4] In New Brunswick there is much greater prosperity in the commercial centre of Moncton than in the resource-based north. This same disparity exists between Cape Breton and Halifax in Nova Scotia, and West Prince county and Charlottetown in Prince Edward Island.[5] Throughout Canada there are similar poorer regions — for example, northern and northwestern Quebec, the Interlake Region of Manitoba, parts of rural Saskatchewan and the Interior of British Columbia, and vast sections of the North. In general, the most depressed areas are dependent upon primary industries, and therefore on international price arrangements that are beyond local control. These industries are also increasingly capital intensive and therefore less able to sustain local populations. As a result there has been an ongoing pattern of migration to urban centres with more stable economies. Given that vast parts of Canada are already sparsely populated, this migration poses a threat to nationhood. Not only are people moving from poorer to wealthier parts of the country, but the same is also true of capital. A 1990 study by the Economic Council of Newfoundland and Labrador indicates that many potential sources of investment capital flow out of the province to be managed through the money markets in Toronto and Montreal. Among these lost sources in 1987–88 were $59 million in RRSP contributions, $78 million in Canada Savings Bonds, $380 million in public pension funds, and a portion of the $100 million Workers' Compensation fund.[6]

In general then, there is a pattern of movement of people, financial savings and raw materials from relatively poorer parts of Canada to more prosperous, urban commercial centres. Most of the movement has been to the south-central parts of the country, but also to the West Coast and to Calgary and Edmonton in resource-rich Alberta. But charting the mosaic of economic inequality goes beyond general regional or sub-regional descriptors, for within the relatively wealthy urban centres like Toronto and Vancouver, there are pockets of poverty that can be even more severe than in smaller communities with lower housing costs and informal social structures for providing services that must be paid for in urban centres. And similarly within rural areas, there is great unevenness in the standard of living, the greatest poverty often found on native reserves, where unemployment can be 80 to 90 per cent of the labour force, and where the amenities of modern life may be absent.[7]

GOVERNMENT STRATEGIES

There is a lengthy tradition of federal intervention in the economy in an effort to reduce regional disparities in wealth. One form of intervention has been social assistance programs, such as unemployment insurance and job training, for people without jobs in the formal economy. These programs are tilted toward underdeveloped regions since these are where there is a relatively greater proportion of unemployed. In Newfoundland, for example, federal transfer payments to individuals have represented about 30 per cent of personal income.[8] These payments are particularly important to workers in seasonal industries who scramble to find employment for 10 weeks in order to qualify for unemployment insurance during the rest of the year when they participate in the informal economy (that is, economic activity outside of the formal labour force).

A second type of federal assistance has been equalization payments to the poorer provinces. Encouraged by the Rowell-Sirois Commission, the provinces and the federal government signed a tax equalization agreement in 1956 designed to bring the per capita tax revenues of the poorer provinces to the standard of the richer provinces.[9] In Newfoundland, for example, total federal payments in 1987–88 represented about half of provincial government revenue.[10]

A third type of intervention by the federal government has been assistance to business so as to offset the tendency by private-sector companies to concentrate in either the industrial heartland of southwestern Ontario or in other commercial centres of the country. This assistance is designed to encourage capitalism with geographic roots. In general, federal business-assistance programs have attempted to support existing regional enterprises, to assist the development of new enterprises, and to encourage businesses to shift their operation to poorer regions. This type of business assistance goes back to the 1930s when the federal government started the practice of aid for prairie farmers as part of a broader federal program to assist provincial governments bankrupted during the Great Depression.[11] Saskatchewan alone received $140 million in federal relief in 1938.[12]

In the post–World War II period, there were many *ad hoc* initiatives such as the Atlantic Development Board (1962) and the Area Development Incentives Act (1965) that gave capital grants and tax incentives to businesses locating in poorer areas of the country.[13] By 1969 these programs were consolidated within the federal Department of Regional Economic Expansion (DREE). DREE's programs were targeted at regions of the country designated as being in need of assistance. With the advent of the Conservative government in Ottawa in 1984, the administrative arrangements underwent further transformations so that federal programs to assist businesses in underdeveloped regions were decentralized, with the Atlantic Canada Opportunities Agency (ACOA) in Moncton controlling programs for the four Atlantic provinces, and the Western Diversification Initiative dealing with the western provinces.

An illuminating evaluation of federal attempts to promote capitalism with geographic roots comes from the 1991 study of Enterprise Cape Breton, an offshoot of ACOA that focused specifically on Cape Breton Island.[14] Located in eastern Nova Scotia, Cape Breton has had a chronically depressed economy with low participation rates in the labour force (52 per cent in 1989),[15] per capita income at 70 per cent of the Canadian average and 84 per cent of the Nova Scotia average,[16] and an unemployment rate (17.7 per cent in 1989),[17] which exceeded the average in all four Atlantic provinces. The full impact of Cape Breton's depressed economy has been attenuated by a sizable out-migration to other parts of Canada and by transfer payments from the federal government, which by 1988 represented 25 per cent of the Island's per capita income.[18] A thriving informal economy also helps the unemployed to cope.

Cape Breton, like other economically depressed regions of Canada, has relied heavily upon primary industry as its economic mainstay. The decline of coal mining and the fisheries and the downsizing of the Island's steel industry has had a negative effect on the local economy. From the early 1960s, various government initiatives have been oriented toward stimulating business development in Cape Breton, one being Enterprise Cape Breton (ECB), operating from 1985 until its absorption by ACOA in 1991. ECB had a variety of programs to assist business, including a 60 per cent investment tax credit, direct payment of costs, and low-interest loans. By November 1990, ECB had authorized $365 million of financial assistance, and $110 million had actually been paid out.[19] ECB's primary strategy appeared to be to entice large corporations to establish subsidiary operations in Cape Breton. It ran advertisements in the *New York Times* promising "free money, less tax and no red tape."[20] Of its total assistance, 88 per cent went to only 52 companies, only 29 per cent of which were still functioning by November 1990.[21] Interestingly, the success rate for projects that received assistance of between $100,000 and $1 million was 55 per cent, and projects receiving assistance of less than $100,000 had a 72 per cent success rate.[22]

For expansions of existing companies, the success rate increased to 86 per cent.[23]

The statistics foretell the conclusion of the ECB evaluation:

> Ownership directly influenced success rates. Projects owned either wholly or partially by Cape Bretoners or Atlantic Canadians show a much higher success rate than those owned outside of Atlantic Canada. Companies with at least partial local ownership ... are often owner-managed enterprises, and their owners have a personal financial interest and a vigorous commitment to the success of the project. ... The generous up-front and topping-up financing built into the programs reduced the equity required from the client to an extremely low level and attracted a disproportionate number of high-risk companies. Some of these companies proved unwilling or unable to see their projects through difficult times. ... Branch-plant operations approved by ECB have had a low rate of success.[24]

While the conclusions of the ECB are particular to the last five years of federally funded business development in Cape Breton, there are components that can be applied generally. A large American study of plant closures, recently published by the National Council for Urban Economic Development, also notes that branch plants of larger corporations are most vulnerable to shutdown.[25] In other words, companies controlled from outside the local community tend to make decisions without considering the impact upon the local populace. Newfoundland, too, has been embarrassed after giving money to off-shore capitalists to get involved in large, well-publicized ventures in the province. Its Economic Council has recommended ways of improving equity financing for the indigenous entrepreneurs in small- and medium-sized businesses. Developing local business is seen as a vehicle for reducing economic problems that parallel those of Cape Breton.[26]

Both the report of the Economic Council of Newfoundland and the evaluation of ECB look to the indigenous small-business class as the vehicle for lifting these regions of the country out of their economic doldrums. The Economic Council of Newfoundland emphasizes the importance of a financing vehicle for local micro businesses requiring less that $100,000 and the importance of education and training to nurture indigenous entrepreneurs.[27] The evaluation of ECB also points in the same direction:

> It must be clearly understood that money alone is not the answer. The reshaping and rebuilding of the Cape Breton economy must come from within, through the efforts of Cape Bretoners. There must be a concerted effort to shift from dependence to enterprise and to nurture entrepreneurship. We must recognize the vital role that education and training and, in particular, the University of Cape Breton, must play in effecting this shift.[28]

In its advocacy of the indigenous small-business class, the ECB evaluation attempts to overcome the tendency of private-sector enterprises to make decisions without consideration of their consequences for local communities. The exceptions are businesses tied to a natural resource (oil or forestry, for instance), businesses with a geographically specific product (for example, a publisher of Canadian books), and very small enterprises. In fact, micro businesses tend to straddle the line between the private sector and the social sector. Like social enterprises, they provide a service specific to a geographic community, and the revenues of the business go either to labour or to the business itself. Unlike a social enterprise, however, the assets (usually small) are privately rather than socially owned, and the governance is less likely to be democratic.

Community Development Corporations (CDCs)

Neither the evaluation of ECB nor the report of the Economic Council of Newfoundland deal with the relatively recent movement to use CDCs as a mechanism for local development, though there are many parallels between the CDC and the direction advocated by these reports. The CDC may be seen as a creation of the social economy. CDCs are non-profit corporations designed to assist the development of the communities in which they are located. Originating as part of the American civil rights movements of the late 1960s, and particularly in the desire to overcome the poverty experienced by blacks living in the ghettos of decaying cities, the CDC has become a vehicle through which groups and individuals can channel their energies toward developing the local community.[29] The goals are both social and economic.

In Canada, the first CDCs were started by co-operative activists who wanted to assist local communities to overcome their economic problems.[30] In contrast to co-operatives that tend to focus on specific services for a defined group within the community ("unifunctional" organizations), the community economic development strategy attempts to take the perspective of the entire community.[31] This strategy, while including co-operatives, involves support for community businesses in general, which in some cases includes small businesses in the private sector. This broader strategy means that the constituency base for CDCs is not as clearly defined as in co-operatives. As such, the membership and the governance can be *ad hoc* and may lack the representative structure of co-operatives.

Although CDCs vary in their organization and programs, they have the common feature of providing a social support system for local entrepreneurship. In some cases, the CDC may actually plan local development itself and control the assets, either directly or through subsidiary corporations. New Dawn of Sydney, Cape Breton, is a good example of such an arrangement.[32] Believed to be the oldest CDC in Canada (formally incorporated in 1976), New Dawn was rooted in the Atlantic co-operative movement. Its spiritual leader has been Greg MacLeod, a coal miner's son who became a priest, and then a philosophy professor and community activist. New Dawn has six subsidiary corporations:

- The Cape Breton Association for Housing Development — the builder of 216 apartment units
- New Day Ventures — a construction company for small jobs
- Cape Care — a homecare and home nursing service
- Home Living — a service to match seniors with families
- Highland Resources — a training and consulting company that assists local projects to obtain federal funds
- The Volunteer Resource Centre — organizing volunteers for Meals on Wheels, snow shovelling, and so on.

Among New Dawn's most recent projects is Pine Tree Park, a residential community built on an abandoned Department of National Defence radar base. Seniors live alongside families who are paid a salary by New Dawn to care for the seniors. At present there are 35 seniors and 12 families.

New Dawn has created 90 full-time jobs and part-time jobs in the economically depressed Sydney area. It also organizes 200 regular volunteers to provide services to the community.

The $14 million of assets within this network are controlled by the CDC as a form of social property. Surplus revenues (profits) are retained and reinvested in the community. As such, New Dawn operates as a non-profit corporation engaged in social entrepreneurship or developing the local community. The Economic Council of Canada refers to New Dawn as "one of the most successful CDCs operating in Canada."[33]

Another CDC with a similar arrangement to New Dawn is the Human Resource Development Association (HRDA), a non-profit organization launched by the city of Halifax largely through efforts by the municipal social planning department. [34] HRDA was originally intended to provide employment for people on social assistance as an alternative to welfare. In 1982, it underwent a major reorganization so that it could become self-sufficient. It established a subsidiary company, HRDA Enterprises Ltd., which currently runs five small businesses: Magna Industrial Services (janitorial work and window cleaning); Nova Sewing Contractors (contract sewing); HRDA Property Division (building maintenance and management); Skyline Industrial Painters; and Enviro-Care Services (collection, processing, and marketing of recyclable products).

In 1992, 10 years after it was set up, HRDA Enterprises is employing 150 people full-time, 60 per cent of whom have been recipients of social assistance.[35] The annual revenues of HRDA Enterprises have reached $415 million, and in the last fiscal year it turned a profit of $200,000.[36] As of 1987, HRDA no longer received a block grant from the city of Halifax; rather, it was paid a fee for every person it serviced who would have otherwise been on social assistance.[37] In addition to employment in HRDA Enterprises, the services include job training for 300 people annually. HRDA also operates a low-interest loan fund for micro businesses in Halifax's Gottingen Street inner city area.

HRDA's enterprises are set up to help an urban underclass to participate in the economy and to break its dependence upon social assistance. A similar trend is found in other urban centres, for example, in enterprises supported by the Learning Enrichment Foundation in the City of York[38] or in A-WAY Express, a courier service staffed by the psychiatrically handicapped that was started by a social service agency in Toronto.[39] The A-WAY Express model has been used in six other businesses in Ontario for the psychiatrically handicapped.[40]

These examples reflect community-development initiatives structured primarily around social enterprises. Other CDCs have assisted the development of private-sector enterprises. The Great Northern Peninsula Development Corporation (GNPDC), located at Plum Point, in one of the economically poorest areas of Newfoundland, has organized a consortium of local independent sawmillers to win a contract from Newfoundland Hydro to provide 50,000 tons of wood chips per year for a plant just built in the area.[41] Unless these local sawmillers worked as a group, the contract would have gone to a large business from outside the region.

In response to the collapse of Newfoundland's fish industry, the GNPDC is participating in an Arctic Char hatchery project in Daniel's Harbour. Part of its role over the next years is to train local residents in fish farming techniques.[42]

In general, the GNPDC is striving to form partnership arrangements with the private sector, although it turned down an opportunity to become a one-third owner in a privately owned fish plant, because it would lack sufficient control. Its policy in joint ventures is 51 per cent ownership for the CDC.

The Kitsaki Development Corporation (KDC) of the La Ronge Indian Band in northern Saskatchewan has joint ventures with the private sector for six businesses. According to general manager Dave McIlmoyl, Kitsaki was formed in 1981 as part of an effort by the La Ronge Indian Band to create its own economic system so that there would be job opportunities for Band members and others living in the area.[43] Kitsaki is incorporated as a limited company owned by the Band. Therefore, profits from the companies that are owned either in part or in whole by this CDC go to the Band. At present, the companies owned by Kitsaki are generating about 200 full-time jobs and $14 million of gross revenues. [44] Kitsaki also runs training programs for management of its companies.

KDC's ventures include an insurance company, a catering firm, Saskatchewan's largest producer of wild rice, a rice-marketing company, La Ronge's largest hotel, and a meat company. Its largest venture, Northern Resources Trucking, is a partnership with a Calgary company. Northern handles about 80 per cent of the heavy bulk fuel trucking in northern Saskatchewan.

Kitsaki was formed in a context of chronic economic problems, reflected in an unemployment rate of about 85 percent among the La Ronge Indian Band. Through its various businesses, Kitsaki has been able to create some job opportunities in the La Ronge area and has earned the recognition of the publication *Saskatchewan Business*, which referred to it as the third fastest growing business in Saskatchewan between 1986 and 1989.[45]

New Dawn, HRDA, GNPDC and KDC are only a few of the CDCs operating across Canada. In general, they are operating in areas where the existing economy is inadequate to meet the employment needs of the community. To overcome this problem, the CDC becomes a substitute entrepreneur that considers opportunities and formulates plans for the local community. These skills come primarily from a general manager — the manager's particular experience often giving direction to the business opportunities that are pursued. New Dawn's first manager, a former real estate agent, helped that CDC acquire most of the properties that form the bulk of its current assets.[46]

The CDC centralizes business planning, an important aspect of entrepreneurship. However, arranging financing, another key component of a social-entrepreneurship strategy, can be problematic for CDCs. The CDC's objective to maintain a satisfactory degree of social control reduces the likelihood of partnerships with private-sector enterprises. Also, many community-development projects are micro enterprises, and as such have difficulty obtaining adequate financing through conventional sources, which view these projects as too risky. The problem of adequate financing for very small businesses is noted in a 1988 paper published by the Canadian Federation of Independent Business.[47] It is also emphasized by the Economic Council of Newfoundland and Labrador.[48] With respect to the financing needs for projects sponsored by CDCs, the Economic Council of Canada states that only one of the 12 programs under the large Atlantic Canada Opportunities Agency actually provided any funding.[49]

FINANCING REGIONAL DEVELOPMENT

Recently, there have been some innovative proposals and programs to assist micro entrepreneurship, particularly in regions of economic hardship. The Federal Business Development Bank (FBDB), a lender of last resort in Canada, has been considering a proposal, based on a successful program in the United Kingdom, for a participating debenture, through which money is lent to businesses with no repayment until finances reach a break-even point.[50] Then, the lending agency would make a claim on earnings reflecting the risk associated with the loan and the business's ability to pay. The idea would be to maintain the debt payments at a manageable level.

Another innovative finance program is the First Peoples' Fund started by the Calmeadow Foundation, a Toronto-based foundation that provides technical and financial support for micro enterprises in poor communities in Canada and internationally.[51] The First Peoples' Fund, based on the Grameen Bank of Bangladesh, a credit union that provides micro loans for poor people who are self-employed, is directed at native communities. Like Grameen, the very small loans (up to $3,000) are made to poor people who want to start up a micro business or to expand an existing one. The innovative feature of this program is that the loans do not require collateral. Instead the repayment, including commercial rates of interest, is enforced through a "borrowers' circle" of four to seven people who approve and guarantee each other's loans. These circles meet regularly to decide upon loan requests, to provide social support for participants and to administer the repayments. The circle represents a form of peer control to guarantee that financial responsibilities are maintained. For a native community to join the fund, participation must be approved by the band council, and it must provide security for 25 per cent of the loan fund. The Calmeadow Foundation guarantees 50 per cent, and the bank assumes 25 per cent of the risk. The band appoints an administrator who is trained by the Fund. The Grameen Bank of Bangladesh, the prototype of micro credit for the poor, has 700,000 members with loans averaging $75.[52] Similar micro-credit programs are functioning in Bolivia, Columbia and Peru. It is still premature to determine whether the First Peoples' Fund will achieve the success of the Grameen Bank of Bangladesh.

The First Peoples' Fund deals strictly with very small loans. A program providing finance on a somewhat larger scale is the Community Bonds Program enacted by the government of Saskatchewan in 1990.[53] The purpose of this program is to encourage people to invest in local enterprises through a Community Bonds Corporation. To encourage participation, the provincial government guarantees the principal portion of an investment in a project to a limit of $2 million. The return on the investment is the only financial risk to the bondholder. To be eligible for investment from a Community Bonds Corporation, an enterprise must be in the following market sectors: commercial water and irrigation, tourism, export services, manufacturing or processing of raw materials, and environmental improvement. The investments are treated as equity, and their normal term is five years. The arrangements for establishing a Community Bonds Corporation are quite loose. Such a corporation may be started by either a provincial rural development corporation or any group of six or more individuals, provided that at least one director is a mayor, reeve or a designate of the local council, and the arrangement is approved by the province. The bondholders are residents of Saskatchewan, either individuals, corporations or municipalities.

In its first year of operation, 74 Community Bonds Corporations were started, with 2,946 investors subscribing $4.4 million.[54] Although it is too early to evaluate the economic impact of the program, Community Bonds do appear to be effective in channelling the savings of Saskatchewan residents to local development. In doing so, the program endeavours to overcome the pattern prevalent throughout the hinterlands of Canada whereby local savings flow to the main commercial centres for investment by money managers in those locations. The Community Bonds Program, although applicable to finance social enterprises, is directed primarily towards the private sector. It is another example of a program to stimulate capitalism with geographic roots. The voting arrangements for Community Bonds Corporations are based upon property rights, that is, bond holdings.

Recently some community development corporations have attempted to create their own venture capital funds to gain greater control over the development process. New Dawn, which pioneered the CDC concept in Canada, has also become the leader in this approach by starting the venture capital fund,

BCA (Banking Community Assets) Holdings.[55] BCA Holdings is based upon the same idea as Community Bond Corporations — that is, to channel local finance to local development. The member-organizations of BCA are New Dawn, a nearby CDC called New Deal, and some credit unions. BCA is largely a social-sector financial organization operating in conjunction with local CDCs. Whereas CDCs socialize business planning, BCA socializes venture capital. The intent is to broaden the social infrastructure in support of local development. Greg MacLeod, a driving force behind BCA Holdings as well as New Dawn, has been influenced strongly by the Mondragon model in Spain as a community-based development system.[56] The infrastructure that he has helped to develop in Cape Breton has taken on some of the key features of Mondragon.

REGIONALLY BASED CO-OPERATIVE SYSTEMS

The Mondragon Model

The Mondragon model, developed in the Basque region of Spain, has had great influence in Canada and internationally.[57] Mondragon is a community economic development model utilizing co-operatives. However, it departs from the co-operative tradition in that each co-operative not only provides specific services to a defined membership but is also part of an integrated system of regional development. Since its beginnings in the mid-1950s, the Mondragon group has evolved into one of the most impressive community development systems in the world. Because of its financing mechanisms and its approach to entrepreneurship, Mondragon has been able to develop medium-sized corporations that are competing effectively in international markets. At this point there are about 100 worker co-operative firms with about 20,000 workers in the Mondragon group, including FAGOR, Spain's largest household appliance manufacturer. The Mondragon worker co-ops also produce industrial components for appliances, electrical components for telephones and televisions, machine tools, computer software and a range of agricultural products.

The Mondragon worker co-operatives are supported by about 65 educational and service co-operatives. The system includes a large consumer-retail co-op (Eroski), a social and life insurance co-op (Lagunaro), a technical-research institute (Ikerlan), schools and a polytechnical institute, and housing co-ops. The hub of the system has been the Caja Laboral Popular (the Working People's Bank), a financial co-operative with nearly 200 branches throughout the Basque country and about $3 billion of assets in 1990. The Caja channels about one-third of its investments to assist the financing of new co-operatives and the expansion of existing ones, often at concessionary interest rates. The co-ops in turn enter into a 'contract of association' with the Caja, part of which includes depositing their earnings in the Caja.

Originally, the Caja also provided technical and business planning assistance through its empressarial or consulting division, now a separate co-operative called Lankide Suztaketa. Through this approach, the Mondragon group has been able to develop medium-sized industries, using modern technologies. It has broken out of the ghetto of small, labour-intensive firms in low-wage market sectors, which is typical for community economic development in Canada.

The Mondragon approach has centralized in part the entrepreneurial function. American economist David Ellerman appropriately labels this approach, "the socialization of entrepreneurship,"[58] in that the key aspects of entrepreneurship — financing and business planning — are organized through social enterprises.

The Mondragon group has another important feature: it functions as an integrated system. Each co-operative transfers some control to a central council (Co-operative Congress), which acts as the governance for the entire system. Jesus Larranaga, a founder of the first Mondragon co-op, suggests that through shifting control to a central organization from workers in the individual enterprise, Mondragon has become a "neoco-operative" system.[59] Without this centralization of control, he believes Mondragon could not compete with multi-national corporations in the European Economic Community and internationally.

The Evangeline group of Co-operatives

There is nothing on the scale of Mondragon in Canada's experience with community economic development. The closest approximation is the Evangeline group in southwestern Prince Edward Island. This small Acadian community in the Evangeline region of P.E.I. consists of 2,500 people in three villages — Wellington, Mont Carmel and Abram's Village — all within a 20-square-kilometre area.[60] In the period since the mid-1970s, this community has built a system of co-operatives that has earned it the title, 'uncontested co-op capital of North America.'[61]

In a region of P.E.I. with substandard earnings, high unemployment and high out-migration, the 15 Evangeline co-operatives employ 369 people in providing services to the community.[62] The range of activities involved is impressive: a credit union; a fish-processing plant; a supermarket/mall; a health clinic; a seniors' home; a tourist facility (Acadian Pioneer village) including a hotel, restaurant, theatre and tour company; a handicraft enterprise; a forestry business; a potato chip producer (Olde Barrel); a cable television service; a funeral service; and a youth co-operative.

In total, the Evangeline group has 6,159 members (many people belonging to several co-ops) and earned $4.8 million in revenues in 1989–90. The co-ops have $23 million in assets and have become a vehicle for retaining local savings in the development of the community.[63]

As in Mondragon, Evangeline has socialized entrepreneurship within a co-operative community. The Evangeline Caisse Populaire/Credit Union, the only financial institution in the area, has 3,200 members and $17 million of assets, as compared to its founding in 1970 when it had 1,309 members and $548,000 of assets.[64] The credit union was created from three small parish credit unions dating back to the 1930s.

Evangeline had been influenced by the Antigonish movement which started in the 1930s in the Catholic parishes of eastern Nova Scotia, utilizing adult education to galvanize the poor into mutual self-help. Evangeline took up the Antigonish tradition of holding kitchen meetings to decide upon a course of action to overcome the community's economic problems. In addition to the parish credit unions, a fishers' co-operative was formed at that time. Although the kitchen-meeting tradition has continued, the real impetus to developing a co-operative infrastructure occurred in the 1970s when Léonce Bernard, subsequently the Minister of Community and Cultural Affairs in Prince Edward Island, became the first manager of the Evangeline Credit Union. Like the Caja Laboral Popular in the Mondragon group, Bernard encouraged the credit union to take a leading role in financing local development.[65] By 1984, the Baie Acadienne Venture Capital Group was established to assist with financing new enterprises.[66] A portion of the financing for the Venture Capital Group comes from members of the credit union foregoing part of their patronage dividends (their share of the year-end surplus).

Since the mid-1970s the credit union has been assisted in its entrepreneurial role by the Conseil de la coopération de l'Île-du-Prince Édouard, a second-tier co-operative whose members are the first-tier co-operatives.[67] Like the Co-operative Congress in Mondragon, the Conseil is the political arm of the movement, and it also handles promotion, co-ordination and some business planning. Its role is analogous to community development cor-porations like New Dawn, but its membership base in allied organizations is more clearly defined.

Evangeline, the subject of a recent National Film Board of Canada production, We're the Boss,[68] has provoked a rethinking of the purpose of co-operatives in Atlantic Canada and in other economically depressed areas of the country. The objective ac-cording to Lynden Hillier, executive director of the Canadian Co-operative Association, is "developing a broad policy frame-work for describing the role of co-operatives in economic devel-opment."[69] Essentially that means extending the co-operative tradition of simply organizing a group of people around a partic-ular service to a model whereby communities use various forms of co-operatives to meet their needs. A unique feature of the Evangeline group is that the credit union is not simply relating to other credit unions, and the supermarket co-op is not just relat-ing to the food co-op retail system, as is usual for co-operatives, but they are both relating to their community and the other co-operatives in the community. Thus the Olde Barrel potato chip business, a worker co-op employing 20 local people, was initiated with the support of the credit union, the venture capital fund and the Conseil.[70] There were also investments from the worker-owners and from the provincial and federal govern-ments.

Other Models in the Atlantic Region

The Atlantic co-operative movement has been strongly influ-enced by Evangeline. There is also a similar community-based system of co-operatives in the Acadian community of Chéticamp on Cape Breton's Cabot Trail,[71] and the Acadian Co-operative Movement of New Brunswick has recently started a similar development strategy in the Caraquet area.[72] Co-op Atlantic, the wholesaler for the network of consumer co-ops in the Atlantic, has adopted *A Proposal for Renewal,* which would see it extend its role from the food and dry goods market to that of promoting an "interdependent network of co-operative enterprises" in communities throughout the Atlantic.[73] Essentially, *A Proposal for Renewal* is projecting a vision of a social economy for local communities in the Atlantic.

In Co-op Atlantic's view, the co-operative movement is too tied into a membership based upon agriculture and fishing — industries which are increasingly coming under the control of large private-sector corporations. *A Proposal for Renewal* would see Co-op Atlantic channelling a portion of its resources to assist the development of a community-based system of co-operatives. The key institution, or development mechanism, will be the local co-operative community council, like the co-op Conseil in Evangeline. It will be a second-tier organization, with first-tier co-operatives as members. *A Proposal for Renewal* also recommends that co-operatives depart from their tradition of one type of member — usually either users or primary producers — and that they include employees of the co-operative as a distinct membership group.[74] Using these approaches, Co-op Atlantic seeks to encourage a community-based system of democratic social enterprises throughout the Atlantic provinces.

Even though Co-op Atlantic is a large corporation with 1990 sales of $408 million,[75] it recognizes that investment capital is a problem for the realization of its goals. It is studying a proposal for an investment fund based on "some form of levy linked to sales."[76] However, in implementing such a proposal, it is faced with the problem of every co-operative: proposals must have the members' support. This strength becomes a weakness when enlisting the members' backing to develop other co-operatives which are less directly related to their own interests.

There's one other aspect of *A Proposal for Renewal* which merits some comment. To date the most striking examples of community-based systems of co-operatives are in locations where the people are a minority group, united by a common culture, religion and language. This is true of Mondragon, where Basque culture is the unifying force, and also true of Evangeline and Chéticamp, where the people are Acadians. In order to develop an integrated co-operative system, is it necessary to have as a prior condition a tightly knit community with people who have a tradition of working together? The answer to this question is not clear, though as Co-op Atlantic proceeds with its plan it will be interesting to see whether it takes hold generally in communities throughout the Atlantic or if implementation is limited to communities based upon minority cultures.[77]

ORGANIZED LABOUR

Worker Buyouts

The traditional role of organized labour has been to represent the interests of members organized through locals in collective bargaining with employers. However, with the epidemic of plant closings across Canada, organized labour has been forced to broaden its role to consider strategies for preventing closings, which in selected cases includes organizing worker buyouts.

These buyouts represent an important community economic development strategy, particularly when they occur in underdeveloped regions of the country. If the definition of worker buyouts is limited to those companies in which workers have majority and effective ownership (as opposed to the more usual scenario of managerial buyouts with expanded employee ownership in some cases), there is not a large number in Canada. A 1990 study counted 39 worker buyouts,[78] the oldest being the 1978 buyout, Northern Breweries in Sault Ste. Marie.[79]

It is extremely difficult for a union local acting on its own to undertake a worker buyout, particularly if the plant is under threat of closure. A buyout involves organizing a group of workers to consider playing a role with which they are unfamiliar and which usually requires a financial investment from them. It also involves organizing a feasibility study and a new business plan, as well as acquiring new sources of financing. All of these tasks involve time — time which may not be available when the opportunity for a buyout exists.

Not surprisingly then, organizing a worker buyout usually requires some central union support for the members of a local. In cases where an industry's closure threatens the future of a community ("one-industry towns"), the community itself may rally behind a buyout. The purchase of Spruce Falls Power and Paper Company in Kapuskasing at the end of 1991 is a recent illustration of a community, with support from the provincial government, rallying to save its sole major employer.[80] Without the buyout, Kapuskasing, a town of 12,000 in northeastern Ontario, would have lost much of its population, and surrounding communities would also have been affected.

Where a buyout involves a union in a company of significant scale, the pattern in Canada has been for the union local to be supported by its central. As such, the buyouts involving unions have tended to be clustered around particular labour organizations. On the West Coast, for example, the International Woodworkers have been involved in three worker buyouts since 1984, supporting two and opposing one.[81] The United Steelworkers of America has assisted about 10 employee buyouts in the United States since the 1980s in steel companies under the threat of closure.[82] The buyout strategy was encouraged by the steelworkers' head office in Pittsburg, including its Canadian president Lynn Williams.[83] More recently, the Ontario District of the United Steelworkers has assisted locals to evaluate potential worker buyouts, as it too is faced with closings of major plants. After backing off on a worker buyout of the Inglis plant in Toronto in 1989 because the company refused to sell its closing operation, in 1992 the Steelworkers organized the employee purchase of Algoma Steel in Sault Ste. Marie (see Chapter 2)[84] Apart from its size (involving about 6,000 employees), this buyout was also significant because, like the one in Kapuskasing, it represented a community with the support of the provincial government, rallying behind its major industry.

Quebec's Confédération des syndicats nationaux (CSN)

Perhaps the most systematic example of a Canadian labour organization becoming involved in a buyout strategy is the Quebec-based Confédération des syndicats nationaux, a confederation of 2,075 public- and private-sector union locals with 250,000 workers. In contrast to most unions that have considered worker ownership only as a last resort, the CSN's approach represents a throwback to the nineteenth-century Knights of Labour, when that labour organization was involved in promoting an alternative economic vision. Léopold Beaulieu, the CSN's treasurer and a driving force behind the initiative, views it as part of a broader program of building economic democracy, including financial co-operatives, social housing and community projects: "The unions affiliated with the CSN have always promoted tools for economic and social action over which they have control."[85]

In 1987 the CSN created an in-house consulting group in Montreal of seven professionals with specializations in marketing, finance, accounting and management, aided by support staff. The consulting group (*groupe conseil spéciale*) monitors the companies in which CSN locals are involved, looking for early signs of plant closings (such as a lack of investment by the owners). Its main objective is to work with existing owners to prevent closings. However, upon request from groups of workers, the consulting group assesses the feasibility of a buyout of their place of work.

Originally, the consulting group was funded by a federal Innovations grant, but at present it covers the costs associated with feasibility analysis and business planning through fees charged to workers, job retraining monies and through funding from the CSN itself. As for financing of businesses purchased by the workers, the CSN has turned to two large financial co-operatives affiliated with it — the Caisse d'économie des travailleuses et des travailleurs de Québec and the Caisse populaire des syndicats nationaux de Montréal — for business loans, which in 1990 totalled $25 million for 11 enterprises with 1,300 workers. Investments from the workers have been $1.7 million, another $2 million has come from private-sector lenders, and of the loans, $7 million has been guaranteed by the provincial Société de développement des coopératives.[86] Five of the completed projects have created ambulance co-operatives out of many small private-sector services for Quebec's urban centres, and these now embrace one-half of the province's ambulance services.

The CSN has avoided salvage operations of failing companies, believing they are too risky. Rather, where workers at a closing company are interested, the CSN has attempted to start a new enterprise that makes use of the workers' skills and possibly some assets (buildings and equipment) of the original operation. An example is a rubber recycling plant for workers formerly employed by Uniroyal in Montreal.

The CSN has utilized a central funding mechanism, partially underwritten by the Confédération itself, to assist the financing of worker-owned social enterprises. The CSN consulting group also monitors carefully the progress of each enterprise and provides ongoing advice to deal with problems. Through these processes, the CSN also has "socialized entrepreneurship and finance," thereby providing ongoing support for each of its enterprises. Its consulting group and financial co-operatives play similar roles to the infrastructure in Evangeline, Chéticamp or Mondragon. However, the integration of these enterprises into a system is more limited than in these other community-based models. In part, this is because the CSN is a labour confederation dealing with the workplace, rather than a geographic community with a *gemeinschaft* social configuration.

Other Initiatives by Organized Labour

As will be discussed in Chapter 8, the CSN is not the only labour organization to become involved in a regional development strategy. The Quebec Federation of Labour and more recently the British Columbia Federation of Labour and the Manitoba Federation of Labour have established investment funds to help develop business in their provinces. The Manitoba Fund, as will be noted, also encourages workers' control of its investments.

Organized labour has also been involved in developing social housing since the mid-1970s. The Canadian Labour Congress was one of the founding members of the Co-operative Housing Foundation, the forerunner to the Co-operative Housing Federation of Canada, and the CLC was one of the key lobbyists for a federal social housing program in 1973.[87] The Toronto and District Labour Council and the Canadian Auto Workers also have sponsored resource groups that develop co-operative housing projects.

An innovative variation of labour's involvement in social housing has been the program undertaken by Local 1115 of the International Labourers Union in Glace Bay (Cape Breton).[88] The union has organized a construction company, the Labourers' Development Company, which builds modestly priced houses for its members. Houses are financed through a revolving loan fund which receives revenues through 25-cent-per-hour deductions from each workers' pay cheque, as well as donations from religious organizations and local businesses. Both the pay deductions and the mortgage loans from the fund are interest-free. As the mortgage is repaid, the fund can finance other houses, thereby creating both low-cost housing and jobs in the local community.

Both in housing and in preserving local industries, labour is broadening its traditional role of collective bargaining. These initiatives not only involve union locals but central labour organizations. The support of labour centrals parallels that of central organizations in other community economic development initiatives. It appears to be a key element for success of development schemes.

CONCLUSIONS

Federal government policies of attracting large corporations to economically depressed regions of the country have not proven to be a very effective strategy for overcoming economic disparities. Evidence suggests that financial incentives are most effective when directed at local entrepreneurs in small businesses.

There are some interesting experiments within the social economy which seem useful in attacking regional disparities. These include community development corporations and communities with a co-operative infrastructure. Financing has been an obstacle to development strategies in economically depressed regions. Community development corporations such as New Dawn in Sydney, Nova Scotia, are developing their own venture capital pools. This same strategy has been pursued in the Evangeline group of co-operatives in southwestern Prince Edward Island, which has used a second-tier co-operative and its credit union to spearhead its development strategy. Co-op Atlantic, the wholesaler for food retail co-ops in the four Atlantic provinces, is looking to encourage the development of similar co-operative communities throughout Atlantic Canada.

Organized labour is another important player in community economic development strategies. The large number of plant closings has forced it to become involved in organizing buyouts of closing plants. Of the labour organizations in Canada, the Confédération des syndicats nationaux has created the most systematic approach to community economic development. Although the many types of community economic development projects discussed in this chapter differ, a key element for success appears to be strong central organizations to assist with business planning and finance. This is referred to as the "socialization of entrepreneurship."

Social Housing

Another type of community with a growing role within the social economy is social housing. Primarily an urban phenomenon, social housing is a type of mutual association that involves a common housing arrangement. Social housing may be seen as a cross between a geographic community and a mutual non-profit based upon a specific interest. Housing is an important part of people's lifespace, and one which involves much living time each day. Therefore, it is a type of association requiring greater analysis than others.

Social housing evolved during the 1970s and '80s in response to the inability of a growing number of people to pay the costs (either rent or ownership expenses) of the private market and the perceived failure of government or public housing. Social housing represented a middle way. Before looking at some basic organizational models of social housing, this chapter discusses the context for its evolution.

THE AFFORDABILITY CRISIS

Traditionally, Canada has had a good standard of housing with a relatively high percentage of private ownership, good quality stock and a relatively low rate of homelessness.[1] However, social changes have led to a lack of affordable housing for a growing sector of the populace over the last two decades. The inability of the private sector to solve this affordability crisis has given birth to a social housing movement.

Although there have been many analyses of the housing problem, the social forces leading to it are neatly captured by Statistics Canada in a publication, *Affordability of Housing in Canada*.[2] Previous research by Canada Mortgage and Housing Corporation (the federal Crown corporation responsible for implementing government housing policies) determined that when housing costs exceed 30 per cent of a household's income, it is necessary to cut back on other essentials.[3] Using that criterion, Statistics Canada estimated that, based on 1986 census data, 35.6 per cent of all renter-households and 13.4 per cent of home-owners were experiencing affordability problems.[4] The greater affordability problems among tenants were not due to larger expenditures than home-owners (the opposite was the case), but rather to lower incomes. Half of tenant-households were earning less than $20,000 (in 1985), whereas only 22 per cent of home-owners were in a similar situation.[5] In addition, the affordability problems are concentrated among tenants with one-parent families (55 per cent of people in that circumstance, usually single mothers) and single persons (45 per cent of that group).[6]

Age is also a correlate of affordability.[7] Problems are concentrated among the young, usually new entrants to the labour force with low incomes, and the elderly. While elderly home-owners have the lowest percentage of affordability problems because their mortgages have been paid off, more than 40 per cent of elderly tenants are using a disproportionate share of their income for housing. This is because rents increase annually, whereas pensioners' incomes usually decline once they are out of the labour force, and often do not keep pace with rent increases.

Another striking correlate of affordability is location.[8] Affordability problems in housing are concentrated in metropolitan areas, particularly among renters in those areas. In every census metropolitan area in Canada, at least 30 per cent of tenants had affordability problems. At the extreme, in Victoria it was 48 per cent and in Vancouver 45 per cent, because of the large numbers of pensioners in these cities.[9] Moreover, in large cities like Toronto and Vancouver, the price of housing is so high that average tenants would have to increase their incomes more than five times to purchase average-priced houses.[10] "In these circumstances," according to Statistics Canada, "average tenant households have little chance of becoming home-owners, unless they can draw on substantial savings."[11] Put differently, the av-

erage tenant has been effectively frozen out of the home ownership market in Canada's large urban centres — and particularly
in Ontario, Quebec and British Columbia, where a 1990 CMHC
study indicates that 91.8 of renter-households with incomes
above the core-need category could not afford home ownership.[12] These trends may have been altered somewhat by the
decline in housing prices during the recession of the early 1990s.
However, for most tenants in Canada's large cities, the cost of
home ownership remains forbidding.

In spite of this affordability problem, the post-war shift in
population to large urban centres continues. Within every province except New Brunswick, the growth of the census metropolitan areas exceeded the provincial averages between 1981 and
1986.[13] These demographic changes are increasing the pressure
on the housing market in those areas. This pressure has been
further increased by an ongoing pattern of reduced household
size.[14] In 1961, the average household contained 4 persons, but
by 1986 the comparable figure was 2.81. In other words, in the
period 1961–86, the Canadian population grew by 39 per cent,
and the number of households increased by 97 per cent.[15] Such
factors as more divorces, fewer and later marriages, more elderly
people, fewer children, less doubling up and earlier home leaving have all led to smaller households. The higher-income households were moving into urban areas, buying large, old houses
and renovating them. This process, called "gentrification," has
led to higher prices and a loss of rental units, putting pressure on
the rental market.[16] In general, the price of housing in urban
areas has greatly outpaced average incomes.

The severity of affordability problems of people in Canada's
cities varies, the least problematic being the "nouveau poor,"
people with good incomes attempting to realize the Canadian
dream of home ownership by taking on a large mortgage. The
most serious affordability problems are experienced by households with low incomes, and, at the extreme, people who are
homeless ("no fixed address"). As Alex Murray notes, estimating
the exact numbers of homeless in Canada's urban centres is very
difficult.[17] A survey by the Canadian Council on Social Development in 1987 identified 472 shelters with 13,797 places.[18] More
numerous are the numbers of households that are cutting back
on food and other basic necessities in order to pay their rent. In
Ontario alone, a 1988 study by the Ministry of Housing estimates

that as many as 100,000 households, or 9 per cent of renters, are at risk of homelessness because of extreme difficulties in affording rental accommodation.[19]

Although there are differing analyses of what's to be done about the lack of affordable housing, there is broad agreement that government intervention is required to assist in housing those with affordability problems. The "economic rent," the price at which new accommodation can be rented or sold in order for the developer to recover all costs, exceeds the financial means of the average household in large cities. The private housing market functions well for luxury housing, for people with high incomes and for people with substantial equity in existing dwellings. For others, government financial intervention is necessary.

GOVERNMENT INVOLVEMENT

The government presence in the Canadian housing market predates the current crisis. In 1938 it passed the National Housing Act,[20] and, in order to administer the NHA, three years later it created a Crown corporation, Wartime Housing Limited, the forerunner of Canada Mortgage and Housing Corporation (formerly Central Mortgage and Housing Corporation).[21] From the inception of the government presence in housing, the primary thrust was supporting the private sector.

"From 1945 through 1964," according to housing analyst Albert Rose, "the Government of Canada was strongly in favour of the attainment of home ownership by every family. This goal was enunciated from time to time in Parliament and in the speeches of federal ministers."[22] Home ownership was not simply a social goal, but a primary aspect of economic policy, which by the mid-1960s directly involved 500,000 jobs.[23] To support the industry, the government made mortgage money available through the NHA by lowering interest rates, increasing the amortization period, reducing down-payment requirements — in short, doing anything that would encourage home ownership.[24] Moreover, even with the end of the golden era of housing in Canada — an era in which home ownership appeared realizable to most households — the primary thrust of government policy through the 1970s and '80s has been to assist the private market, for both home ownership and rental accommodation, through a variety of subsidies and tax expenditures, detailed by

David Hulchanski, a housing professor at the University of Toronto.[25] The initiatives have included a capital gains exemption for home-owners, various mortgage subsidies, grants and tax exemptions for first-time home buyers, the Canada Mortgage Renewal Plan, and subsequently the Mortgage Rate Protection Program to protect owners against sharp fluctuations in interest rates. The private-sector rental programs have included accelerated Capital Cost Allowances, the Multiple Unit Residential Building (a tax shelter for wealthy individuals), the Canada Rental Supply Program (a subsidy to builders of rental units) and shelter allowances to subsidize low-income earners in the private market.

In spite of these expenditures to assist the private sector, the supply of affordable accommodation in large cities remains a problem. With low vacancy rates throughout the 1980s in many cities, there was pressure to increase rents, thereby forcing provincial governments to intervene with rent controls. These controls, builders argued, reduce the incentive for new development. However, without controls, rents would have risen sharply, producing greater hardship for tenants who have become a strong voice in society, and therefore producing an unacceptable political fallout for any government abolishing controls.

SOCIAL HOUSING

The inability of the private sector, even with government assistance, to meet the need for affordable housing has given rise to the social housing or non-market housing movement. Canada's social housing sector is one of the smallest among the Western countries,[26] but it has grown in importance, largely because it offers a solution to the affordability problem.

The roots of the social sector are in housing directly owned by government. Referred to as "public housing," it was an attempt by government to meet the needs of the poor by building projects to house them. The first major public housing project in Canada was Regent Park North in Toronto, built after municipal taxpayers endorsed a $6 million dollar levy in 1947.[27] By the mid-1950s public housing projects had also been built in Saint John's, Halifax, Hamilton, Windsor and Vancouver. There was strong opposition at the municipal level, both on social grounds (creating "urban slums") and on financial bases, because under federal-provincial cost-sharing programs municipalities had to pick up the cost of support services.[28] Nevertheless, public housing appeared to be the most practical approach for housing the poor, and an infrastructure was gradually put in place for developing such projects. From 1949, a total of 206,000 units were built.[29]

From a high point of more than 20,000 units in 1971, public housing has declined to be replaced by a system of non-profit social housing developed by organizations independent of government — municipal non-profit housing agencies, and church, labour, native and co-op groups.[30] Since the mid-1960s, when the first pilot projects in social housing were initiated, about 300,000 units of social housing have been built.[31] This estimate includes non-profits under various federal programs, co-ops, native non-profits, and provincially funded social housing. To put this figure in perspective, in the period between the 1979 and 1989 when the vast majority of social housing was built, about two million houses of all types were built in Canada.[32] Social housing is still a small part of the housing market in Canada, but nevertheless it is significant.

Although there are many types of social housing, all have the common feature of being produced for use only and not as a commodity that would financially benefit the owner, as when private-sector housing is sold for a profit. The benefit to the tenants is secure tenure in good quality housing at a reasonable charge. When a tenant leaves a social housing unit, it is simply leased by the management to someone else. A major advantage of social housing over private-market rentals is that housing charges rise only to meet increased operating costs. With time, therefore, there is an increasing gap in the charge to tenants between social housing and private rentals. Without rent controls, which generally have pegged rent increases to the cost of living, this gap would be even greater.

Like private-sector housing that is not for the luxury market, social housing requires a supply-side subsidy in order to be built at a cost that tenants can afford. Again this is because the costs of building in large urban centres lead to housing charges that exceed the paying capacity of the average tenant. In response to this problem there have been a variety of federal initiatives, and, as housing responsibility has shifted to the provinces, they too have become involved and recently have assumed the primary initiative. Prior to 1973, social housing consisted of experimental demonstration projects with *ad hoc* funding arrangements. During 1973–74, when the Liberal minority government in Ottawa depended upon the NDP for support, amendments to the National Housing Act were passed "to make it easier for non-profit housing organizations to develop housing projects."[33] The main features of these initiatives were to enable the Canada Mortgage and Housing Corporation to make loans of an amount equivalent to the total cost of a project to non-profit corporations, including co-operative resource groups, and to make available financing for development services provided by non-profit housing associations and co-op resource groups.

In 1978 there were additional amendments, which led to the government shifting from providing financing to subsidizing and insuring financing arranged through independent financial institutions.[34] The subsidy reduced the effective mortgage rate, thereby making it possible for the housing charge to be set at the low end of market for the area in which a development was built. In addition, there were rent-geared-to-income supplements for people whose incomes were too low to meet the housing charge. This has been the basic arrangement through the 1980s, with several provinces — Ontario, Quebec, Manitoba[35] and very recently Alberta (through its Heritage Fund)[36] — becoming involved in financing their own developments. Since the Conservatives formed the federal government in 1984, more financing has shifted to the provinces and less financing has been provided federally. In addition, the government has placed greater pressure on social housing to move from mixed- to low-income communities, thereby obscuring one of the differences between it and public housing. The government sees itself as responding to the greatest social need rather than assisting the supply of an alternative social form.

CO-OP HOUSING

Of the social housing programs, the one that has received the roughest political ride is non-profit co-operative housing. As noted in Chapter 2, most co-operatives are self-reliant enterprises financing themselves from member investments and from revenues earned either from services paid for by members or from transactions in the market. Housing co-operatives are a form of user co-operative, the residents being the users of the service, and as such paying a charge that covers the operating costs of the development not subsidized by government. Subsidies from government, however, differentiate housing co-operatives from most other forms of co-operatives.

There are also some fundamental differences between housing co-ops and other forms of non-profit housing. Non-profits are based upon a rental relationship between tenants and a landlord, represented by the sponsoring organization which also forms the board. In housing co-operatives the tenants are also owners-in-common and members of the co-operative in which they live. The tenants, as members, control the development through electing a board from among themselves according to the principle of one-person/one-vote, and they also staff committees that work with hired management in operating the co-operative.[37] In a housing co-operative the residents have the same rights of ownership as in the private market, except the right to sell the development for a profit. The members lease their housing unit from the co-op and return it when they leave, at which point it is leased to a new member.

At year-end 1989 there were 65,000 units of co-op housing — primarily in Ontario, Quebec and British Columbia — with about 200,000 residents.[38] Housing co-operatives are being developed by about 60 resource groups across the country, including 30 in Quebec alone. The resource groups receive a fee-for-service payment for each project based upon the capital funding under the mortgage. Thus, these resource groups are examples of social enterprises that derive their income primarily from contracts with government.

In addition, there are 18 federations (regional and provincial) and a national federation (the Co-operative Housing Federation of Canada). The co-operative housing movement is the best organized within the non-profit housing sector, and for that reason the most threatening to private-housing developers. Co-operative housing has caused some rethinking among other forms of non-profits about encouraging greater tenant participation, both on the board and in management, largely because of lower operating costs in housing co-operatives. A 1990 Canada Mortgage and Housing Corporation evaluation of co-operative housing indicates that the operating costs per unit are much lower than in other forms of non-profits, and the housing co-ops are more successful at community-building than other non-profits.[39]

The dependence upon government financial assistance has made co-operative housing vulnerable to criticism from private-sector lobbyists. The nub of the criticism is that the supply-side subsidy which makes it possible to build affordable accommodation is benefiting other than the very needy. The criticism was expressed strongly in an evaluation by Canada Mortgage and Housing Corporation in 1983: "The programs do not support the government's social priority to serve those most in need."[40] Only 33 per cent of households in co-op housing, according to this CMHC evaluation, were in "core need."[41] This criticism was challenging a primary social objective of housing co-ops — the creation of mixed-income communities. In fact, the actual income mix in co-op housing is skewed toward low-income households, on average about 40 per cent having incomes of less than $20,000 and only about 20 per cent having incomes of more than $40,000.[42]

In spite of evidence showing that residents of co-op housing are predominantly of modest incomes, in the 1990s the federal government introduced a series of policy changes (including a cap on incomes of those eligible for co-op housing[43] and an increase in housing charges) that culminated in 1992 with the cancelling of its co-op housing program. The provinces have now become the only source for underwriting the costs of new co-op projects.

Out of concern about its dependence upon government, the housing co-op movement has taken a number of initiatives since the mid-1980s to become more self-sufficient. The Co-operative Housing Federation of Canada's lobbying of the Canada Mortgage and Housing Corporation resulted in the introduction in 1985 of an index-linked mortgage which pegs the interest rate on a mortgage to the rate of inflation.[44] In contrast to regular mortgages which front-load the interest payments, and therefore reduce the payment in constant dollars as the outstanding balance is reduced, an index-linked mortgage makes the payment in constant dollars similar throughout the term. The index-linked mortgage is appealing to government because it reduces the projected cost of financing, and it is appealing to the housing co-operative movement because it means that members coming in at different points in the life of a 35-year mortgage will have a similar financial burden.

Housing co-operatives in Toronto and Ottawa also have introduced land trusts.[45] Through this practice the land upon which a co-operative is situated is held in a trust and leased to the co-operative. During the life of the mortgage, the lease rate is nominal. However, once the mortgage is paid off, the lease rate increases so that the housing charge to members is maintained at a level equivalent to what it has been. Otherwise, members of the co-operative could have housing charges at an unjustifiably low rate.

The need for index-linked mortgages and land trusts also reflects a weakness in the control structure of co-operative housing. In giving exclusive control of a development to its residents, there is the risk that they will put their self-interest for a low housing charge above all other considerations. A resident moving into a housing co-operative in the latter years of a mortgage in which interest-payments are front-loaded, or even more so after the mortgage is paid off, is likely to inherit very low housing charges. Yet the government, not residents, bears the financial risk involved in developing the housing, and a new member in year 35 of a development, for example, has not even put sweat equity into the co-operative. The index-linked mortgage ensures that during the life of the mortgage the housing charges will be relatively constant, and the land trust ensures that the same will happen once the mortgage is paid off. As well as helping to avoid private-sector complaints that co-op housing costs are too low, these financing schemes also support the fundamental tenet of the co-op movement that responsibilities as well as benefits are shared equally by members.

The land trust, in effect, alters the control structure of the co-operative by introducing another stakeholder — the trustees of the land. The land trust, which is controlled by the housing co-ops whose land is held and by resource groups in the area, also provides a vehicle for financing new developments. It collects payments from individual co-ops and holds assets which can be mortgaged. In theory, it should be possible to accomplish the same objectives of financing expansion of the movement and keeping housing charges relatively constant by an individual co-operative remortgaging itself as the original mortgage is paid down. Doing so would probably require a multi-stakeholder board structure of which the residents would be but one component and in which organizations representing the movement —

resource groups, federations, a housing co-op bank (which is being contemplated to handle financial matters) — would also be involved. Such a model would have the disadvantage of reducing member control in any given development, but also the advantage of involving a broader array of participants who have a commitment to the expansion of social housing. This model might also be considered by other forms of non-profit housing that normally maintain control in the sponsoring organization and do not give sufficient influence to the residents. The multi-stakeholder arrangement, therefore, could lead to a common control structure for all forms of social housing, and therefore might unify the movement in its efforts to win support from governments.

However, the more fundamental problem is reducing the dependence upon government — the Achilles heel of social housing — and gaining greater self-sufficiency within the movement. Using index-linked mortgages as a means to financing, and land trusts to finance expansion are steps in that direction.

Another innovation is to have residents participate in financing their development — referred to as either limited equity or resident-financed non-profits.[46] Although this concept is still in the pilot phase, the general principle is to have non-profit housing (not sold on the market) in which each resident makes an investment and upon leaving receives it back. There still is a debate about whether there should be a rate of return and, if so, whether it should reflect only inflation or in addition a portion of any increased value of the project. There is also a debate about whether residents should finance the project in total or only in part. Two limited equity co-operatives have been formed to date, both involving seniors in Surrey, British Columbia.[47] Seniors with equity in a home who want security of tenure in a supportive community appear to be the most likely target group. However, the model is being assessed for other groups as well.

CONCLUSIONS

The trends that are pricing people out of the private housing market have continued throughout the 1980s. CMHC put the waiting list numbers for co-op housing alone at more than 40,000 in 1990, and many co-ops have closed their waiting lists.[48] The situation is similar for other non-profits. Governments are caught in the dilemma of having to provide incentives for increasing the supply of affordable housing, but also recognizing that there is little incentive for building such housing in the private sector because the economic rent which builders need to earn a profit is higher that what most people can pay. The decisions by the federal government to reduce the down payment required on new housing to only 5 per cent of the total cost and to allow people to use savings in RRSPs for that purpose are recent examples of the effort being made to broaden the range of the private market.

However, there is also a great need to increase the supply of social housing. Projecting current trends ahead, one can foresee a private-housing market serving the well-to-do and a social housing sector for households with middle and low incomes. With governments experiencing a financial crunch, tough choices will have to be made as to whether to continue to expend monies (tax expenditures and subsidies) in support of private housing or to invest more heavily in building new social housing and converting private rental accommodation to the social sector where it is freed from cost increase associated with speculative gain. At present about 95 per cent of Canada's housing stock is in the private sector.[49] However, about 10 per cent of the housing built between 1979–89 was social housing,[50] and the indications are that the trend toward more social housing will continue.

Within the social housing sector itself, co-operatives which are controlled by their residents appear to provide the most innovative model. However, a multi-stakeholder arrangement involving resource groups and federations could offset some of the weaknesses in resident-run co-ops. It could also lead to a more uniform arrangement with other types of social housing which would make efforts to gain government support for such housing more effective.

Social Service

This chapter analyzes two key areas of social service: healthcare and childcare. During the post-war era, both of these services have undergone fundamental changes in organization, and in recent years both have been the subject of fierce debate, as the public and governments search for appropriate delivery models. Among those that have emerged are non-profit models in which people with a common interest participate in centres which provide the service. These models are part of Canada's social economy.

This chapter starts with a discussion of healthcare, the context that has led to questioning of the private-sector approach, and then the alternative of a non-profit delivery system based upon community clinics. Subsequently, the chapter turns to childcare, again analyzing the context for change and the emerging delivery system of non-profit childcare centres.

HEALTHCARE

Like housing, healthcare is an essential service that a humane society makes available to all its citizens at a reasonable cost. And like housing, the actual costs of providing basic healthcare services have outstripped the means of people with lower and middle incomes, as well as those with chronic needs. Therefore, the governments of Canada, like many other governments in the West, have had to intervene and become a primary participant in financing healthcare.

The first actual plan became operational in 1947, after the Saskatchewan CCF government passed the Hospitalization Act providing government insurance for hospital care.[1] By 1957, the federal government had enacted its own plan that paid money to any province introducing comprehensive hospital insurance that was accessible to all residents and portable throughout the country.

Saskatchewan again was the laboratory for government-funded medical services, when it enacted the Medical Care Insurance Act (medicare) in 1962. The federal government followed suit when it legislated the National Medical Insurance Act in 1966. Since that time, there has been negotiations over the specifics of cost-sharing between the federal government and the provinces[2] and negotiations over issues such as users' fees charged by doctors, but government finance has remained a pillar of Canada's healthcare system. Since the mid-1970s, governments have paid for about three-quarters of all healthcare costs — the remainder coming from private insurance (extended coverage, dental and drug plans) and user fees.[3] By comparison, governments in the United States pay about two-fifths of healthcare expenditures.[4]

Yet in spite of this strong government presence in finance, the delivery of healthcare remains largely private, under the control of physicians working on a fee-for-service basis, and using facilities paid for by government and by donors both to hospital foundations and other healthcare organizations. This delivery system has been subject to criticism, the nub being that costs have risen to a point where governments burdened by debt can no longer afford them, and that the results are not commensurate with the increased costs.[5] The spiral in costs is unmistakable, moving from only $12.2 billion in 1975 to an estimated $60.2 billion in 1990.[6] When these figures are adjusted for inflation, healthcare costs have doubled in 15 years.[7]

Nor is the picture any different when viewed relative to population increase and the increase in the Gross National Product (GNP). On a per capita basis, healthcare costs have gone from $120 in 1960 to $1,912 (estimated) in 1990, and have increased almost four-fold in the past 15 years.[8] Relative to the GNP, healthcare has gone from 5.5 per cent in 1960 to 9.2 per cent in 1990, with about a 25 per cent increase since the mid-1970s.[9] When these figures are analyzed, the primary factors appear to be hospital and other institutional costs, which represent about 50 per cent of the total, physicians' fees representing about one-fifth, and drugs involving about one-tenth.[10] As these statistics show, healthcare in Canada is largely a disease-oriented system in which physicians help patients recover from illness, with hospitalization and drugs serving as important features of the model.

In the 1970s and 1980s, numerous government commissions criticized this disease-oriented approach to healthcare. In 1989, a provocative best seller, *Second Opinion*, by Michael Rachlis and Carol Kushner, drew public attention to the issue. The authors point out that a primary factor in increased healthcare costs has been the supply of physicians, which has increased from 1 for 800 Canadians in 1964 to 1 for every 465 by 1987.[11] Cost increases, according to Rachlis and Kushner, have been propelled by a fee-for-service payment system, which provides incentives for tests, prescriptions and hospitalization, and which "is oriented almost entirely toward treating and curing illness."[12]

Community Clinics

Rachlis and Kushner are among those advocating a socially controlled delivery system, which places greater emphasis on health promotion and disease prevention, and which encourages homecare as an alternative to hospitalization and nursing homes. The community health clinic has become the focal point for this alternative view of healthcare.

The roots of the community health model in Canada can be traced to the Victorian Order of Nurses, started in 1897, when Lady Aberdeen (the wife of Canada's governor general at that time) was granted a charter by Queen Victoria to proceed with an organization of nurses who, inspired by Florence Nightingale, would treat those in need of healthcare in their homes and in "cottage hospitals."[13] The first of these, established in Regina in 1898, might be seen as the pioneer community health clinic (CHC). By 1924, when the VON turned its cottage hospitals over to local authorities, 43 more had been established in communities and isolated areas across Canada to provide care to settlers.

The VON was born because there was a lack of basic health services at the turn of the century. The impetus for the more recent CHC movement was also a lack of basic health services, but for different reasons. When medicare was introduced in Saskatchewan in 1962, many doctors went on strike in protest, forcing local communities to organize the provision of their own healthcare by forming Community Health Service Associations.[14] Some of these associations went so far as to start actual clinics, five of which (Prince Albert, Saskatoon, Regina, Lloydminster and Wynyard) are still operating today.[15] According to Robin Badgley and Samuel Wolfe, authors of *Doctors' Strike*,

> Out of the pressure groups that arose during the medical conflict, only one, the community clinic survived. The concept of a consumer-sponsored group practice has captured the imagination of many of the general public and a sizeable number of doctors in recent decades. In Saskatchewan this movement developed as a direct consequence of the doctors' strike.[16]

The Saskatchewan community health clinics operate as consumer co-operatives, with many users of the service also being members with the right to exercise a vote in the affairs of the organization. About 50,000 of the 100,000 active patients are members.[17]

The birth of socially controlled healthcare in Saskatchewan lacked the same fanfare as government-financed insurance (medicare). Its movement onto the national stage has also lagged behind medicare. Like medicare, though, its birth was painful and strongly opposed by the private-delivery system controlled by doctors. However, unlike medicare, which doctors embraced when its financial benefits became clear, the opposition to a socially controlled delivery system has continued because it is perceived as a threat to doctors' autonomy. The Saskatoon Agreement, which concluded the doctors' strike in 1962, spelled out the rights of the citizens of Saskatchewan to establish community clinics.[18] Nevertheless, there was deep-seated animosity in the medical profession toward community clinics. For example, some doctors employed by the clinics were denied hospital privileges.[19] The provincial government, for its part, offered no particular support for community clinics, and it was not until 1972 that the clinics were funded directly for their services by the Department of Health.[20] Up until that time, the Saskatchewan clinics were dependent upon their doctors' billings to support their services.

The Quebec Model

The community health movement was given a major boost when Quebec introduced in 1972 a publicly funded province-wide system of Local Community Service Centres (CLSCs).[21] There are currently 158 CLSCs, each servicing a region of the province ranging from 53,000 people in urban centres to 14,000 in rural communities. The CLSCs combine primary healthcare and social services, with a strong emphasis on homecare. With the exception of child protection services, CLSCs have a full range of social services. The homecare programs emphasize prenatal and infant care. Of 70 full-time staff in the average CLSC, about half are nurses and social workers. These are supplemented by 6,000 homecare workers, or auxiliaries, often working part-time.

At present there is an average of four doctors per CLSC providing primary healthcare. These tend to be young general practitioners, disproportionately women, who are prepared to work on salary for a 35-hour week. In that respect they differ from most self-employed doctors who bill the government for each service they provide (fee-for-service). Eight regional CLSCs (Centre de santé) have specialists offering minor surgical services with in-patient facilities. Others hire psychiatrists on contract.

The participation of doctors remains a major problem for CLSCs. Newer clinics in particular have an insufficient number of doctors; recruitment is a problem, and there are high turnover rates. The resistance by doctors to participate in CLSCs goes beyond individual choice. From the beginning there has been strong resistance from doctors' organizations and hospitals, both of which appear threatened by CLSCs. On May 21, 1991, Montreal doctors conducted a one-day strike, which, among other issues, was to protest a provision coercing doctors with fewer than 10 years of practice to work in CLSCs.[22]

The organizational structure of CLSCs is perceived as a threat to the private delivery system. The CLSC is a non-profit corporation with a unique stakeholder board, which was modified in 1991 to consist of: five representatives elected by the public in the region served by the CLSC; two public representatives with specialized skills chosen by other public representatives; a representative elected by each of three staff groups

(medical, clinical and clerical); a member of a sponsoring foundation (if one exists); a representative of a related nursing home;
and the director, who is a non-voting member. The board structure is an attempt to create a balanced representative governance
of all the stakeholders involved in the CLSC. The medical staff
have much less control in the CLSC governance than in a private
practice. In effect, the CLSC — like other community health
clinics — provides the opportunity for greater public influence
over health policy and enshrines clinical staff such as nurses and
social workers with greater authority than private delivery systems.

In contrast to most CHCs in Canada, which have evolved
from the initiative of community activists, the CLSC system has
been a creation of Quebec's government. For that reason there is
a tendency among CHCs in the rest of the country to view the
CLSC as a government-controlled rather than community-con-
trolled system. Yet this interpretation seems misleading.
Through CLSCs, the Quebec government has been attempting to
decentralize the planning and co-ordination of health services
within 12 regional councils. Each CLSC operates within provincial and regional policy frameworks, but it has its own board,
which appears to have as much autonomy as that of CHCs in
other parts of Canada.

In fact, the health policy orientation of CLSCs and CHCs are
very similar. There is a difference, however, in the board arrangements. CHCs tend to base their governance on users of
their services who are also members. This is the general rule
among the 5 Saskatchewan clinics,[23] the 36 CHCs in Ontario,[24]
the 14 in Manitoba[25] and a small number in British Columbia
and Nova Scotia.[26] Some CHCs have staff on their boards, but
this tends to be done in an inconsistent manner rather than in a
carefully balanced approach as in Quebec. Regardless of their
official status on the board, staff have a more active role in CHCs
than users of the service, who on average tend to be a passive
group. A primary innovation of the community health movement is that it gives a stronger hand to both nurses (often referred to as 'practitioners') and social workers than other
delivery systems. In the official governance of the CLSC, they are
seen as equals to medical doctors. Another strength of the structure is that it removes any incentive for doctors working on

salary to undertake unnecessary tests or to hurry their diagnoses, as doctors on fee-for-service may do.

However, these strengths can also become weaknesses in that they make many doctors, and particularly specialists, reluctant to participate. Doctors prefer to be independent practitioners billing the provincial insurance plans for each service. This is not simply a problem for the CLSCs in Quebec, but for some community health clinics in other parts of Canada as well.

Another difficulty lies in the perception of the CHC's role in the healthcare system. A telling criticism of CLSCs by the Quebec government's Brunet Commission is that the public perceives them more as social service agencies providing homecare services than as primary healthcare clinics.[27] The broad social service emphasis of CLSCs makes them different from other community health clinics. But other CHCs, regardless of their success in providing primary healthcare, have also been perceived as merely a supplement to a healthcare system based on the private practice of doctors and a hospital system largely controlled by doctors. With the exceptions of Quebec and Saskatchewan, in order for a CHC to be funded it must undergo a feasibility assessment to demonstrate that it is meeting a need not being serviced through existing healthcare systems. The target groups are low-income earners, seniors, women, natives, teens, that is, groups with special needs that the CHC, with its ties to the community and its broad array of preventive services, might be better positioned to meet than the more impersonal regular system with its emphasis upon the treatment of disease. The politics of funding CHCs, therefore, has been to find a particular arrangement that is not perceived as threatening by the medical establishment. Rather than support community healthcare for the entire public, provincial governments — with the exceptions of Quebec's — have slipped this model into the system quietly and unobtrusively. The policy, it would appear, is based upon politics.

The Comprehensive Health Organization

Recently, three provinces — British Columbia, Ontario and Quebec — have conceptualized a non-profit model that might be more acceptable to both the medical profession and hospitals, but which also incorporates some ideals of CHCs. In Ontario and British Columbia this model is referred to as a Comprehensive

Health Organization (CHO),[28] and in Quebec it is called Organisations de soins intégrés de santé (OSIS).[29] The B.C. Ministry of Health is proceeding with a demonstration project in Victoria, and the Ontario Ministry of Health has approved plans for 12 sites in the province, with the first openings expected in the Rainy River and Northern Algoma districts.[30]

The workplan for the CHO incorporates much of the CHC agenda, with an emphasis on health promotion, disease prevention and at-home care. Because of the anticipated participation of the medical profession and hospitals, the CHO covers a complete range of medical services and could even include services not insured under medicare. From the perspective of government, a selling point for the CHO is the anticipated reduction of costs through funding approaches that are other than fee-for-service and through an anticipation of fewer referrals to hospital because of the auxiliary services. Such cost reductions have been demonstrated for other community models (in a study of Saskatchewan's community health co-operatives in 1983[31] and similar research in Ontario and the United States[32]). In 1989, when Ontario's health minister Elinor Caplan announced the CHO program, she emphasized the anticipated cost savings and the community philosophy designed "to foster independent living for all members, an approach that reflects our new, broader understanding of health."[33]

Until CHOs become operational, it is not clear whether they will provide an adequate balance among all stakeholders in the healthcare system or whether they will be a variation of doctor-controlled community clinics such as the Health Service Organization in Ontario or the polyclinic in Quebec. At this point, the board structure for the CHO is vague, though in Ontario at least 50 per cent of board members must be users of service.

Some critics of the healthcare system remain skeptical of the CHO. Douglas Angus of Queen's University and Pran Manga of the University of Ottawa, strong proponents of community health, have expressed their concerns:

We doubt that the nature of community participation in the CHO delivery system will be like that for the CHCs. ... There is also too great an emphasis on healthcare services and too little on other services. While capitation and salary payments may be preferred by government, the

CHO can and will concede physicians fee-for-service methods of payment. We suggest that these aspects of the CHO model are functionally related to its vertically integrated feature, that is, it involves both primary ambulatory care and specialized institutional care. The more vertically integrated and complex the delivery system, the more power could be invested in the medical profession and the administrative-managerial personnel.[34]

The concerns expressed by Angus and Manga have to be balanced against the weaknesses of the CHC created by the lack of co-operation of the medical profession. A possible remedy might be to raise doctors' salaries within the CHC model. If governments are contemplating a shift to the CHO, more evidence is needed to determine whether that model will strike a balance that incorporates the ideals of community health with a structure in which the medical profession is willing to work.

In Ontario, at least, the government seems intent on giving the CHO prominence, projecting that 15 per cent of the population will be enrolled within 10 years. In Quebec, which has made a commitment to its CLSC model, the OSIS (the parallel to the CHO) has been put on hold.[35] It would appear that the Quebec government has decided to attempt to strengthen the primary health services of CLSCs by pressuring more doctors to participate. The goal is for each CLSC to have eight doctors.

The struggle to create a healthcare delivery system based upon democratic social organizations is ongoing. Although there is public acceptance of the private-sector delivery system, rising costs are forcing its re-evaluation. As a result, in early 1992 Canada's health ministers agreed to promote alternatives to the fee-for-service method of payment, which forms the foundation of the private system.[36] These alternatives will involve either salary or capitation methods — approaches which are likely to give greater impetus to social organizations such as community clinics. Thirty years after the introduction of medicare in Saskatchewan, which began a revolution in the financing of medical services in Canada, there are signs that the methods for delivery of healthcare are also about to be transformed.

Conclusions

Through the models discussed in this chapter, Canadian governments are attempting to encourage a socially controlled healthcare system that will function in concert with government financing. It has often been said that Canada has a system of "socialized medicine." It would be more accurate to say that systems of socialized healthcare are struggling to emerge from a for-profit delivery system controlled by the medical profession. This struggle in socializing the delivery system began with the introduction of medicare and has gained momentum because of the escalating healthcare costs of the private delivery system. Although Canada's healthcare costs remain lower than those of the U.S.,[37] the cost increases are of concern to government. Because of this and a related belief that greater emphasis on health promotion and disease prevention will lead to better results, systems of socialized healthcare are gradually emerging. Of these, the CLSC model in Quebec is the most extensive, as it is province-wide and covers a broad range of primary health and social services. Its multi-stakeholder governance is innovative and could be a model for other social organizations. Yet a weakness in the CLSCs and CHCs in other provinces is the reluctance of the mainstream of the medical profession to work on salary. Recently, the Ontario and British Columbia governments have started pilot projects for CHO, a community-based model that might prove more attractive to doctors and hospital administrators. It is still too early to know whether the CHO will incorporate the ideals of the CHC, both in its approach to healthcare and its governance.

COMMUNITY-BASED CHILDCARE

While community healthcare is gaining more public support because of the spiralling costs associated with private-sector delivery models, community-based childcare is evolving for different reasons. Before discussing some community-based models for childcare, this section analyzes the context from which they have evolved.

Traditionally, childcare in Canada has been a private concern of the family. The exception is when child abuse occurs, in which case legal authorities and child protection agencies such as the Children's Aid become involved. In the last two decades there has been a revolution in childcare, with licensed centres assuming much greater responsibility. Social childcare (or daycare) has a tradition dating back to the nineteenth century when, for example, religious communities in Quebec established *salles d'asile* for as many as 1,000 children whose parents worked outside the home.[38] These children's shelters were financed primarily through Christian charity as a means of helping the poor.

As social forms of childcare have become more widespread, the social welfare tradition from which it arose has been called into question. Yet Canada still lacks a national policy for childcare. The need for such a policy is tied to the modernization of society, and particularly to the changing role of women. Statistics indicate that there has been a steady increase throughout this century in the participation of women in the paid labour force. From 1901–1961, the participation rate of women doubled from 14.4 per cent to 29.3 per cent,[39] and it had almost doubled again by 1990, when 57.6 per cent of women were employed. By 1990, women made up about 44 per cent of the paid labour force.[40]

This rapid change has included women with young children.[41] By 1988, 58.3 per cent of women whose youngest child was less than three years old were in the paid labour force, compared to 65 per cent of women with a youngest child of 3 to 5 years, and 72.6 per cent of women with a youngest child 6–12 years. Except for women over 55 years, the participation rates are very high, and continue to increase, regardless of whether the family has young children. The *Report of the Task Force on Child Care* aptly summarizes this change: "The typical Canadian family today has only one or two children, and mother works outside the home, usually in a full-time job, even when her children are young."[42]

Not only is the role of women changing, but the family unit and its relationship to society are changing as well.[43] The family is becoming smaller and thereby losing the supports from within itself traditionally used to maintain childcare, particularly when the mother is working. The shift away from an extended family involving multiple generations in the same household has meant the loss of an unpaid source of childcare. Similarly, the trend to having fewer children has led to a loss of childcare support from older siblings. Today's family unit is much less permanent, more mobile and in much greater need of external institutional assistance in childcare. External assistance, while it benefits the entire family, is most needed by women. Even though the participation rate of women in the labour force and social structure of the family have changed very rapidly, the tradition of patriarchy that forms the context for childrearing has remained unchanged. Data from the National Child Care Survey in Canada indicate that as of 1988 "working men are responsible for childcare in only six per cent of families."[44] Not only are women responsible for childcare, but also for meal preparation, housecleaning and laundry.[45] In other words, it appears that women are now carrying a double workload — in the labour force and in the household. This burden falls most heavily on the 7.1 per cent of women who are lone parents.[46]

Patriarchy is also underlined by the lower earnings of women in the labour force[47] and the sexual division of labour which places women in "pink ghettos." Childcare is one such job. It is almost exclusively a female profession, and like so many other female-dominated professions, the pay is very low.[48] A national daycare system is needed to address these issues.

Not only do daycare centres provide women in the labour force with the vital support of reliable, trained staff to care for their children; they may also, in some cases, give children a head start in their education, a contribution which is of particular importance to families where the parents have not enjoyed successful experiences at school. At minimum, children have an opportunity to meet with peers and to learn about sociable play. At centres where parents are part-time volunteers, children can also play with parents, and parents can meet each other, building up an informal support system.

Current Policies

Although there is a strong need for childcare centres, at present the arrangements are a hodge-podge, reflecting a lack of careful government policy.[49] The federal government participates in financing childcare through the Canada Assistance Plan, a cost-sharing arrangement with the provinces to subsidize placements for families with low and moderate incomes.[50] In 1989–90, the federal government spent $240 million on daycare through the Canada Assistance Plan, far short of the need. In addition, the federal government expended an estimated $530 million in 1989–90 on two tax measures — the Child Care Expense Deduction and the Child Care Tax Credit.

For the most part, childcare policy in Canada is being enacted at the provincial level, and there too the arrangements vary greatly and appear to be a makeshift response to dire need rather than based upon a coherent plan. In 1988–89, the provinces spent about $660 million on childcare, including cost-sharing under the Canada Assistance Plan, start-up grants, salary supplements, administrative grants and funding for children with special needs.[51]

This patchwork of funding programs — differing from province to province — is reflective of an inconsistent national policy that places the initiative on the individual family to make its own arrangements. According to the National Childcare Survey undertaken in 1988, the predominant mode of childcare was a "sitter."[52] In 1988, 814,000 Canadian families left at least one child with a sitter, about 40 per cent of whom were relatives, usually grandparents or aunts and uncles. The sitter arrangement is low-cost — one-third paying nothing and 85 per cent paying less than $50 per week. When a relative is the sitter, the payment is probably based on what parents can afford. Unlike childcare centres, there is a lack of regulation of sitters, a factor which may adversely affect the standard of care.

About 128,000 Canadian mothers sent at least one child to a childcare centre in 1988.[53] Eighty-nine per cent of these children were less than six years old, and almost one in five was from a lone-parent family. The average time that children spent in a centre was 31.4 hours a week, whereas the average sitter arrangement was only 20 hours.

Childcare centres are used primarily by families of low and modest incomes who can obtain subsidies — either total or partial — and the well-to-do who can afford to pay the going rate. According to the National Childcare Survey, 6 per cent of users pay nothing, about half pay less than $50 per week, and only 6 per cent are paying more than $100 per week.[54] The payments, of course, are lowered by the substandard wages of staff, thereby creating an indirect subsidy.

The trend in Canada is to rely less on privately owned commercial childcare centres. Research indicates that commercial centres do not provide as high a standard of care as non-profit centres, and that commercial centres pay lower salaries to already low-paid staff.[55] Many policymakers have accepted the view that the non-profit approach is preferable as a delivery system. The annual report of the National Child Care Information Centre indicates that the proportion of spaces in the commercial sector has shrunk from 75 per cent of the total in 1968 to 34 per cent in 1990.[56] The remaining spaces are in non-profits, except for about 9,300 municipally operated spaces, almost exclusively in Ontario.[57] Of the non-profits there are about 800 co-operatives located primarily in Ontario, Manitoba and Saskatchewan.[58]

In general, childcare co-operatives are based upon parents as the members. They form the board and also provide volunteer labour to assist the staff. Among other non-profits, there is much less consistency in the structure.[59] Quebec, which has encouraged non-profits through its funding policies, and Saskatchewan both require that at least 51 per cent of the board of directors be parents of children in the centre. Manitoba, New Brunswick and the Northwest Territories also specify minimums for parent participation on the board of a centre. Other provinces such as British Columbia, Alberta, Newfoundland and Ontario do not require parent involvement in the board. In Ontario, the current lack of a clear definition of the required structure for non-profit childcare centres has, according to the Ontario Coalition for Better Daycare, "encouraged the growth of pseudo non-profit operators" (privately controlled businesses using non-profit legislation), taking advantage of government grants. [60]

The crux of the childcare problem is that most families are unable to afford the going rates for licensed centres, and at present governments do not regard childcare as a service that should be available to everyone. In contrast to education and healthcare, government-funded services to which everyone is entitled, childcare is still seen as the responsibility of the family. When governments become involved in financing childcare, it is characterized as social welfare, in much the same way as social housing. This point was emphasized by the Report of the Task Force on Child Care:

> The present state of childcare in Canada is on a par with the state of education in this country in the late 1800s and healthcare in the 1930s. In a global perspective, Canada's childcare and parental leave programs lag far behind systems operating in most western industrialized countries.[61]

The Task Force recommended a government-funded system, cost-shared between the federal government and the provinces, and with national criteria, as for healthcare.[62] The estimated cost would be \$11.3 billion by 2001, the federal share consisting of \$6.2 billion.

At this point, this proposal, supported by advocates across Canada, remains a far-off dream, the federal government having backed off a 1984 election-campaign commitment to enact a national policy. In 1990, the National Child Care Information Centre estimated that for families with parents working full-time, only a minority of children were being served through licensed childcare centres (19 per cent of children 18 to 35 months and 10 per cent of children who were younger, for example[63]), and the Information Centre estimates "that about 50 per cent of those not using formalized care would do so if provided the opportunity."[64]

Nevertheless, the Information Centre also notes that there has been an eighteen-fold increase in the number of spaces for children in the last two decades, and the annual rate of growth over that period has been, excepting a few years, between 10 and 16 per cent.[65] More important, perhaps, in the arrangements created to date, one can find the embryo of successful models that may form the basis for a national policy.

Models for a Childcare System

As noted, the trend in Canada is away from childcare centres operated on a commercial basis by the private sector. However, within the non-commercial models, there is a debate about whether to encourage parent-controlled non-profits, including co-operatives, or to integrate childcare centres within the school system, albeit with parent advisory boards.

Although parent involvement is seen as desirable in both of these approaches, independent non-profits rely more strongly on parents, not simply for involvement with respect to childcare policy, but also for administrative and financial arrangements. The concern is whether those responsibilities present an unfair burden to working parents. This point is highlighted in the 1989 policy statement by the Ontario Coalition for Better Daycare.[66] In that statement the Coalition reversed its position on non-profit childcare, criticizing it as an "underfunded cottage industry."[67] The Coalition pointed out that the current arrangement depended upon the volunteer labour of overburdened parents, usually mothers already responsible for a job in the labour force and the household, to assist staff who are poorly paid, overworked and who, as a result, turn over rapidly. Put differently, childcare policy in Canada is grounded in patriarchal traditions in which poorly paid women care for children whose mothers are working, most often in low-paid jobs. Under those circumstances the volunteer aspects of co-operatives and other nonprofits can become quite onerous. The Ontario Coalition for Better Daycare labelled this arrangement an "administrative nightmare ... replicated in many non-profit centres across the province. ... While many parents may be interested in their children's program, few are interested in being a director of a corporation that may be administering a half-million dollar budget and employing many staff!"[68]

The Coalition's analysis of this point is consistent with research in Quebec which shows a lack of parent involvement in non-profit childcare centres.[69] Only 44 per cent attended annual general meetings at which the board was elected, and only 56 per cent attended meetings with the centre's staff. This lack of parent involvement formed the basis for a re-evaluation of the nonprofit model in Ontario. The Ontario Coalition, which up until its 1989 discussion paper had been advocating the non-profit, parent-controlled model, changed its position and started encouraging a "publicly-operated universally accessible system ... for children 3.8 years and over, that would be introduced through the public school system over the next five years."[70] Childcare would become an extension of public education — a right to which every child is entitled — rather than a service to parents in need. At the same time, the Ontario Coalition maintained its concern about parent involvement, suggesting that each school board establish a Parent Council and an Early Childhood Services Committee.[71]

This proposal followed a direction taken in other jurisdictions, particularly Quebec and France. During the 1980s, Quebec created a system of school-based childcare — *milieu scholaire* — for school-age children who require after-school childcare while their parents are at work.[72] The care is provided on the school's premises from 7 a.m. to 6 p.m. and is administered through the school and the local Board of Education, with a parents' committee having an advisory role. A school starts a *milieu scholaire* program when a minimum of 10 children require care. Start-up and operating grants are provided through the provincial Department of Education. Users of the service pay a fee of $1.50 per hour — the users' fees covering staff salaries. This program is in elementary schools throughout Quebec. When a new school is built or an old school is renovated, space is now set aside for childcare. A lack of space and difficulty in co-ordinating with school bus schedules are the primary obstacles to making this program universal throughout Quebec. In the school year 1990–91, the *milieu scholaire* program served 30,000 children in 715 schools.[73] The number of spaces has grown steadily over the past decade from only 1,649 in 1980.[74] Nevertheless, the provincial unit responsible for childcare — the Office des services de garde à l'enfance — estimates that only half of the need is being met.

There are other school-based after-school childcare programs in Canada. The York Board of Education in Metropolitan Toronto had programs in 21 of its schools in 1990–91.[75] However, Quebec's *milieu scholaire* program is the only example in Canada of a province-wide approach. The 1989 policy statement of the Ontario Coalition also proposed a province-wide, school-based system, but from 3.8 years, the age at which the Ontario government has mandated the province's school boards to provide half-day kindergarten by 1995.[76] The Ontario Coalition's proposal piggybacks on the government's plan, suggesting that there be a "seamless day" merging childcare and education.

There is a similar arrangement in France, where publicly funded *écoles maternelles* serve about 85 per cent of children three to five years old and publicly subsidized private schools serve an additional 13 per cent.[77] France's *écoles maternelles* program covers both the school day and a "wrap around" (*services périscholaires*) for children who have to be dropped off early or picked up late. Parents pay $210 annually for this extended care. In the French system, staff are highly educated with college degrees plus specialized training in early childhood education. In other words, public education has been extended to age three.

Although the school-based model for childcare centres has some practical administrative and financial advantages, advocates of independent, non-profit centres are concerned about the lack of parent control. Judith Martin, a leading Saskatchewan activist and the founding chair of the Canadian Daycare Advocacy Association, is blunt in her criticism:

The school system is anything but a model to advance. We all know what happens to many children, and especially working-class children, in that system. ... It makes a difference for the centre to be "yours," even if you don't participate on the Board. You have some power.[78]

Parent involvement is a common theme running through the presentations of all leading childcare advocacy groups. However, as Martin points out, for parent control to work, there has to be appropriate funding and administrative support. Therefore, she has advocated a parent-controlled, non-profit model with "community co-ordination" bodies providing an infrastructure.[79] These community co-ordination bodies would be analogous to resource groups in the social housing model, providing assistance to establish new centres, relieving the individual centres of some administrative responsibilities, such as bookkeeping and equipment maintenance, and serving as a liaison between the individual centres and the provincial government. The community co-ordination bodies would have a representative structure of key stakeholders in the childcare area, including the individual centres, government and advocacy groups.

There is currently one organization operating in Canada that provides a type of infrastructure for preschool childcare centres. Parent Co-operative Pre-School International assists preschool co-operatives with start-ups and ongoing problems through councils in Ontario, British Columbia and Quebec.[80] The councils are second-tier co-operatives to which about 800 local centres belong. The local centres are both part-time nursery schools and preschool daycares. Parents of children using the centres make up at least 50 per cent of the board of directors, and according to Pat Fenton, president of Parent Co-operative Pre-School International, total parent control of the board is quite common. Fenton believes that a parent board is important to balance the influence of staff in daily affairs.

The preschool co-ops also require parent participation in their programs, particularly in the nursery schools. For parents working at full-time jobs, the level of participation may be too taxing for some. The general strategy adopted by childcare activists at this point is to create structures that will encourage parents to participate but at a manageable level. This is where the community co-ordination bodies would help by taking over some of the centres' administrative and financial functions.

An example of this type of program has been operating on a small scale in Quebec, where CLSCs have taken an active role in organizing non-profit childcare services for young children.[81] These include full-day centres in some CLSCs, stopover centres for those requiring intermittent care, self-help groups for parents of children with special needs, and such homecare arrangements as babysitting co-operatives. In effect, Quebec is piggybacking parent-based childcare within local communities upon its network of CLSCs already spanning the province. The staff of the CLSCs also use childcare centres for healthcare promotion and disease prevention, thereby making those programs more effective.

In Ontario, daycare advocates are now proposing a model that would make participation in non-profits less onerous for working parents by relieving each individual centre of financial administration. According to this 1990 proposal of the Ontario Coalition for Better Child Care, the financial administration of licensed centres would be done through the provincial government, with parents participating in the program being billed monthly by the government department administering the program.[82] The charge per child to parents would be adjusted for income. With that type of administrative support and with improved funding for centres, the Ontario Coalition now suggests that a non-profit model would be best.

In the non-profit models, maintaining parent involvement is a primary concern. Ironically, staff involvement is assumed but rarely highlighted. Among the non-profit centres in Canada, nine in Ottawa have created a governance based upon both parents and staff.[83] The Ottawa group consists of co-operatives with 125 staff serving over 500 children. The ratio of staff to parent representatives in the governance varies among the centres, but in all cases the parents are in a majority (at least 51 per cent), and the president of the corporation is a parent. The staff is also unionized through CUPE (the Canadian Union of Public Employees). This group of centres has formed its own association, the Ottawa Federation of Parent Day Care Centres, to promote the parent/staff co-operative model. These nine Ottawa centres are structured on the premise that parents and staff are the key stakeholders.

Conclusions

The increased participation of women in the labour force has led to the need for more childcare centres. The existing number of spaces is much less than the demand, resulting in parents making arrangements with a sitter, usually a family member or neighbor. There is government assistance for lower income users of centres, but in general the cost of the service is a financial burden to parents. The low earnings of staff, usually women, help to subsidize the costs.

The trend in Canada for childcare centres is toward non-profit models, based upon parent volunteer participation, including the governance. For many working parents, this model represents an unfair burden to them, particularly if they are expected to participate in financial administration. As a result, the Ontario Coalition in 1989 advocated integrating childcare centres within the public school system from 3.8 years of age. This proposal was based upon a similar program in France. The most extensive example of school-based childcare in Canada is *milieu scholaire* program in Quebec, an afterschool program for school children throughout the province.

However, the predominant model advocated across Canada is the parent-controlled non-profit centre. To make that model work, advocates agree that parents must be relieved of a portion of the administrative responsibility and that centres must be funded properly. In Saskatchewan a community co-ordination body has been proposed to work with groups of five centres. The Ontario Coalition is proposing that financial administration be run through the provincial government, rather than each centre. A group of nine centres in Ottawa has a dual-stakeholder model consisting of parents and staff.

8

Social Capital

As noted throughout this book, financing is a problem in the social economy. For development to proceed more rapidly, there have to be sources of investment capital. In this chapter, key sources are discussed, some of which are located within the social economy itself, and therefore referred to as social capital, and some of which are in the private sector, but could have some affinity to the social economy. The chapter begins with a discussion of pension funds, a vast pool of investment capital for the economy, much of which also represents the savings of working people. The rules governing pension funds also raise some basic issues regarding investment in the social economy.

PENSION FUNDS

In Canada, as in other capitalist countries, not only is most capital invested within the private sector, but its control is concentrated in a small number of hands. This pattern of concentrated ownership has been documented by a number of researchers over the years,[1] one of the more recent and provocative being William Carroll.[2] Carroll notes that from the mid-1970s "the centralization of capital already under indigenous control reached dizzying heights" through a frenzy of takeovers of weaker companies by stronger corporations.[3] By 1985, only 46 corporations controlled 71 per cent of industrial assets in Canada. Carroll argues further that through interlocking relationships in corporate control and directorships, there are nine dominant group-

ings, largely familial in nature, which control companies representing 46 per cent of the stock value on the Toronto Stock Exchange.[4] The names of these "empires" are quite familiar —
Bronfman, Thomson, Demarais, Weston, Black, Reichmann.

Canada's corporate empires include both industrial corporations and financial institutions, an important component of
which are the savings of workers, primarily pension monies.
According to Statistics Canada, the total reserves of retirement
savings plans in Canada at year-end 1987 were $367 billion.[5]
About two-thirds of this total was in "employer-sponsored pension plans" and the remainder was in Canada/Quebec Pension
funds and Registered Retirement Savings Plans (RRSPs). The
scale of these savings becomes apparent when they are compared to the total assets of industrial corporations in Canada. In
1990, these were $625 billion, at least a substantial portion of
which was the pooled savings of workers, often administered
through insurance and trust companies that are part of these
same corporate empires.[6]

The role of workers' savings in corporate financing is documented in a 1989 book by Richard Deaton, a researcher with the
Canadian Union of Public Employees (CUPE).[7] He argues that
"institutional investors" (of which pension funds are an important part) "are now the dominant force in the securities market
and have the largest holding of corporate shares."[8] Since the
mid-1960s, pension funds have averaged about 25 per cent of all
equity investments in Canada. Not only are pension funds leading investors in Canadian companies, but because of their
managers' concern about reliable returns they have also tended
to be concentrated in blue chip investments, thereby coming to
dominate some large, publicly traded corporations.[9] "Pension
fund shareholdings are generally held in 20 of the 872 listed
companies, accounting for nearly 50 per cent of the value of the
TSE (Toronto Stock Exchange) Composite Index," a Wood
Gundy study shows.[10]

Pension funds are also important players in financing the
takeovers which have led to the centralization of control. In fact,
pension funds, according to Deaton, have accelerated this process "by generating a significant portion of the required cash for
these activities."[11] This practice — referred to as "pension fund
socialism" by Peter Drucker[12] — has become so pronounced in

the United States that the Federal Department of Labor has been attempting to restrict it.

There is an irony in utilizing pension monies to finance takeovers that deserves comment. Pension funds are the deferred earnings of workers invested to provide income after they retire. Quite often takeovers lead to so-called corporate restructuring and the reduction of company workforces. Assuming that increasing job opportunities is in the interests of employees as a whole, it could be argued that the liberal use of pension monies to finance corporate takeovers is contrary to the interests of their beneficiaries. However, the increasing of job opportunities is not generally a criterion that is applied to evaluate the benefit of pension fund investments. Where funds are administered by trustees, they are guided by the "prudent person principle" in determining investment policies. Although there are differing interpretations of "prudence," legal opinion has tended toward a narrow interpretation based upon maximizing the financial return to the beneficiaries. This concern about financial obligations has also shaped investment policies, pushing them in the direction of bonds and debentures with a fixed rate of return, and, where equity investments are taken, toward blue-chip corporations which have paid regular dividends.

However, within the widely accepted view that the primary obligation of a pension fund is to generate the revenue needed to achieve the benefits expected by participants, a fierce debate has developed about the extent to which social and ethical criteria should enter into investment decisions. This debate pertains not only to pension funds but also to other forms of investment funds, which will be discussed subsequently.

The lightning rod for ethical debate concerning pension funds was from a 1984 decision by the Court of the Queen's Bench in England (Cowan vs. Scargill), a decision that has been cited in Canada as well.[13] In that case, union trustees for the coal miners' fund insisted that there not be investments in energy industries in direct competition with coal. Essentially, the union was attempting to place some social criteria on the investment policies of its members' pensions. Justice Megarry, writing for the court, ruled against the union trustees:

When the purpose of the trust is to provide financial benefits for the beneficiaries, as is usually the case, the

best interests are normally their best financial interests. ...
Trustees may be firmly opposed to any investment in
South Africa or other countries, or they may object to any
form of investment in companies concerned with alcohol,
tobacco, armaments or many other things. ... Yet under a
trust, if investments of this type would be more beneficial
to the beneficiaries than other investments, the trustees
must not refrain from making the investments by reasons
of the views they hold.[14]

The Megarry rule was cited by Malcolm Rowan, the chair of
Ontario's *Task Force on the Investment of Public Sector Pension
Funds*, as a basis for guiding investment policies.[15] In general he
argued for less investment in government bonds and a greater
emphasis on the "capital market," including equity investments,
in order to yield a higher return.

The Megarry judgement, and the recommendations following from it, have also been subject to much criticism. Patricia
Lane, the former Director of Research and Legislation of the
British Columbia Federation of Labour, points out that the trustees of several British Columbia union pension funds have already been using ethical and social criteria in making investment
decisions.[16] For example, the International Union of Operating
Engineers Local 115 has invested pension monies in social housing and the construction of a hotel in Nanaimo. Furthermore, all
of its projects involve unionized contractors. The Carpentry
Workers Pension Fund has created a subsidiary corporation, The
Western Development Co-operative, to build affordable housing, of which it either retains ownership (as an investment) or
which it sells on the open market. It too deals only with unionized workers. The Telecommunication Workers Union Pension
Fund instructs its trustees to refrain from investing in South
Africa and other countries with repressive régimes. Citing these
examples, Lane makes the more general point:

Why, if we have in our control this large pool of capital
that could be used to improve the overall standard of
living in our community, to set up, low cost housing, or
senior citizens' homes or healthcare clinics or long-term
permanent job creation and at the same time improve
pensions — why should we send this money to increase

profits of large companies who do not have fair wage policies or who manufacture munitions.[17]

An important part of the argument in favour of the investments advocated by Lane is that financial returns have been excellent. This same point is emphasized by other advocates of "ethical investment" policies.

In summarizing Canadian legal opinion on the issue, Edward Waitzer (a partner in law firm Stikeman, Elliott) issues a blunt warning:

> If ethical choices do not lower investment returns, the practical (and legal) reality is that trustees are unlikely to face judicial interdiction, regardless of their motivation. If investment returns are lowered, trustees are in trouble.[18]

Waitzer reflects the predominant view about the investment of pension monies. But Waitzer (like many others) assumes that only some types of investment reflect ethical choices. By comparison, conventional investments in government bonds or in the private sector are assumed to be neutral and not based on any particular ethical point of view. This is a questionable interpretation of ethics, but more important, it raises the concern that investments of pension monies in the social economy are more likely than conventional investments to be scrutinized carefully and subject to criticism if the return is poor.

But in spite of this concern, there is nevertheless a tradition, well accepted not only by unions but also by governments, of using social criteria with respect to the investment of pension monies. For example, the federal government permits each of the provinces to utilize for its provincial budget its share of Canada Pension funds held to meet future pension obligations. Ontario has used its share ($15.8 billion by year-end 1987) primarily for general government expenditures, though $1.1 billion has been borrowed specifically by Ontario Hydro, a provincial Crown corporation.[19] In 1988 Ontario also borrowed $3 billion of its share of the CPP monies to finance 30,000 units of social housing (the Homes Now program).[20] That investment, albeit a departure from tradition, is an example of how pension funds could be used to develop the social economy. Since CPP monies are loaned to the provinces at preferred rates of interest, it was financially advantageous to tap this source. Arguably, Ontario's financial gain is the federal government's loss in that the Canada pension funds it administers are not yielding the best financial return. However, return can also be defined more broadly to include the social impact of investments, for example, in meeting the needs for affordable housing in communities. That type of impact can be evaluated through a social audit — an evaluation of the social consequences of an investment — as opposed to the more typical financial audit that focuses strictly on financial impact. Social impact is not only important in its own right but it also affects financial impact. For example, there is a financial spin-off from building social housing projects, in that residents with affordable housing charges are less likely to depend upon welfare and therefore more likely to become gainfully employed.

The Quebec Model

Probably the best Canadian example of the application of social criteria to the investment of pension monies has occurred in Quebec where, since 1966, the government has consolidated all of the public pension funds (including the available monies in Quebec Pension) into one fund, the Caisse de dépôt et plaçement du Québec. With holdings of $36.7 billion at year-end 1989, and with new investments of $2 billion each year, the Caisse de dépôt has become one of the largest pools of investment funds in Canada.[21]

Like other pension funds, the Caisse de dépôt is concerned with the financial return on its investment so that it can meet its obligations to about 4 million Quebec pensioners whose money it holds. However, within that constraint it endeavors to meet a social goal of promoting "Quebec's economic development."[22] It does this in a number of ways: about half of its portfolio is in bonds, primarily Quebec institutions such as the province, Hydro-Québec, municipalities and school boards; about 6 per cent of its portfolio is in mortgages — residential, commercial and industrial; and another 5 per cent is in developing large- and medium-sized real estate projects, including partnerships with development companies (such as the Société immobilière trans-Québec). The Caisse is also the largest Canadian investor in the stock market, holding shares in more than 350 Canadian companies and investing heavily in about 30 large corporations.

In another type of investment, the Caisse de dépôt has entered into arrangements (referred to as "partnerships") with dynamic small- and medium-sized businesses in Quebec.[23] In these arrangements, Caisse representatives become members of the board of directors to ensure that company decisions are not creating undue risks for its investments. The Caisse is also a stakeholder in nine investment companies that have invested $275 million in 45 Quebec businesses. In addition, the Caisse has invested $226 million directly in another 61 such enterprises, thereby promoting its objective of "creating benefits for small- and medium-sized Quebec partners."

The Caisse de dépôt's policies are a clear illustration of how social criteria are being used to guide pension fund investment decisions. The influence of its policies is apparent in the Rowan report on Ontario public pension funds, which advises the province that it "could pursue a more indirect approach similar to the way the Quebec Government's economic development objectives are served by the Caisse de dépôt et plaçement."[24]

The policies of the Caisse de dépôt run counter to the predominant tendency of modern capitalism to give investors a free hand in seeking the best return. The Caisse is channeling the deferred earnings of Quebecers into investments that are intended primarily to develop that province, and arguably in support of Quebec's nationalist aspirations. The Caisse's policies therefore are oriented toward a type of social investment, that is, investment guided by both social and financial criteria. In light of modern trends, there is some controversy surrounding such policies. The need for justification would become even greater were these investments to move beyond government bonds and stock in private sector companies and into corporations in the social economy.

Labour-Sponsored Funds

Labour-sponsored funds are pools of investment capital that are similar to other mutual funds but are unique in that their sponsoring organization is a major labour federation, and, as a result, unionized workers belonging to the federation are more likely to participate. These funds therefore are harnessing a pool of investment capital which other funds might not attract.

In Canada, the prototype of the labour-sponsored fund is the Quebec Federation of Labour Solidarity Fund (Fonds de solidarité des travailleurs du Québec [FTQ]), started in 1984. By 1990 its net assets had climbed to $300 million, spurred by 20 per cent tax credits from both the federal and provincial governments.[25] The objectives of the FTQ are "to encourage the development of Quebec business enterprises by inviting labour to participate in such development by subscribing to shares of the Fund."[26] The investors in the FTQ are Quebecers, about 70 per cent of whom are unionized and predominantly from locals affiliated with the Quebec Federation of Labour. The investors purchase a share based upon a value determined by the board, which they are expected to hold until retirement or death, thereby also making them eligible for the tax advantages of an RRSP (in addition to the federal and provincial tax credits).

The FTQ calls itself "the largest development capital corporation in Quebec,"[27] investing primarily in "small- and medium-sized business enterprises, which are the source of the greatest number of jobs in Quebec."[28] Unlike a pension fund, the FTQ does not have to realize a return sufficient to meet a defined benefit level. People purchasing shares in the FTQ know that investments in small businesses can be risky. In view of the fund's mandate, therefore, shareholders in the FTQ may not see the best rate of return as the primary criterion for evaluation. But the FTQ still has to realize a return that will make it attractive to potential investors. To assure that its investments are effective, the FTQ has a staff of 30 financial specialists who scrutinize each prospective business and who monitor subsequent performance. The FTQ is an activist investor, viewing itself as a "partner" with board positions, that intervenes when dissatisfied with performance and suggests steps that may be taken to overcome the problem. The Fund's most high-profile project has been organizing the consortium and investing $5 million to keep the Montreal Expos baseball team in the province.

The FTQ has been criticized for its performance. In its first six years, share values increased from $10 to only $12.57,[29] though with tax credits the benefit to investors was far greater. The FTQ's general manager and president, Claude Blanchet, acknowledges that performance could be better, but argues that the Fund's mission also involves creating and sustaining jobs: "There's an equilibrium between job creation and return on capital."[30] Investing in small- and medium-sized businesses can be risky, and in a competitive market some of these ventures fail.

Blanchet's principle (the balance between job creation and financial return) differs from the Megarry rule, with its singular preoccupation with financial return. Blanchet's principle also opens the door to a broader social audit, including environmental impact. The FTQ has focused its social audit on jobs in Quebec, and preferably in unionized companies, though its dealings with small businesses also involve non-unionized workers.

Of the FTQ's current investments, all are within the private sector, though two involve employee buyouts.[31] The Director of Communications, Jean-François LeBrun, says that the FTQ "looks favourably at employee ownership and in general tries to encourage workers and owners to co-operate."[32] It has established an educational foundation that offers two-day courses to workers on the economics of business. LeBrun also indicates that the FTQ would consider investments in worker co-operatives and other social enterprises, though it has none at present.

The FTQ has inspired the formation of a number of similar funds by other labour organizations. The Canadian Federation of Labour (an organization of construction unions not affiliated with the Canadian Labour Congress) has a small ($2 million in 1990) nationally-incorporated fund, Working Ventures. But, unlike the FTQ, its policy is based on the Megarry rule of "maximum return for investors," and its investments are not restricted by social considerations.[33] The Ontario government announced in 1991 that it will provide tax credits for a Labour-Sponsored Investment Fund that, like the FTQ, will target small- and medium-sized businesses based in the province.[34] It is unclear whether the Ontario Federation of Labour will make use of this opportunity. At its 1989 convention, it agreed in principle to a fund that would invest in social housing, community economic development and environmental technologies, but it balked at including worker buyouts, largely because of objections from unions such as the Canadian Auto Workers that argued that such investments are not in the best interests of workers.[35] A proviso restricting the Ontario fund to minority positions in its investments might satisfy the OFL's opposition to total worker buyouts.

Another labour-sponsored fund just getting underway in 1992 is the Working Opportunity Fund in British Columbia.[36] Projected to have $100 million of assets in five years, it will focus on investments in the non-resource industries, thereby encouraging greater diversification of British Columbia's economy. The fund is being directed by David Levi, a founder of VanCity Credit Union's very successful Ethical Growth Fund.

Of the labour-sponsored funds started to date, the one that emphasizes social criteria most strongly is the Crocus Investment Fund, sponsored by the Manitoba Federation of Labour, and just underway in 1991.[37] The Crocus Investment Fund was set up as a response to the closing of businesses and the resulting flight of jobs and capital from Manitoba. The Fund intends to enter into joint ventures with businesses in the province in an effort to assist their development. In particular, it targets family businesses in which there is no heir for a retiring owner, unionized publicly traded companies which may be the target of leveraged buyouts from out-of-the province, and selected start-ups. Many of its goals are similar to the FTQ; however, the Crocus Fund also emphasizes workers' control of its investments.

The Crocus Fund was designed largely by Sherman Kreiner, a Philadelphia-based consultant, who took a leading role in organizing worker buyouts of closing A&P supermarkets in the Philadelphia area in the 1980s. As such, the design of the Crocus is influenced in part by the American experience in Employee Stock Ownership Plans (ESOPs). However, unlike ESOPs, which are largely benefit plans set up by corporations for their employees and often lacking in full voting rights for employees, the Crocus Fund encourages workers' control of the workplace. Like ESOPs, the Crocus Fund structures its purchases through a voting trust. Stock that the Fund purchases in a company will be held in trust, and the voting rights (not the stock itself) are assigned to the employees, each having one vote in instructing the trustees on how to vote on the stock. Through this procedure, voting rights are separated from property rights, which remain with the Fund.

The employees of a company being purchased through the Crocus Fund do not have to make out-of-pocket allocations for stock purchases. They are encouraged to invest in the Fund itself, though they are not required to do so. By investing in the Fund rather than their place of work, the double jeopardy of worker-investors who, in the case of a business failure, lose both their jobs and their investments is avoided. Also, like investment funds in general, Crocus spreads its investors' risks by diversifying its portfolio.

The Crocus Fund (as with ESOPs) allows for a gradual trans-fer of stock to the employee trust within a company. In addition, the trust is structured so that the assets which it controls can be levered for loans to purchase additional stock. The Fund antici-pates that the tax advantages of a Deferred Profit Sharing Plan (DPSP) can be utilized in purchases where the company has been paying a dividend on its stock, thereby permitting the loan to be repaid in pretax dollars.

In transferring voting rights to the workers of a company under purchase, the Crocus Fund has adopted a philosophy that is markedly different than other labour-sponsored funds. The FTQ has entered into partnerships with private-sector entrepre-neurs, taking board positions to protect the interests of the fund. The Swedish Wage Earner Funds (no longer receiving additional monies but owning about 5 per cent of shares in publicly held Swedish corporations) divides the voting rights associated with its purchases between the fund itself and the employees of a firm in which it invests.[38] The Crocus, by comparison, is more ex-treme, opting for complete control by the employees. In that respect it is embracing the philosophy of the worker co-operative movement and stating, at least implicitly, that control of the workplace ought to reside with employees according to the dem-ocratic principle of one-worker/one-vote. In companies in which Crocus is a partial investor, the structure will be similar to the worker-shareholder co-operatives in Quebec (see Chapter 2).

To realize this principle of workers' control in practice, the Crocus Fund intends to be involved in the organizational devel-opment of companies in which it invests so that employees will be prepared to assume the responsibilities entrusted to them. In practice, the Fund itself will still retain much control because of its financial arrangements with the trust within a company and because of its in-house expertise, which will be used to assess the feasibility of each project and to monitor its progress. The Crocus will become like the Caja for the Mondragon co-operatives or like the consulting group and financial co-operatives used by the Confédération des syndicats nationaux for its related social en-terprises in Quebec. Like these other models, the Crocus will represent a "socialization of entrepreneurship."

Nevertheless, the question of where control ought to reside is an interesting one to consider. The Crocus takes the position, espoused by the co-operative movement in the nineteenth century (by the Rochdale Pioneers in England), that labour should take precedence over capital. This position was a reaction against capitalism, which was seen as representing the domination of labour by capital. Should the Crocus be able to demonstrate a rate of return on investments comparable to other funds, while permitting the workers' trust fund to control the stock in their company, it may indeed have a major impact on the philosophy of labour-sponsored funds.

Social Funds

There is capital within financial institutions in the social economy — credit unions, caisses populaires, mutual and co-operative insurance companies — that represents an important source of investment funds. At the end of 1989, the assets of credit unions and caisses populaires amounted to $63.2 billion, and there was another $31.3 billion in other financial co-operatives such as insurance and trust companies.[39] Some of these funds could form the basis for investments in the social economy, but only a small portion is actually used for this purpose.

In part this is because the use of these funds is restricted by their purpose and by the philosophy of financial co-operatives. Rather than seeing themselves as part of a co-operative system, or of a social economy, financial co-operatives are independent organizations that tend to pride themselves on servicing their members' needs better than the competition. The hallmark of financial co-operatives, then, has become small, personal loans to members for consumer purchases, mortgages or small business investments. The small size of individual financial co-operatives and the needs of their clientele, who are also their members, encourages this course of action.

There is also a select group of financial co-operatives which, in their philosophy and investment practices, have supported social enterprises. The Evangeline Credit Union in the Acadian region of western Prince Edward Island has been the financial linchpin for a system of 15 co-operatives (see Chapter 5).[40] The Caisse populaire des syndicats nationaux de Montréal and the Caisse d'économie des travailleuses et des travailleurs de Québec provide much of the financing for the CSN's investments in social housing, worker ownership and community economic development projects (Chapter 5).[41] Bread and Roses Credit Union in Toronto and the CCEC Credit Union in Vancouver also have focused on investments in projects structured as co-operatives and non-profits.

In addition to these select financial co-operatives, some initiatives have been undertaken by central organizations. For example, Co-op Trust has provided much of the mortgage money for co-operative housing and has also invested in mortgages for non-profits such as seniors' housing and nursing homes.[42] Much of this money comes from The Co-operators, the holding company for Co-operators Insurance. The Co-operators, whose members are co-operative organizations from across Canada, has traditionally given priority to other co-operatives and credit unions in its investment policies.[43] Recently, it established a small venture capital fund to assist emerging co-operatives.[44] Similarly, the Credit Union Central of Canada, the national organization for Canada's financial co-operatives, has invested in larger co-operative ventures. That organization created some controversy when it decided in 1988 to call its loan on the United Maritime Fishermen's Co-operative (UMF), that subsequently went into receivership.[45] UMF took the Credit Union Central of Canada to court over its decision, but was not successful.

There has also been some effort on the part of financial co-operatives to assist the financing of community economic development projects. VanCity (the largest credit union in Canada) has established a special foundation "which provides housing and services to lower income groups, usually considered too risky by other financial institutions."[46] This foundation also has a special "Peer Group Lending Program" modelled after the Grameen People's Bank of Bangladesh, which makes small loans to lower income people lacking the collateral normally demanded by the lender (see Chapter 5).[47]

There are other examples: Universities and Colleges Credit Union in Toronto is recommending that "credit unions should strive to be the preferred financial institution for community-service organizations and the non-profit sector;"[48] the Saskatchewan Credit Union Central is studying ways that it can assist community development in the depressed economy of rural Saskatchewan;[49] and the Désjardins group, the central organization for Quebec's powerful financial co-operatives, donates generously to various community initiatives,[50] such as educational projects, sponsorships of sports and recreational activities (the Quebec Summer Games), and grants to theatre and religious groups. Similarly, the Mouvement coopératif acadien of New Brunswick (the central organization for that province's francophone co-operatives) has established a $2.6 million venture capital fund to assist in developing employment in Acadian communities.[51]

However, financial co-operatives wanting to assist community projects have also encountered frustrations. The Sudbury Regional Credit Union disbanded a small investment fund established for this purpose because there was no demand for its services.[52] The directors of projects that applied were reluctant to make personal guarantees for loans from the fund, in part because government money was available more cheaply and without the same personal risks.

Notwithstanding these many examples (and only a sample have been cited), the capital in financial co-operatives directed to business investment goes predominantly to the private sector. The Société d'investissement Désjardins, a holding company of the Désjardins financial co-operatives group, has made $145 million of equity investments (1989) in "medium-sized industrial and commercial enterprises" in Quebec.[53] It is also instructive that the most publicized equity investment funds administered by financial co-operatives — the VanCity Ethical Growth Fund and the Désjardins Environment Fund — are providing capital for private-sector businesses meeting particular social criteria. These funds fall into the broad category of ethical investment, a growing movement that has attempted to encourage private-sector corporations to become more responsive to concerns such as the environment, health and safety conditions, and employment equity.[54] The performance of ethical investment funds has been very good (VanCity's fund was the third highest Canadian mutual in 1988, and all the ethical funds were above average that year[55]), making them attractive to investors.

In its advertising, Désjardins highlights Megarry's rule, "Profitability will always be the Fund's number one investment criterion."[56] There is an irony in this statement because Alphonse Désjardins, the man after whom the Désjardins movement was named, was a visionary who, through financial co-operatives, desired to place finance within a social context. As with many other social movements, the ideals have been weakened as the original leaders move on. This is true not only for the Désjardins movement, but for financial co-operatives in general. Even though they are democratic social enterprises, and they are inter-connected with other social enterprises that use their services for deposits and loans, for the most part their investments are con-ventional. With some exceptions, they are not behaving as though they are part of a movement designed to build a "co-operative commonwealth," or even a social economy. Rather, they are financial enterprises with the objective of providing the best possible service to their users, who also happen to be its members. For most, the concept of membership is parenthetical, with service and convenience being the priorities.

To assist financial co-operatives in making more investments in the social sector, the Canadian Co-operative Association and the Conseil canadien de la coopération (the apex organizations for co-operatives) have lobbied the federal government for a co-op RRSP "that would encourage long-term deferred invest-ment in co-operatives" through tax deferral provisions similar to other RRSPs.[57] Thus far only Quebec treats co-op investments as tax deductible. Through the Régime d'investissement coopératif, investments in co-operatives are entitled to the same 125 per cent tax deduction as investments in other enterprises.[58]

While such attempts are being made to make investment in social enterprises more attractive for financial co-operatives, there are some investment funds designated specifically for the social economy. Their activities fall into the broad category of what Eugene Ellman refers to as "alternative investment," that is, "investors who want to build an economy based on collective human needs, rather than the motive of private, individual profit."[59] In contrast to ethical investment which involves pas-sive investors seeking a good return, alternative investment in-volves participants with an active interest in building democratic social enterprises. One of the largest of these funds is the Cana-dian Alternative Investment Co-operative (CAIC), founded in 1984 by 10 Catholic religious institutions such as the Jesuit Centre for Social Faith and Justice. CAIC's investments focus on mort-gages for social housing, but it also invests in community eco-nomic development projects and other co-operatives. There are also a number of small, specialized alternative-investment funds across Canada, often with a regional focus. These include the Tompkins Fund (Cape Breton), Atlantic Co-operatives Develop-ment Fund (sponsored by Co-op Atlantic, the wholesaler for consumer co-operatives in the Atlantic), Community Works (eastern Ontario) and WomenFutures Loan Guarantee Fund (British Columbia).

These funds may be seen as part of the same general group as the specialized funds among financial co-operatives. Their primary purpose is their social objective, which takes precedence over the rate of return, albeit not to such an extreme that it would jeopardize the fund's value.

Heritage Funds

Heritage funds are government-sector funds using revenues from natural resources to save for the future and to help diversify provincial economies. Alberta's fund was established in 1976, Saskatchewan's in 1980. By 1989–90, the Alberta fund had accumulated assets of more than $12 billion, and the smaller Saskatchewan Heritage Fund had assets of $1.7 billion.[60]

The Alberta fund has actually shrunk since the mid-1980s because the oil economy went into decline. Originally the province was transferring 30 per cent of resource revenues to the Heritage Fund, but in 1983–84 the transfer was reduced to 15 per cent, and since 1987 no revenues have been transferred. From 1982, also, because of the economic slowdown caused by the recession of that time, Alberta started using its Heritage Fund for the province's general revenues, a use for which the fund was not originally intended. By 1989–90, $10.8 billion had been used for that purpose. At present, Alberta's Heritage Fund is not growing, as all non-renewable resource income and income from investments are being transferred to general revenues to help reduce the province's deficit.

The Heritage Fund is an important player in Alberta's economy. As of the end of the 1989–90 financial year, it had invested $5.8 billion in five of Alberta's Crown corporations — for example, the Alberta Opportunity Agency, which provides financing for small businesses; the Alberta Agricultural Development Corporation, which assists family-owned farms; and the Alberta Mortgage and Housing Corporation, an important lender for affordable housing. In addition, Heritage has made substantial investments in the province's energy industry (Lloydminster, the OSLO Oil Sands Project, Syncrude).

The Saskatchewan Heritage Fund is much smaller than Alberta's because that province never had a resource boom comparable to that experienced by Alberta. The Fund receives all revenues raised through taxation and royalties from non-renew-able resources, income from investments, and revenues from the lease and sale of agricultural lands. Its investments are handled through divisions — resources, energy security, environmental protection, agriculture, and research and development.

These two Heritage Funds assist government finance through general revenues and loans to Crown corporations. In that respect, they provide a type of social investment. The Alberta fund has also started investing in social housing. However, with those exceptions, the funds invest in the private sector with the expectation that the investments will produce jobs and a reasonable rate of return.

Strategies for Change

In reviewing the sources of investment capital in Canada, it becomes apparent that only a very small part is being channelled to the social economy. Practically speaking, there simply aren't the investment opportunities in social enterprises to make use of existing sources of capital. With respect to the vast pension funds, Richard Deaton states that they "effectively become 'locked in' to the relatively narrow range of leading 'blue-chip' corporate investments, limiting the extent of portfolio diversification available to them to satisfy their fiduciary responsibility."[61] In other words, the concern about attaining the returns needed for promised benefits has directed pension monies to the pillars of the economy, which pay relatively predictable dividends and have a track record that satisfies the trustees.

Changing these practices is primarily a political problem and can only be undertaken gradually. Part of the solution lies in creating opportunities for social investment and building confidence in those investments. Inevitably, this involves governments and other political players who will support the social economy, in much the same way as they provide incentives for private enterprise. There are already isolated examples of such initiatives: the federal government's insured mortgages for social housing through Canada Mortgage and Housing has attracted capital, not only from the social sector but also from conventional financial institutions; and Quebec government loan guarantees through the Société de développement des coopératives have greatly assisted the development of worker co-operatives in that province.[62] These are only a few illustrations of how social capital will flow to the social economy, where appropriate supports are in place. Many other initiatives could be taken by governments, labour leaders and leaders of the social sector who have the political will to see an expanded social economy.

There are, in addition, some issues related to both the control of capital and taxation policies encouraging its formation. At present, much investment capital is in employer-sponsored pension funds. As noted, these funds represent deferred wages that workers have set aside for their retirement. Therefore, organized labour has argued that workers and their representatives (union locals) should have some control over these plans through electing 50 per cent of the trustees. "Co-determination" was the position of the Ontario Federation of Labour presented to the Rowan Commission on that province's public pensions.[63] The employer's right to participation is based upon its obligation to meet defined benefits.

Yet even though co-determination is an important principle to implement, it's not clear that giving workers voice and vote with respect to their pensions will lead to different types of investments than at present. A British study of this issue indicates that "whenever trade union representatives become trustees, they are just as keen, if not more so, to act in a capitalist fashion."[64] In addition, trustees of pension funds, like corporate directors in general, too often defer to management's advice and fail to assume a level of independence in decision-making which they have the right to exercise.[65]

Therefore, the problem is far more complex than simply having workers gain some control over their savings. Just as a labour-based investment fund can be bereft of any social criteria other than the best return for investors (the Canadian Federation of Labour's Ventures Fund, for instance), the same is possible for a labour-controlled pension fund or the investment capital in financial co-operatives. Control provides an opportunity, but it does not guarantee different policies.

There is another important issue. Government policies have provided major tax incentives to encourage people to save for retirement, thereby creating a large pool of investment capital. These tax incentives are regressive, bringing the greatest benefit to those with relatively greater wealth, who obtain a greater tax benefit both because they usually have larger annual savings for their retirement and because the deduction is against income, thereby bringing a relatively increased benefit as income increases. A way of reducing this problem is to expand the Canada/Quebec Pension Plan so it is the major pension fund for everyone (instead of a secondary plan as at present) and to apply a progressive contribution structure pegged to income, but with benefits that are equivalent for all contributors. This policy, supported by organized labour,[66] has been enacted by social democracies of Scandinavia and Western Europe. Aside from reducing the regressive tax benefits of current policies and improving the pension benefits of lower- and middle-income earners, shifting pension monies from employer-sponsored plans and private savings to a national (or bi-national) plan would put a greater pool of capital in government hands.

The funds available for investment in an expanded Canada/Quebec Pension Plan could be dealt with, as at present, by each of the provinces in proportion to contribution, and in addition controlled through an agency operating at arm's length from government (as Quebec's Caisse de dépôt)[67] but with incentives for investment in social enterprises (as in the Homes Now program for social housing in Ontario). By these means there would be many pools of capital for investment purposes, and control would be widely dispersed. These investment pools could work with governments desiring to encourage the continued development of the social economy.

These same objectives could also be achieved under current pension arrangements if organized labour asserted greater control over pension funds for unionized employees. Such a strategy has been followed on a small scale by the International Union of Operating Engineers and the Carpentry Workers Pension Fund in financing social housing in British Columbia. In addition to a greater number of direct investments in the social economy, union-controlled pension funds could channel a portion of their investment monies into labour-sponsored investment funds, particularly those, such as the Manitoba Federation of Labour's Crocus Fund, that accentuate social criteria. Although such funds bear greater risks for investors than most pension funds (as the performance of Quebec's Solidarity Fund [FTQ] suggests), they are protected in part by federal and provincial tax credits and by tax credits for RRSPs. The return to the investor is also enhanced by the creation of jobs and services in the local economy through organizations that are rooted in the community. In other words, the rate of return to investors can be defined more broadly than mere dollars in hand: the development of one's society pays dividends to its members, too.

This same strategy could be followed by individuals as well, through self-directed RRSPs. Rather than surrendering control over their RRSPs to financial institutions, people could direct them toward the social economy, either through particular investments or through specific funds with social objectives that the individual wishes to support.

Ultimately, "the bottom line" for these proposals is whether people, either in organizations or as individuals, want to direct their savings into investment vehicles utilizing social criteria, or whether their only concern is the rate of return, regardless of the investment policies that generate it. Developing greater public responsibility requires both education and strategies for change — matters to which we turn in the final chapter.

CONCLUSIONS

The difficulties in channelling investments into the social economy can be seen in the context of the entire economy. Funds tend to use the Megarry rule, which is to obtain the highest return for their investors. Where the fund has to meet a defined benefit level, it becomes locked into investments with a predictable rate of return, either government bonds or equities in leading blue chip corporations.

Some investment funds, such as those that are labour-sponsored, also utilize social criteria that go beyond the rate of return. The Solidarity Fund sponsored by the Quebec Federation of Labour (FTQ) attempts to encourage unionized jobs in Quebec, and the Crocus Investment Fund of the Manitoba Federation of Labour encourages both unionized jobs in the province and workers' control over Fund investments in their place of work.

The funds directed specifically at the social economy tend to be located within the social economy, with financial co-operatives, credit union centrals, co-operative insurers, and non-profit groups. These funds are small, and reflect to some extent the general lack of vision about building a social economy.

Changing these practices can only be a gradual process requiring education and a willingness of individuals and organizations such as unions to assert greater control over the investment policies associated with their members' savings through electing trustees and giving them policy guidelines.

4
Overcoming the Obstacles

Building a Social Economy

The social economy includes some of the most important facets of society: healthcare, higher education, religion, politics, culture (in its many dimensions), sports and recreation, a broad array of social and humanitarian services, and various forms of economic associations and enterprises. In the analyses of Canada's economy, the vital role of the private sector and the more controversial role of government as a partner to the private sector are often highlighted, but the social economy as a unique form of organization is lost in the shuffle.

Yet is it possible to imagine a society without the services of the social economy? If people were to log on a daily basis the organizations with which they interact, would the social economy be seen as "the third sector?" Furthermore, if this log also included interactions to which people attached a lot of importance, how would the social economy rank? There is little doubt that the organizations of the social economy are among the most vital in society. Some might argue, however, that these organizations are *social*, not economic. Religious congregations, unions or humanitarian organizations like the Red Cross are not businesses in the same sense as General Motors or Mac's Milk. They are simply services, with an indirect economic impact.

One problem with that argument is that services are the predominant type of business in the private sector. Why should a service which is privately owned be viewed as economic, whereas a service in the social economy is considered strictly social? There is, as discussed in Chapter 1, a difference between the private and social sectors in the balance between economic and social objectives. The private sector places service within the context of earning a profit, while for the social sector service is the priority. The Canadian Red Cross does not function in order to make money; it spends money in order to serve the public. However, in doing so, it employs 5,950 people, mobilizes 2.5 million volunteers, and has an operating budget of $346 million.[1] Like any other organization that spends money, it has an impact upon its suppliers. In other words, in the context of its social objectives, the Red Cross also serves an economic purpose.

In the case of the Red Cross much of its money comes from government, generally as contracts for specific services in Canada (such as the blood and homemakers' programs) or as project grants for international work. As noted in Chapter 1, organizations in the social economy range from enterprises that are financially self-reliant (co-operatives, commercial non-profits, business associations) through to others which are totally dependent upon either government grants or private donations. Most social organizations, like the Red Cross, fall between the two extremes, having some combination of income derived from direct payments for service and also income from external grants and donations. The tendency is to dismiss the economic import of organizations depending even in part upon external finance because that income is not earned through the market. However, given that the services they provide are often essential, these have to be arranged either through social organizations or by the private sector or government. One way or another, these services must exist. If they happen to be provided through a social organization, why should the service's economic impact be ignored? The same point could be made with respect to other services offered through the social economy that are also available from the private sector. The basis for funding should not be a criterion for economic impact. Hospitals, for example, derive most of their funding from government and employ about 450,000 people.[2] Their economic impact is unquestionable.

The economics of organizations in the social economy are more open to conjecture with respect to the role of volunteers. Except for out-of-pocket expenditures by volunteers — estimated at $841 million in 1987 — and expenditures on training, volunteers are not operating within the cash economy. Yet they affect the cash economy because without their contribution, people would have to be hired to do their work. Therefore, it seems reasonable, as David Ross and Richard Shillington have done, to estimate the economic impact of volunteers at about $12 billion in 1987.[3]

Estimating the total economic impact of the social economy in Canada is a difficult undertaking. Statistics Canada does not consider the social economy as a distinct category, and there is no overall survey of the estimated 175,000 organizations in this sector. By using global figures of government expenditure on services, Samuel Martin estimated that "31 per cent of the country's national income ... flowed through the humanistic sector in 1980."[4] Martin also estimated that "the humanistic sector employed more people — and higher-priced people — than were on the direct payroll of all governments combined."[5] Martin's conception of the humanistic sector overlaps largely with the social economy as described in this book. He includes some organizations such as school boards which this book defines as governmental. On the other hand, he does not include economic organizations such as co-operatives, unions, business and professional associations or advocacy groups.

Martin admits that the method of calculation through which he derived his estimates has been challenged.[6] However, it appears that he is quite justified in his conclusion that the humanistic sector has become "big business."[7] In the main, the social economy consists of a large number of small labour-intensive organizations that in total have a considerable economic impact and an immense social contribution. Throughout this book figures have been presented to underline the number of organizations in particular services and, where possible, the scale of their economic contribution. The reason for doing this was to highlight the point that there is an important economic dimension to the social economy — a dimension that should not be ignored merely because of the social orientation of the organizations that are involved.

WHY IS THERE A SOCIAL ECONOMY?

There does not appear to be one hard and fast rule to explain why some services are offered through the social economy and others by private enterprise or government. Economists have theorized as to why services end up in particular sectors of the economy, but the explanations are highly speculative.[8]

Many organizations in the social economy — particularly charitable organizations — have been created to assist people with low incomes who are unable to purchase adequate services in the private sector. However, a determination of when a social need cannot be met through the private sector is not simply economic. It has much to do with tradition and politics. The chapters on regional development, housing, healthcare and childcare show that there is much conjecture about the degree to which such needs can be met through private enterprise. Conservatives, more than people on the political left, argue that the latitude of the private sector should be quite broad. The recent decision by Ontario's NDP government to give financial incentives to private-sector daycare operators to convert to non-profits reflects one point of view. The decision by the federal Conservatives to kill its co-operative housing program and to attempt to stimulate the private housing market reflects another viewpoint.

These differences are in degree only. It is generally recognized even by its staunchest advocates that the private sector has its limitations in serving people with very low incomes. However, the social economy is not the only alternative when the private sector does not meet needs adequately. Services offered through social organizations could also be offered by government (municipal daycare, government housing or family services available in some provinces). And again there is not a good explanation why some gaps in the market economy are met by government and others through the social economy or by some combination of the two. The role of the social economy and government in these cases may be seen as complementary, their combined impact being the creation of a minor adjustment in the distribution of wealth caused by market forces. [9] Together they create a community infrastructure through which basic services are delivered to people.

Having services for people in need undertaken by non-profits is advantageous for government because it is not directly responsible for the quality. Also the use of volunteers by non-profits reduces the costs. The public may also prefer this arrangement since financial contributions to a specific social organization are targeted, often tax-deductible and optional, as opposed to taxes which are general and compulsory.

The emergence of non-profits in humanitarian service may also be in response to government failings and injustices. Amnesty International is an excellent example of an organization responding to inhumane government policies. Food banks and rape crisis centres, for example, reflect other types of weakness in government policies, though they are also supported in part by government because they provide an essential service in an effective, cost-efficient manner. Government solutions to overcoming hunger, for example, such as increasing welfare payments or a higher guaranteed income, albeit more desirable, would also be more costly.

Therefore, it could be argued that non-profits meeting most basic humanitarian needs have carved out a niche between the private and government sectors that quite often both of those sectors accept. With the increasing criticism of public debt, government appears to accept having more services undertaken by non-profits.

However, the emergence of the social economy goes beyond serving those on low income or those unable to help themselves for other reasons. In other words, the social economy is not simply a response to weaknesses of the private and government sectors, but also reflects a preferred model for organizing services. Some business people prefer the non-profit structure — the Canadian Automobile Association or Blue Cross, for example. For certain organizations (religious, ethno-cultural), it just seems more appropriate.

Consumers, too, may under some circumstances prefer non-profits because they are more trusting[10] of them or they feel that the service is better. Consumer preferences can be based on a gut feeling, like many choices in the market, or it can be based on hard evidence of better quality. For example, because of evidence that blood banks run by private enterprise in the United States until the early 1970s were not screening samples properly for impurities, there was a loss of market share and eventual legislation precluding private enterprise for this service.[11] Consumer preferences for a non-profit organization may go to the point that people will pay additional costs, as in a private school, because they feel the service is better.[12]

These preferences can lead consumers to organize a co-operative. This may be also done in response to excessive prices, to the inadequacy of services in the private sector, or it can be done because of a desire by consumers for greater input and control. The consumer co-operative is but one form of mutual association in the social economy. In theory, these associations can be organized as private-sector businesses. The non-profit form is usually chosen because it is suited to the social objectives of the organization. However, these examples also underline a paradox about many organizations in the social economy: the people who are involved in them do not necessarily perceive themselves as being part of an alternative social form. Even more so, in the case of business associations, they may simply view themselves as an extension of the private sector since the members' purpose in forming an association is to promote and enhance their personal business interests.

ADDRESSING THE PARADOX

Yet in forming a mutual non-profit, the members of a business association have organized themselves differently than in the private sector. Their association is based on the democratic principle of one-member/one-vote, rather than control according to shares or some other proprietary form. In that respect, they are organized in the same way as the members of a union local, a co-operative, a religious congregation, a ethno-cultural club, an Alcoholics Anonymous group, a recreational or environmental group, and much like the citizens of a political democracy.

Organizations in the social economy extend democracy from the political to the social realm, in effect, building a social democracy — not in the sectarian political sense, but quite literally the building of a democratic society. The citizens of social organizations are the members. Like the members of a political democracy, they may fail to exercise their responsibilities and, as noted in Chapter 3, in some social organizations the membership is a closed group, a type of family compact, to use an historical analogy. However, the social economy offers greater potential for improving the standard of democracy than the private sector because unlike the latter, membership is not tied to proprietary rights. Rather, membership is taken on because people support and benefit from the objectives of the organization. The benefits can be direct, as from the services that mutual association or co-operatives provide to members, and indirect, through the social interactions within these organizations. The organizations of the social economy support geographic communities by providing services that their residents need, and they also help to create communities of common interest. Through giving voice and vote to members and through providing opportunities for meaningful participation in furthering their goals, social organizations become building blocks for people to overcome the alienation of modern life, an alienation supported by private-sector corporations lacking in geographic allegiance and in loyalty to staff.

Although there are some commonalities between organizations in the social economy, it would be a mistake to suggest that there is a common identity or purpose. Rather each organization has its own objectives, which tend to be the focus for their members' commitments. At times, organizations within the social economy can come into conflict with each other, as may be the case, for example, with business and labour associations, or between different religious denominations. Even organizations with similar roots, such as unions and co-operatives, can have their differences. This point is underlined in a study by researchers Kurt Wetzel and Daniel Gallagher, who found that in Saskatchewan between 1974 and 1985, "co-operatives accounted for 32 per cent of total strikes and up to 50 per cent of the total person-days lost ... while employing about 6 per cent of the province's unionized workforce."[13]

The lack of common purpose between organizations in the social economy can be attributed in part to their emphasis upon meeting their own members' needs. Democratic control by members can cause an organization to look inward and be only concerned that members are satisfied. Democracy therefore can serve as a brake upon an organization channelling its energies into a broader social context. When organizations in the social economy do relate to each other, it generally involves those with similar functions working together to strengthen their common purpose. Credit unions, for example, belong to credit union centrals. Religious congregations are part of a tiering arrangement both within their denomination and in some cases between denominations. This type of functional integration is common throughout the social economy. The integration not only involves organizations with very similar functions but also organizations with different services having a common need (as in fundraising through the United Way).

This functional integration tends to have practical objectives, usually to help social organizations strengthen their services.

Achieving that goal, it could be argued, also helps to build a movement, in that a movement depends upon strong organizations. However, a movement also has objectives which go beyond the self-interest of each organization and involves an outreach to help organizations with a different purpose. In order to achieve such self-transcendence, there has to be a unifying vision — that is, a view that even though organizations have different services, there's a goal shared in common.

Within the co-operative sector, the goal in the latter half of the nineteenth and the early twentieth centuries was the creation of a "co-operative commonwealth." Like visionary ideals in general, the co-operative commonwealth was not clearly articulated. But at minimum it provided a message to all co-operators that they share something in common — the building of a society based upon co-operation — and they ought to reach out and help each other.

There were also unifying visions among labour organizations and religious denominations — visions which the modern world with its emphasis on rational realizable goals have buried in cynicism. Social movements in the modern age tend to be based on specific issues embedded in focused values. Even broad coalitions of social organizations tend to focus on specific issues (opposition to free trade, for example).

The implication to be drawn from this discussion is there are limits to the degree of co-operation within the social economy. Nevertheless, there is probably greater potential than has been realized, for example, in both building coalitions around specific issues and creating ongoing forums for participation through organizations such as the social planning councils in communities across Canada.

Whether or not organizations within the social economy coalesce into a broadly based social movement with a common identity, the social economy represents a quiet revolution, in that democracy has been extended, without much fanfare, into a broad array of community organizations. In a world where people feel they have neither voice nor control of the institutions to which they relate, this accomplishment is very important. Moreover, if the building of democracy in community organizations is seen as a gradual movement — that is, democratization — then what has been accomplished to this point lays the groundwork for further advances.

THE ROLE OF EDUCATION

Inevitably, education becomes a critical component in advancing the social economy. The role of education in social change was recognized by John Dewey in his classic text *Democracy and Education* when he argued:

> A society which makes provision for participation ... of all its members on equal terms ... must have a type of education which gives individuals a personal interest in social relationships and control, and the habits of mind which secure social changes without introducing disorder.[14]

Dewey was a leading proponent of the role of education in social change, which he suggested, was merely "an educative change."[15]

> We may produce in schools a projection in type of the society we should like to realize, and by forming minds in accord with it, gradually modify the larger and more recalcitrant features of adult society.[16]

Dewey's assessment of the power of schools is somewhat exaggerated. Nevertheless, his general point that schools do have some influence is well taken. For the social economy to advance, there must be some recognition of its existence and the encouragement of compatible values within the formal education system.

There are some components of the education system that are consistent with democracy. Parents elect trustees who serve as a corporate governance, parents have the opportunity to participate in home and school associations, and at the secondary level and beyond, there are student-elected councils which can give voice to student concerns.

However, in spite of these building blocks, the public schools remain largely hierarchical institutions under the control of professional administrators. In many respects schools reproduce the hierarchical social relations into which students enter once they graduate.[17] The curriculum is virtually bereft of analysis of experiments in the social economy. Entrepreneurship, one of the buzzwords in the business curriculum, is seen as a private-sector phenomenon and not a talent that is applicable to the social economy. Students seldom are introduced to the many interesting examples of social entrepreneurship in our society. Recognizing these biases, the co-operative movement has developed its own curriculum modules, and its staff run workshops for teachers who want to include these topics in their curriculum.[18]

There are also interesting experiments in the practice of co-operation in schools. In Quebec alone, there are 43 student co-operatives belonging to an organization, the *Fédération des coopératives québécoises en milieu scolaire*.[19] These co-operatives — all but one in colleges and universities — have 400,000 members (students who use the service), and in 1989–90 had $36.1 million of sales, in such services as book stores and student supplies, cafeterias, tobacco stores and driving schools.[20] Three hundred students are employed full-time and 150 part-time in these student co-operatives, largely administered by other students.

There are similar projects outside of Quebec, though not as extensive. At the post-secondary level, these are predominantly student housing co-operatives.[21] At the secondary level these include worker co-operatives in Saskatchewan[22] and New Brunswick,[23] both during the school year and the summer, and summer camps in Saskatchewan and Ontario. The Evangeline Group in southwestern Prince Edward Island has even extended the practice of co-operation to the elementary level, where students become members of a school-based credit union and continue in this capacity through the secondary level.[24] It is not coincidental then that the Evangeline Credit Union has such strong community support.

In general, education about organizations in the social economy is a very minor component within a school system which equates business with private enterprise. Work/Study programs and supplementary initiatives such as Junior Achievement focus upon the private sector. This is ironic because public education evolved as part of a progressive movement that broadened the use of schooling from a narrow set of private interests, to make it available to everyone regardless of wealth or ability to pay. In that respect public schooling is embedded within a democratic context. However, schooling also seems to mirror the social relations of the society of which it is a part. Its capacity to reproduce the existing conceptions seems greater than its ability to project images and to develop skills which would push back the frontiers by experimenting with alternatives.

Arguably, the best instruction in democracy is in the practice, that is, actually participating in the democratic process. In that respect an experiment in the Toronto elementary schools since the mid-1970s is noteworthy. This initiative has involved key stakeholders in creating a staffing and program plan for Toronto schools.[25] At the central level, the Toronto Teachers Federation representing the teachers and the board representing its community each elect three representatives and a co-chairperson to a committee, which creates a staffing plan for the board and considers such issues as class size and the staffing of new functions. At the school level a committee is established with representatives of the staff (at least 10 per cent of that group), the principal, and representatives elected by the school's parental organization (not to exceed 50 per cent of the staff representatives). The school's committee develops a staffing plan for the school, which is then submitted to a committee of the school's staff, whence it proceeds to the area superintendent.

This exercise attempts to involve the primary stakeholders in the school (save the students) in the process of making staffing decisions. It may be seen as part of a broader move toward decentralization of control in education to school councils comprised of parents, teachers, principals and, in some cases, students.[26] Similar experiments have been in place in Edmonton since the mid-1970s, as well as in Langley, British Columbia, and Chicago in the United States. They are also found in the State of Victoria, Australia, in Denmark, and in parts of France, England and Wales.[27] Although the models vary, the intention is to give greater control to the local school and for that control to be exercised in part through a council representing the key stakeholders in the community and the school.

Inevitably, it becomes problematic to involve parents who have full-time jobs and family responsibilities in school councils. Payment for participating, as is done for elected school trustees in many jurisdictions, could serve as an incentive. This point speaks to a fundamental weakness in the governance of social enterprises. The role is considered to be voluntary, as compared to elected political representatives or directors of a private-sector corporation, who are paid for the responsibilities. The voluntary nature of social enterprise governance is reflective of its importance in a society which attaches a monetary value to most functions outside of the household. But social democracy, like political democracy, takes time, and it should cost money.Given the financial constraints upon many organizations in the social economy, this payment for service could be in the form of a tax credit, much as Revenue Canada currently gives a tax credit for financial donations. In other words, the donation of service ought to receive, at the very least, the same tax benefit as the donation of money.

THE ROLE OF FINANCE

Some organizations in the social economy control major sources of capital and have the potential to direct its usage. Pension funds representing the savings of Canadian workers are a major source of investment capital. Labour-sponsored venture capital funds and mutual funds sponsored by financial co-operatives and church coalitions also are playing an important role in business development. These funds could be used to promote such social criteria as democracy.

Nor is such a proposal a radical departure from tradition, since some mutual funds are already applying social criteria to their investments. Therefore it is not outlandish to suggest that funds controlled by socially conscious organizations could insist upon a minimum threshold of democracy in businesses in which they invest, as is being done for example by the Crocus Investment Fund of the Manitoba Federation of Labour. Corporations with publicly traded stock could be responsive to the influence of socially conscious funds. Funds with large pools of finance could negotiate their social criteria in exchange for investments. Through this type of negotiation, the sharp differences between the social economy and other sectors of the economy might be reduced with time.

There are also financial organizations within the social economy that are channelling their investments toward the development of the social economy. The Caja Laboral Popular in the Mondragon group in Basque Spain, the archetype of such an organization, has set an example which is being followed by a select number of financial co-operatives in Canada (see Chapters 5 and 8), primarily in francophone communities in the Atlantic and Quebec.

A CONCLUDING NOTE

As this book reaches completion, the state-owned economies of Eastern Europe are collapsing from apparent failure to meet the consumer needs of the people. This is being heralded as a triumph for capitalism, particularly since Eastern Europe is being converted to a market economy that eventually might become similar to that in the West. The move to a market economy is being encouraged by the International Monetary Fund and other financial consortiums in the West, in exchange for investment capital. This pattern is a prime example of how investment funds encourage a change of social policy. Although social investment, defined as investment with specific social criteria, is viewed as a relatively recent phenomenon in Canada, in fact it has been part and parcel of our tradition for a long time. The real departure from tradition is in the changing criteria. In recent years, some mutual funds have highlighted different social concerns, such as environmental policies. The proposal made in this concluding chapter is that mutual funds can utilize democracy within a business as a criterion for investment, and the extension of democracy from a narrow political realm to the economy can be encouraged in this manner.

A democratically controlled economy is in effect a social economy. It is an economy beholden to and controlled by the members of a society. Although co-operatives and the various forms of non-profits differ from each other, they often share the common feature of democratic control by their members. Both through education and investment funds, they have the opportunity to promote democracy more broadly in Canada, and thereby strengthen the social economy of which they are a part.

NOTES

Chapter 1

1. For discussions of the social economy in Western Europe see Ian Snaith, "The Economie Sociale in the New Europe," *Yearbook of Co-operative Enterprise* 1991: 67–75; Jacques DeFourney, "De La Coopération à L'Économie Sociale," in *Proceedings of the Congreso de Co-opertivisimo, University of Duesto and the World Basque Congress, 1988* 71–88; Thierry Jeantet, "Economie Sociale et Coopératives," (France]: n.p. [July, 1991]); *Économie Sociale*, ed. Jacques Defourny and José Monzon (Brussels: CIRIEC, 1992).
2. Thierry Jeantet includes informal arrangements as part of the social economy, though the umbrella body in France, the Comité national de liaison des activités mutualistes, coopératives et associatives, and the Commission of the European Community do not include that category.
3. American economist David Ellerman argues this point throughout his writings. See *The Democratic Worker-Owned Firm: A New Model for East and West* (Boston: Unwin Hyman, 1990).
4. The Comité national de liaison des activités mutualistes, coopératives et associatives of France has accepted four defining criteria: democratic management, objectives which go beyond the purely commercial, voluntary membership and independence from the state.
5. "The Regina Manifesto" (Ottawa: New Democratic Party of Canada, 1990); originally published in 1933.
6. Ian MacPherson, "An Uneasy Alliance," *Building the Co-operative Commonwealth: Essays on the Democratic Socialist Tradition in Canada*, ed. J. William Brennan (Regina: Canadian Plains Research Centre, 1983) 182
7. Ian MacPherson, *Each for All: A History of the Co-operative Movement in English Canada: 1900–45* (Toronto: MacMillan, 1989) 189.
8. John Richards and Larry Pratt, *Prairie Capitalism* (Toronto: McClelland and Stewart, 1979) 97.
9. *Ibid.*, 111.
10. *Ibid.*, 253–255.
11. "Statement of Principles: 1983" (Ottawa: New Democratic Party of Canada, 1990) 2
12. Doreen Duchesne, *Giving Freely: Volunteers in Canada* (Ottawa: Statistics Canada, 1989).
13. David P. Ross, "How Valuable is Volunteering?" *Perception* 4 (1990): 17–18.
14. See *Exploring Work and Income Opportunities in the 1980s: Our Future in the Informal Economy* (Ottawa: The Vanier Institute of the Family, 1979); and David Ross and Peter Usher, *From the Roots Up* (Toronto: Lorimer, 1986).

15. Both volunteerism and financial donations may be seen as part of a "dona-tive" culture through which people support organizations in the social economy. See Henry Hansmann, "The Role of Nonprofit Enterprise," *The Economics of Nonprofit Institutions,* ed. Susan Rose-Ackerman (New York: Oxford University Press, 1986).

16. Robert Dahl, *After the Revolution: Authority in a Good Society* (New Haven: Yale University Press, 1970) 126.

17. A similar analogy is made by David Ellerman in the context of democratic worker-owned firms. See David Ellerman, *The Democratic Worker-Owned Firm: A New Model for the East and West* (Boston: Unwin Hyman, 1990) 68–70.

Chapter 2

1. Unless stated otherwise, all the statistics on co-operatives and credit unions are from the annual publication of the federal government, *Canadian Co-operatives: Resource File 1991* (Ottawa: Co-operatives Secretariat, 1991).

2. The Rochdale principles, as adapted by the International Co-operative Alliance in 1966, are Open and Voluntary Membership, Democratic Control, Limited Interest on Shares, Return of Surplus to Members, Co-operative Education and Co-operation among Co-operatives.

3. Ian MacPherson, *Each for All: A History of the Co-operative Movement in English Canada, 1900–1945* (Toronto: MacMillan, 1979) chs. 1 and 2.

4. The historical account of farm marketing co-operatives is taken from *Each for All* chs. 1 and 2.

5. *Ibid.,* chs. 1–3.

6. *Ibid.,* 22.

7. For a good description of co-operative housing, see Joan Selby and Alexandra Wilson, *Canada's Housing Co-operatives* (Ottawa: Co-operative Housing Federation of Canada, 1988).

8. Historical information on financial co-operatives is taken from *Each for All,* 29–32; and Ron Kenyon, *To the Credit of the People* (Toronto: The Ontario Credit Union League, 1976) ch. 1.

9. "Insurance Companies, Canadian and British: Revised Statutes of Canada," Volume 5 (Ottawa: Queen's Printer, 1985).

10. Figures are taken from the "Superintendent's Report 1990" (Toronto: Ontario Insurance Commission).

11. Kenneth Higgins, *Operations of Life and Health Insurance Companies* (Toronto: LOMA, 1986) 33.

12. W.J. Cowlins, J.B. Hawson and J.H. Panabaker, *A Century of Mutuality* (Waterloo: Mutual Life of Canada, 1970).

13. "1990 Annual Report," Mutual Life of Canada.

14. *Canadian Co-operatives,* 38.

15. "Superintendent's Report 1990: Ontario Insurance Commission," 4–10.

16. *Ibid.*

17. John Jordan, *Towards a Multi-Stakeholder Model in Co-operative Insurance* (Guelph: The Co-operators Group, 1990).

18. Jack Quarter, "Worker Ownership: One Movement or Many?" *Partners in Enterprise,* ed. J. Quarter and G. Melnyk (Montreal: Black Rose, 1989).

19. Jacques Gauvin, "Quebec's Forestry Co-operatives Are Adapting," *Worker Co-op* Winter 1991: 20–22.

20. Léopold Beaulieu, "New Ground for Labour," *Worker Co-op* Spring 1990: 26–29.
21. Jack Quarter, "It's Official: the Canadian Worker Co-operative Federation," *Worker Co-op* Fall 1992: 8–9.
22. Alain Bridault and Ginette Lafrenière, "A Social History of Worker Co-operatives in Quebec," *Partners in Enterprise*.
23. Paul Vincent, "James-John Harpell: A Pioneer of Worker Co-operatives in Canada," *Worker Co-op* Spring 1987: 11–16. Vincent's father was a printer at the Harpell Co-operative, and the family grew up in the garden city Harpell constructed for his employees.
24. The information on the nineteenth century history of worker co-operatives is taken from three sources: Greg Kealey, *Toronto Workers Respond to Industrial Capitalism, 1867–1892* (Toronto: University of Toronto Press, 1980); Greg Kealey and Bryan Palmer, *Dreaming of What Might Be: The Knights of Labour in Ontario, 1880–1890* (Toronto: New Hogtown, 1987) and Grant MacDonald, "Organized Labour Encouraged Worker Co-ops in the 19th Century," *Worker Co-op* Summer 1989: 22–24.
25. *Dreaming of What Might Be*, 366.
26. For the Webbs' critique, see Beatrice Potter, *Co-operative Movement in Great Britain* (London: Swan Sonnenschein, 1904); Sidney Webb and Beatrice Webb, *Problems of Modern Industry* (New York: Longmans, Green, 1920); and Sidney and Beatrice Webb, *The Consumers' Co-operative Movement* (London: Longmans, Green, 1921).
27. *Co-operative Movement in Great Britain*, 168.
28. *The Problems of Modern Industry*, 272.
29. Albert Hirschman, *Exit, Voice and Loyalty* (Cambridge: Harvard University Press, 1970) 36–41.
30. William Foote Whyte and Kathleen Whyte, *Making Mondragon* (Ithaca: ILR Press, 1988).
31. John Earle, *The Italian Co-operative Movement* (London: Unwin Hyman, 1986).
32. For an analysis of this restructuring, see John Jordan, "The Multi-stakeholder Approach to Worker Ownership," *Partners in Enterprise*; and Teunis Haalboom and John Jordan, "The Multi-stakeholder Co-operative," *Worker Co-op* Winter 1987: 10–13.
33. Russell Ackoff, *Creating the Corporate Future* (New York: Wiley, 1981) 30–34; Max Clarkson, "Defining and Evaluating Corporate Social Performance: The Stakeholder Management Model," paper presented at the Academy of Management, San Francisco, 1990.
34. Jordan, "The Multi-stakeholder Approach to Worker Ownership," 119.
35. *Ibid.*, 120.
36. *Ibid.*, 118.
37. *Ibid.*, 124.
38. The Fogo Island fishery co-operative near Gander, Newfoundland, and the North Lake Fishing Co-operative in Prince Edward Island are two examples.
39. There is a group of nine daycare centres in Ottawa with a board structure based upon two distinct stakeholders. See David Hagerman and Scott Evans, "Co-operatives, Feminism and the Childcare Agenda: the Case of

the Ottawa Parent/Staff Co-operatives," paper submitted to the Canadian Association for the Studies in Co-operation, May 1990.

40. Sven Ake Böök, "Observations on the Raising of Capital," *Review of International Co-operation* 83, no. 4: 41–42.

41. "The Co-operators Proposal to Ontario for a Program of Driver-Owned Automobile Insurance Co-operatives" (Guelph: The Co-operators, 1991).

42. *Ibid.*

43. Claude Carbonneau, "Quebec Innovates: The Worker-Shareholder Co-op Stirs Controversy," *Worker Co-op* Summer 1991: 26–27.

44. Claude Carbonneau, "New Development Policy in Quebec," *Worker Co-op* Summer 1989: 8.

45. Joseph Blasi, *Employee Ownership: Revolution or Ripoff?* (Cambridge: Ballinger, 1988).

46. Carbonneau, "Quebec Innovates," 27; Claude Carbonneau, "Joint Ventures," *Worker Co-op* Fall 1989: 14.

47. Personal communication with Ken Delaney, Research Dept. of the United Steelworkers of America, Ontario District.

48. Government of Ontario, "Ontario Investment and Worker Ownership Program" (Toronto: Ministry of Treasury and Economics, August 1991).

49. There are some subsidiaries which are incorporated as co-operatives, though this is not the usual arrangement. The Co-operators Group is converting several of its subsidiaries to multi-stakeholder co-operatives, as shall be noted subsequently.

50. George Melnyk, *The Search for Community* (Toronto: Black Rose, 1985).

Chapter 3

1. Henry Hansmann uses the term "mutual non-profit." See his article, "The Role of Non-profit Enterprise," in *The Economics of Non-profit Institutions,* ed. Susan Rose Ackerman (New York: Oxford University Press, 1986) 60.

2. This figure was calculated based upon the information provided by the appropriate department in each of the provinces, territories and the federal government.

3. See *Canada Corporations Act: Part III.*

4. Revenue Canada, "Registered Charities," Information Circular 80-10R, December 17, 1985.

5. Elizabeth Abbott, *Chronicle of Canada* (Montreal: Raincoast Books, 1990) 132

6. *Ibid.*, 187.

7. *Ibid.*, 211.

8. Personal communication with Ken Brewer, the Charities Division, Revenue Canada.

9. Doreen Duchesne, *Giving Freely: Volunteers in Canada* (Ottawa: Statistics Canada, 1989).

10. See David Ross and Richard Shillington, *A Profile of the Canadian Volunteer* (Ottawa: National Voluntary Organizations, 1990) 7; and David Ross and Richard Shillington, *Economic Dimensions of Volunteer Work in Canada* (Ottawa: Secretary of State, 1990).

11. David Ross and Peter Usher, *From the Roots Up* (Toronto: Lorimer, 1986).

12. "Introduction to LETS," 1992 and personal communication with Sat Khalsa, LETS Toronto administrator, 1992.

13. Samuel Martin, *An Essential Grace* (Toronto: McClelland and Stewart, 1985).

14. The Canadian Centre for Philanthropy "Donations by Individuals and Corporations," 1992.
15. "United Way International," 1992.
16. "United Way/Centraide: History and Philosophy," 1992 and personal communication with United Way/Centraide Canada, April 1992.
17. Susan Rose-Ackerman, "United Charities: An Economic Analysis," *Community Organizations: Studies in Resource Mobilization and Exchange*, ed. Carl Milofsky, (New York: Oxford Univ. Press, 1985) 145.
18. The following data on foundations are taken from *Canadian Directory to Foundations 1990–91*, ed. Norah McClintock (Toronto: The Canadian Centre for Philanthropy, 1991) 1–15.
19. Linda McQuaig, *Behind Closed Doors* (Toronto: Penguin, 1987).
20. A primary reference source for the discussion that follows is Goldie Schlanger, *Associations Canada* (Toronto: Canadian Almanac & Directory Publishing, 1991).
21. Personal communication with head office.
22. Personal communication with head office.
23. See *Canadian Automobile Association Annual Report, 1991*.
24. David Macleod, *Building Character in the American Boy: The Boy Scouts, YMCA, and Their Forerunners, 1870–1920* (Madison: University of Wisconsin Press, 1983) 10.
25. The factual information on the Ys, Scouts, Guides, 4-H, Junior Achievement and Boys and Girls Clubs are derived either from annual reports or interviews with management.
26. Personal communication with Margaret Barber, the Sports Federation of Canada.
27. David Ross and Richard Shillington, "A Profile of the Canadian Volunteer," 11.
28. Personal communication with the Canadian Amateur Hockey Association.
29. Mary Cromie, "Performing Arts," *Canadian Social Trends* Winter 1990, 28.
30. Statistics Canada, *Performing Arts 1988–89 Cultural Statistics* (Ottawa: Ministry of Supply and Services, 1991) 9, 18.
31. Communication with Wayne Rutherford of the Canadian Conference of the Arts.
32. Statistics Canada, *Residential Care Facilities for the Aged: 1983–84 and 1985–86* (Ottawa: Minister of Supply and Service, 1987) 1.
33. Figures provided in May, 1991, by Canada Mortgage and Housing Corporation.
34. National Child Care Information Centre, *Status of Daycare in Canada 1990* (Ottawa: Health and Welfare Canada, 1991) 3–5.
35. Sources on the Red Cross are the annual report, 1991, personal communication with the head office and Andre Durand, *From Sarajevo to Hiroshima* (Geneva: International Committee of the Red Cross, 1984).
36. Information on Amnesty is derived from personal communication and from the source documents, *What Amnesty International Does* and *Amnesty International Report 1991*.
37. Information on these clubs was obtained through personal communication with them.
38. Information on the John Howard and Elizabeth Fry Societies is taken from annual reports and personal communication with those organizations.

39. Ryan MacDonald, "Missing Children," *Canadian Social Trends* Spring 1992, 2–5.
40. Jillian Oderkirk, "Food Banks," *Canadian Social Trends* Spring 1992, 6–14.
41. These figures were taken from Table 3 of the *Canada Assistance Plan Annual Report 1988–89* (Ottawa: Minister of National Health & Welfare, 1990) C12, and from personal communication with the federal government.
42. Personal communication with the head office.
43. Canadian Cancer Society, *1989/90 Annual Report*.
44. Personal communication with the head office.
45. Personal communication with the Canadian Conference of the Arts.
46. Personal communication.
47. Personal communication.
48. Personal communication with the Canadian Association of Volunteer Bureaus and Centres.
49. Statistics Canada, *Heritage Institutions: 1988–89* (Ottawa: Ministry of Supply and Services, 1991) 9, 15.
50. Statistics Canada, *List of Canadian Hospitals: 1987* (Ottawa: Ministry of Supply and Service, 1990) 13.
51. Statistics Canada, *Hospital Annual Statistics 1987–88: Services and Finances* (Ottawa: Ministry of Supply and Service, 1991) 78.
52. Statistics Canada, *Residential Care Facilities 1983–84* (Ottawa: Minister of Supply and Service, 1987).
53. Statistics Canada, *University Finance Trend Analysis: 1979–80 to 1988–89* (Ottawa: Ministry of Supply and Service, 1991) 30–31.

Chapter 4

1. Henry Hansmann, "The Role of Non-profit Enterprise," in *The Economics of Non-profit Institutions*, ed. Susan Rose-Ackerman (New York: Oxford University Press, 1986) 60. Hansmann's use of mutuals differs somewhat from mine.
2. A primary reference source for this chapter is *Associations Canada 1991* (Toronto: Canadian Almanac & Directory Publishing Co., 1991).
3. Primary information sources are: Statistics Canada, *Labour Unions Annual Report* (Ottawa: Minister of Supply and Services, 1990); Labour Canada Information Service and the Canadian Labour Congress.
4. Estimate is made from the listings in *Associations Canada 1991*.
5. Information is derived from the *Annual Report* for 1990–91 of the Canadian Chamber of Commerce and a personal communication with its office.
6. Personal communication and *Annual Report 1991* of the Canadian Federation of Independent Business.
7. Business Council on National Issues, *Annual Report, 1991–92*.
8. *Associations Canada 1991* 1–107.
9. Personal communication.
10. The information for this section is derived from *Associations Canada 1991* and supplemented by communication to head offices.
11. Personal communication.
12. Personal communication.
13. Personal communication.
14. *Ethnic Directory of Canada*, ed. Vladimir Markotic and Bob Hromadiuk (Calgary Western Publishers, 1983).

15. *Ibid.*, 86–87.
16. Canadian Ethnocultural Council, *Annual Report 1990–91*.
17. *Yearbook of American and Canadian Churches,* ed. Constant Jacquet Jr. and Alice Jones (Nashville: Abingdon, 1991) 266–269.
18. That figure does not include the Roman Catholic Church. It only lists its "inclusive membership" of 11.3 million.
19. *Yearbook of American and Canadian Churches* 281–291.
20. Information about the United Church of Canada is taken from the publications, "The United Church of Canada: the First Sixty Years," "Structure of the United Church of Canada," "The Statistical State of the United Church of Canada," and personal communication with Doug Flanders of the Church's Division of Communication.
21. *Yearbook of American and Canadian Churches* 281–291.
22. Ross and Shillington, "A Profile of the Canadian Volunteer," 11.
23. *Yearbook of American and Canadian Churches* 281–291.
24. Personal communication with St. John's head office in Ottawa.
25. *Associations Canada 1991*.
26. Personal communication with Greg Hogan and annual report.
27. Personal communication with Rideau Valley Division.
28. Personal communication with the Ontario Genealogical Society.
29. Personal communication with the Doctor Who Information Network.
30. Personal communication with Alcoholics Anonymous.
31. Personal communication.
32. Ross and Shillington, "A Profile of the Canadian Volunteer," 15.
33. Personal communication with Constable Copeland, Crime Prevention Unit, Station 55, Metro Toronto Police.
34. *Canadian Environmental Directory* (Toronto: Canadian Almanac & Directory Publishing, 1991).
35. Personal communication.
36. *Annual Report 1991*.
37. Personal communication.
38. David Ross and Richard Shillington, "A Profile of the Canadian Volunteer," 12.
39. Personal communication with National Action Committee.
40. *Ibid.*
41. Personal communication with the Canadian Peace Alliance.
42. Personal communication with Peace Through Strength.

Chapter 5

1. Paul Phillips, *Regional Disparities* (Toronto: Lorimer, 1982) ch. 2
2. *Ibid.*, 35–39.
3. Peter R. Sinclair, *The Great Northern Peninsula Development Corporation* (Ottawa: Economic Council of Canada, 1990) iii.
4. *Ibid.*, 11–12.
5. Wayne Mackinnon with Jon Pierce, *The West Prince Industrial Commission: A Case Study* (Ottawa: Economic Council of Canada, 1990).
6. Economic Council of Newfoundland and Labrador, *Equity Capital and Economic Development in Newfoundland and Labrador* (Ottawa: Economic Council of Canada, 1990) 16.

7. Michael Decter and Jeffrey Kowall, *A Case Study of the Kitsaki Development Corporation, La Ronge Indian Band, La Ronge, Saskatchewan* (Ottawa: Economic Council of Canada, 1990) 33.
8. *Equity Capital and Economic Development in Newfoundland and Labrador* 6.
9. *Regional Disparities* 82.
10. *Equity Capital and Economic Development in Newfoundland and Labrador* 6.
11. *Regional Disparities* 82.
12. *Ibid.*, 81.
13. *Ibid.*, 83–87.
14. Cape Breton Assessment Team, *From Dependence to Enterprise* (Sydney: Enterprise Cape Breton, 1991).
15. *Ibid.*, 24.
16. *Ibid.*, 33.
17. *Ibid.*, 31.
18. *Ibid.*, 36.
19. *Ibid.*, 109.
20. "Lessons from the Money Poured into Cape Breton," *Globe and Mail*, February 15, 1991, A 16.
21. *From Dependence to Enterprise* 110.
22. *Ibid.*, 22.
23. *Ibid.*, 23.
24. *Ibid.*, 112.
25. Marie Howland, "Plant Closures: Are Local Conditions Responsible?" *Plant Closures and Community Recovery*, ed. John Lynch (Washington: National Council for Urban Economic Development, 1990) 17–21.
26. *Equity Capital and Economic Development in Newfoundland and Labrador.*
27. *Ibid.*, 38.
28. *From Dependence to Enterprise* 119.
29. Stewart Perry, *Communities on the Way* (Albany: State University of New York, 1987) Ch. 1.
30. Personal communication with Greg MacLeod.
31. Greg MacLeod, "Worker Co-ops and Community Economic Development," *Partners in Enterprise*, ed. J. Quarter and G. Melnyk (Montreal: Black Rose, 1989) Ch. 9.
32. The analysis of New Dawn is based upon the following sources: Greg MacLeod, *New Age Business* (Ottawa: Canadian Council on Social Development, 1986) Ch. 2; *Communities on the Way* 23–28; John Hanratty, *The New Dawn Story* (Sydney: Centre for Community Economic Development, 1981); Gert MacIntyre, "Current Frameworks for Economic Development on Cape Breton Island," a doctoral dissertation in preparation, University of Toronto, 1991.
33. Economic Council of Canada, *From the Bottom Up: The Community Economic-Development Approach* (Ottawa: Minister of Supply and Services Canada, 1990) 9.
34. Elizabeth Beale, *Regional Development in Atlantic Canada: An Overview and a Case Study of the Human Resource Development Association* (Ottawa: Economic Council of Canada, 1990).
35. Personal communication with Doreen Parsons, HRDA.
36. *Ibid.*
37. *Ibid.*

38. Personal communication with Lynn Petrushchak, York Board of Education.
39. Karla Hartl, "A-WAY Express: A Way to Empowerment through Competitive Employment," *Canadian Journal of Community Mental Health*, 1992, forthcoming.
40. John Trainor, "Consumer-Survivor Businesses in Ontario," *Canadian Journal of Community Mental Health*, 1992, forthcoming.
41. *The Great Northern Peninsula Development Corporation* 36.
42. Personal communication with Gary Wilton.
43. Personal communication with Dave McIlmoy.
44. *Ibid.*
45. *A Case Study of the Kitsaki Development Corporation* 11.
46. *New Age Business* 22.
47. M.J. Grant & Co. Ltd., *Small Business Views the Banks: The Bottom Line* (Toronto: Canadian Federation of Independent Business, 1988).
48. *Equity Capital and Economic Development in Newfoundland and Labrador* 38.
49. *From the Bottom Up* 14.
50. Cited in *Equity Capital and Economic Development in Newfoundland and Labrador* 25–26.
51. Information on the First Peoples' Fund is taken from the brochure, *The First Peoples' Fund*, published by the Calmeadow Foundation and from the news bulletin, *The First People's Fund*, Vol. 1 (1990).
52. Andreas Fuglesang and Dale Chander, *Participation as a Process: What We Can Learn from the Grameen Bank, Bangladesh* (Oslo: Norad, 1986).
53. Government of Saskatchewan, "The Community Bonds Act," Section 32, Order in Council 663/90, July 4, 1990.
54. G.F. Parsons, "Community Bonds: A New Approach to Community and Economic Development," ([Saskatchewan]: n.p., [1991]) 10.
55. Greg MacLeod, "The BCA Family of Companies," Sydney, Nova Scotia, unpublished, 1991.
56. Greg MacLeod, "Worker Co-ops and Community Economic Development," in *Partners in Enterprise* Ch. 9.
57. This description of Mondragon is based upon an on-the-site tour and the following key references sources: William Whyte and Kathleen Whyte, *Making Mondragon* (Ithaca: ILR Press, 1988); Henk Thomas and Chris Logan, *Mondragon: An Economic Analysis* (London: Allen and Unwin, 1982); Hans Wiener and Robert Oakeshott, *Worker-Owners: Mondragon Revisited* (London: Anglo-German, 1987); and Robert Oakeshott, *The Case for Workers' Co-ops* (London: Routledge and Kegan Paul, 1978).
58. David Ellerman, *The Socialization of Entrepreneurship* (Boston: Industrial Co-operative Association, 1982).
59. Jesus Larranaga, "Neoco-operativism," *Worker Co-op* Summer 1990, 30–32.
60. Georges Arsenault, *The Island Acadians: 1720–1980* (Charlottetown: Ragweed, 1989).
61. Raymond Arsenault, "Evangeline, Prince Edward Island, the Uncontested Co-op Capital," *Worker Co-op* Winter 1988, 7–10.
62. "Evangeline Co-ops Keep Wolf from the Door," *Atlantic Co-operator* February 1991, 1.
63. "Coopératives de la région Evangeline," Unpublished document, 1990.
64. Cécile Gallant, *The Evangeline Region Credit Unions* (Wellington: The Evangeline Credit Union, 1986).

65. Jack Quarter, "Prince Edward Island's Minister of Industry, Léonce Bernard, Talks about Worker Co-operatives," *Worker Co-op* Winter 1988, 11-13.
66. "Notes for the Honourable Léonce Bernard, Minister Responsible for Cooperative Development on Prince Edward Island," Focus on Youth Workshop, Co-operative Resource Centre at the Ontario Institute for Studies in Education, June 26, 1990, 7.
67. *Ibid.*, 56.
68. *We're the Boss* National Film Board of Canada, prod. 1990 (28 mins.).
69. Lynden Hillier, "The CCA View," *Worker Co-op* Winter 1990, 8.
70. Jack Quarter and Paul Wilkinson, "Recent Trends in Worker Ownership in Canada," *Economic and Industrial Democracy, Vol. 11* 1990) 529–552.
71. Tony Scoggins, "The Chéticamp Experience," *Worker Co-op* Summer 1991, 23–25.
72. Maureen Edgett, "New Brunswick Acadians Finance Co-operative Development," *Worker Co-op* Summer 1990, 12.
73. *A Proposal for Renewal* (Moncton: Co-op Atlantic, 1991) 1. See also, Tom Webb, "New Vision from Troubled Times in Atlantic Canada," *Worker Co-op* Spring 1991, 30–32.
74. *A Proposal for Renewal*, Section 3.
75. "Recession Takes Bite but Central Wholesale Co-op Has Satisfactory Year," *Atlantic Co-operator*, April 1991, 2.
76. *A Proposal for Renewal*, 11.
77. This question is being addressed by Paul Wilkinson in his doctoral dissertation, "Themes and Issues in the Formation of Co-operatives in the Evangeline Region of Prince Edward Island," currently in progress at the Ontario Institute for Studies in Education.
78. Jack Quarter and Judith Brown, "Worker Buyouts in Canada: A Social Networking Analysis," *Economic and Industrial Democracy*, February 1992, 13 (1) 95–118.
79. Greg Cameron, "The Northern Breweries Buyout," *Worker Co-op* Spring 1989, 21–22.
80. Fiona Connelly, "Spruce Falls Worker Buyout Successful," *Worker Co-op* Winter 1992, 10.
81. Jack Quarter and Judith Brown, "Worker Buyouts in Canada," 95–118.
82. Warner Woodworth, "Re-Steeling the U.S.," *Worker Co-op* Spring 1989, 13–16.
83. Lynn Williams, "Keynote Speech to the 24th Constitutional Convention in Las Vegas," Pittsburg: United Steelworkers of America, 1988.
84. Stuart Crombie, "Going for Algoma Steel," *Our Times*, March 1992, 22–27; and personal communication with Ken Delaney, Research Dept., Ontario District of the United Steelworkers of America.
85. Léopold Beaulieu, "New Ground for Labour," *Worker Co-op* Spring 1990, 26–29.
86. *Ibid.*
87. Joan Selby and Alexandra Wilson, *Canada's Housing Co-operatives* (Ottawa: Co-operative Housing Federation of Canada, 1988).
88. Greg MacLeod, "Self-Help the Cape Breton Way," *Worker Co-op* Winter 1989, 27.

Chapter 6
1. The rate of home ownership in Canada is just over 60 per cent of the population. It has remained relatively stable for several decades. See Cassie Doyle and David Hulchanski, "Housing in the '90s: Common Issues," Proceedings from the International Conference, University of Illinois, Urbana-Champaign, October 13–15, 1990, 77.
2. Pierre Filion and Trudi Bunting, *Affordability of Housing in Canada* (Ottawa: Statistics Canada, 1990).
3. Canada Mortgage and Housing Corporation, *Report on Estimates of Households with Housing Problems and Those in Core Housing Need* (Ottawa: CMHC, 1985). Updated in 1988.
4. *Affordability of Housing in Canada* 21.
5. *Ibid.*, 22.
6. *Ibid.*, 23.
7. *Ibid.*, 25.
8. *Ibid.*, 27–33.
9. *Ibid.*, 33.
10. *Ibid.*, 31.
11. *Ibid.*, 30.
12. This figure is cited by Canada Mortgage and Housing Corporation in *The Evaluation of Co-operative Housing Programs* (Ottawa: CMHC, September 1990) 303.
13. *Affordability of Housing in Canada* 16.
14. *Ibid.*, 14.
15. *Ibid.*
16. George Fallis, "The Urban Housing Market," *Housing the Homeless and Poor,* ed. George Fallis and Alex Murray (Toronto: University of Toronto Press, 1990) 59–62.
17. Alex Murray, "Homelessness: The People," in *Housing the Homeless and Poor,* 16–48.
18. *Ibid.*, 20.
19. *Ibid.*
20. Albert Rose, *Canadian Housing Policies 1935–1980* (Toronto: Butterworths, 1980) 17.
21. *Ibid.*, 28.
22. *Ibid.*, 35.
23. *Ibid.*, 36.
24. *Ibid.*, 35.
25. David Hulchanski, "Canada," *International Handbook of Housing Policies and Practices,* ed. Willem van Vliet (New York: Greenwood, 1990) 309–313.
26. *Ibid.*
27. *Canadian Housing Policies 1935–1980* 31.
28. *Ibid.* 32.
29. "Canada," 301.
30. Keith Banting, "Housing in a Divided State," in *Housing the Homeless and Poor* 132.
31. Figures provided in May 1991 by Canada Mortgage and Housing Corporation.
32. Canada Mortgage and Housing Corporation, *Canadian Housing Statistics: 1989* (Ottawa: Author, 1990) 23.

33. *Canadian Housing Policies 1935–1980*, 57.
34. "Housing in a Divided State," 131–132.
35. *Facts and Figures about Co-op Housing* (Ottawa: Co-operative Housing Federation of Canada, 1990) 5–6.
36. Alberta Heritage Savings Trust Fund, "Annual Report: 1989-90," 2.
37. For a good description of housing co-operatives, see Joan Selby and Alexandra Wilson, *Canada's Housing Co-operatives* (Ottawa: Co-operative Housing Federation of Canada, 1988).
38. "Facts and Figures about Housing Co-operatives," 10.
39. *Evaluation of Co-operative Housing Programs* 314.
40. Canada Mortgage and Housing Corporation, *Section 56.1 Non-profit and Housing Program Evaluation* (Ottawa: Author, 1983) 321.
41. *Ibid.* 320.
42. *Evaluation of the Federal Co-operative Housing Programs* 78.
43. Andrew Duffy, "Ottawa Puts $60,000 Cap on Co-op Tenant Income," *The Toronto Star* Thursday, May 23, 1991, 1 and 28.
44. Co-operative Housing Federation of Canada, *An Introduction to the Index-Linked Mortgage* (Ottawa: Co-operative Housing Federation, 1990).
45. Personal communication with the Co-operative Housing Association of Ontario. See also: *Land Trust Discussion Round #4* (Ottawa: Co-operative Housing Federation of Canada, 1984).
46. This concept is discussed by Mark Bostwick, *A Guide to Developing Resident-Funded Housing Co-operatives for Seniors* (Ottawa: Co-operative Housing Federation of Canada, 1990).
47. Jeanne Wolfe and William Jay, "The Revolving Door: Third Sector Organizations and the Homeless," in *Housing the Homeless and Poor* 219.
48. *Evaluation of the Federal Co-operative Housing Programs* 57.
49. This figure is cited by Cassie Doyle and David Hulchanski, "The Housing Affordability Gap," Proceedings from the International Conference, University of Illinois, Urbana-Champaign, October 13-15, 1990.
50. This figure is estimated using Tables 13 and 17 in *Canadian Housing Statistics: 1989* 23 & 27.

Chapter 7

1. For a history see Malcolm Taylor, *Health Insurance and Canadian Public Policy: The Seven Decisions that Created the Canadian Health Insurance System* (Montreal: McGill–Queen's University Press, 1978).
2. The federal government pays for about 40 per cent of all government expenditures on healthcare, according to Health and Welfare Canada, *National Health Expenditures in Canada: 1975-87* (Ottawa: Minister of Supply and Services, 1990) 16.
3. *Ibid.* 22.
4. *Ibid.*
5. Michael Rachlis and Carol Kushner, *Second Opinion: What's Wrong with Canada's Healthcare System and How to Fix it* (Toronto: Harper and Collins, 1989).
6. *National Health Expenditures in Canada: 1975–1987* addendum.
7. *Ibid.* addendum.
8. *Ibid.* 18.
9. *Ibid.* 20.

10. *Ibid.* 8.
11. *Second Opinion* 140.
12. *Ibid.* 178.
13. Personal communication with Ruth Meller, the Victorian Order of Nurses, head office in Ottawa, and VON "Annual Report and History." ([Ottawa]: [Victorian Order of Nurses], n.d.).
14. Robin Badgley and Samuel Wolfe, *Doctors' Strike: Medical Care and Conflict in Saskatchewan* (New York: Atherton Press, 1967) 80. The Mount Carmel Clinic in Winnipeg is believed to be the first such clinic in 1926.
15. Community Health Co-operative Federation of Saskatchewan, "Brief to the House of Commons Standing Committee on Health and Welfare, Social Affairs, Seniors and the Status of Women," March 1990, 1.
16. *Doctors' Strike* 102-104.
17. "Brief to the House of Commons," March 1990, 4.
18. *Doctors' Strike* 101.
19. *Ibid.* 102-104.
20. "Brief to the House of Commons," March 1990, 4.
21. Information on the CLSCs is taken from the following sources: Luciano Bozzoni, "Local Community Service Centres (CLSCs) in Quebec: Description, Evaluation, Perspectives," *Journal of Public Health Policy* 1988, 9(3) 346-375; Jean-Pierre Belanger, "Centres Locaux de Services Communautaires," Fédération des CLSCs du Québec, 1990; George Désrosiers, "The Introduction of a Network of Local Community Health Centres: Four Years of Experience," *Canadian Journal of Public Health* Jan./Feb. 1978, Vol. 69, 7–9; and an interview with Jean-Guy Poirier, Assistant Director of the Fédération des CLSCs du Québec, May 1991.
22. André Picard, "Montreal Doctors Walk Out," *The Globe and Mail* Wednesday, May 22, 1991, A5.
23. Personal communication with Judith Martin, Community Health Co-operative Federation of Saskatchewan.
24. Personal communication with Sonny Arrojado, Association of Ontario Health Centres.
25. Personal communication with Patti Sullivan, Manitoba Association of Community Health Centres.
26. Personal communications with John Silver, Reach Community Health Centre, Vancouver, and Joanna Oosterveld, North End Community Health Association, Halifax.
27. This point is discussed in *Second Opinion* 238–239.
28. Information on the CHO in Ontario is taken from the following sources: Ministry of Health, "Comprehensive Health Organization Program," ([Toronto]: n.d.) and an interview with Dave Brindle, CHO program, Ontario Ministry of Health; Information on the British Columbia CHO is taken from: B.C. Ministry of Health, "Comprehensive Health Organization Demonstration Project," July 1990.
29. Yvonne Brunelle, Denis Ouellet and Sylvie Montreuil, "Des Organisations de soins intégrés de santé (OSIS) au Québec," Ministère de la santé et des services sociaux, August 1988.
30. Communication from Frances Lankin, Ontario Minister of Health, Toronto, Summer, 1992.

31. Saskatchewan Health, *Community Clinic Study* (Regina: Policy Research and Management Services Branch, 1983).
32. Evidence is reviewed by Douglas Angus and Pran Manga, *Co-op/Consumer Sponsored Healthcare Delivery Effectiveness* (Ottawa: Canadian Co-operative Association, August 1990) 7–15.
33. Elinor Caplan, "Remarks to the Conference on Comprehensive Health Organizations," Ontario Hospital Association, Toronto, April 5, 1989, 2.
34. "Co-op/Consumer Sponsored Healthcare Delivery," 44–45.
35. Personal communication with Yvonne Brunelle.
36. George Oake, "Health System Reform Targets Doctors' Fees," *Toronto Star* January 29, 1992, A4.
37. In 1989 Canada spent 8.9 per cent of its GNP on healthcare, whereas the U.S. spent 11.6 per cent. Source: *National Health Expenditures in Canada* appendix.
38. This example is cited in Michelle Lalonde-Graton, *Childcare in Quebec: An Overview* (Quebec City: The Special Committee on Childcare, 1986) 4.
39. Statistics Canada, *The Labour Force: Historical* (Ottawa: Minister of Supply and Services, 1990) D 86–107.
40. Statistics Canada, *Annual Historical Labour Force* (Ottawa: Minister of Supply and Services, 1990) 322.
41. Statistics Canada, *Women in Canada* (Ottawa: Minister of Supply and Services, 1990) 80.
42. Status of Women, *Report of the Task Force on Childcare* (Ottawa: Minister of Supply and Services, 1986) 3.
43. *Ibid.* Ch. 1.
44. Susan Crompton, "Who's Looking after the Kids?" *Perspectives on Labour and Income* Summer 1991, 68.
45. Katherine Marshall, "Household Chores," *Canadian Social Trends* Spring 1990, 18–19.
46. "Women in Canada," 8.
47. Abdul Rashid, "Women's Earnings and Family Incomes," *Perspectives on Labour and Income* Summer 1991, 27–37.
48. *Report of the Task Force on Childcare* 114–119.
49. Martha Friendly, "Moving Towards Quality Childcare: Reflections on Childcare Policy in Canada," *Canadian Journal of Research in Early Childhood Education* Spring 1991.
50. *Ibid.* 3–4.
51. This estimate is calculated from *Childcare Information Sheets: The Provinces and Territories 1990* (Toronto: The Childcare and Resource Research Unit, University of Toronto, 1990).
52. "Who's Looking after the Kids?" 70–72.
53. *Ibid.* 72–73.
54. *Ibid.* 73.
55. "Moving Towards Quality Childcare," 10.
56. National Childcare Information Centre, *Status of Daycare in Canada 1990* (Ottawa: Health and Welfare Canada, 1991) 3.
57. "Childcare Information Sheets," Ontario 2.
58. Ken McCready, *The Role of Co-operatives in Childcare* (Ottawa: Co-operative Secretariat, 1990) 1. From 1974 until 1989 nearly all of Saskatchewan's childcare centres were either non-profits with parent-controlled boards or

parent-based co-operatives. In 1989, the Conservative government of Grant Devine introduced legislation supporting private-market childcare centres. See Judith Martin, "From Bad to Worse: Daycare in Saskatchewan, 1982–1989," *Devine Rule in Saskatchewan: A Decade of Hope and Hardship*, ed. Lesley Biggs and Mark Stobbe (Saskatoon: Fifth House, 1990) Ch. 11.

59. "Childcare Information Sheets."
60. Ontario Coalition for Better Childcare, "Discussion Paper," Fall Policy Forum, November 8, 1989, 5.
61. *Report of the Task Force on Childcare* 277.
62. *Ibid.* 331.
63. "Status of Daycare in Canada 1990," 6.
64. *Ibid.* 4.
65. *Ibid.* 3.
66. "Discussion Paper."
67. *Ibid.* 5.
68. "Discussion Paper," 5.
69. *Childcare in Quebec* 86.
70. "Discussion Paper," 9.
71. *Ibid.* 26–27.
72. *Childcare in Quebec* 68–71.
73. Personal communication with the Office des services de garde à l'enfance.
74. *Childcare in Quebec* 68.
75. Personal communication with Lynn Petrushchak of the York Board of Education.
76. "Discussion Paper," 9.
77. *Ibid.* and Gail Richardson and Elisabeth Marx, "A Welcome for Every Child," *Report of the Childcare Study Panel of the French-American Foundation* 1989.
78. Personal communication from Judith Martin.
79. Judith Martin, *Child Care in Saskatchewan: What We Have, What We Want* (Saskatoon: Action Child Care, 1988) 42–44.
80. See Robyn Magee, *Growing Co-operatively: A Reference Manual on Parent Participating Schools* (Toronto: Ontario Ministry of Community and Social Services, 1986).
81. *Childcare in Quebec: An Overview* 75–77; and personal communication with the Office des services de garde à l'enfance, June 1991.
82. Ontario Coalition for Better Childcare, "Making the Shift to the 1990s: A Working Paper," October 1990.
83. David Hagerman and Scott Evans, "Co-operatives, Feminism and the Childcare Agenda: The Case of the Ottawa Parent/Staff Co-operatives," paper submitted to the Canadian Association for the Studies in Co-operation, May 1990.

Chapter 8

1. Some of the key references are: John Porter, *The Vertical Mosaic* (Toronto: The University of Toronto Press, 1965); Wallace Clement, *The Canadian Corporate Elite* (Toronto: McClelland and Stewart, 1975); Peter Newman, *The Canadian Establishment* Vol. 1 (Toronto: McClelland and Stewart, 1975); Jorge Niosi, *Canadian Capitalism* (Toronto: James Lorimer, 1981); *The Structure of*

the Canadian Capitalist Class, ed. Robert Brym (Toronto: Garamond Press, 1985).
2. William Carrol, Corporate Power and Canadian Capitalism (Vancouver: University of British Columbia Press, 1986).
3. Ibid. 164.
4. Ibid. 182.
5. Statistics Canada, Pension Plans in Canada, 1988 (Ottawa: Supply and Services Canada, 1990), 8. See also, Statistics Canada, Trusteed Pension Funds, 1988 (Ottawa: Supply and Services Canada, 1990).
6. Statistics Canada, Industrial Corporations Financial Statistics: Second Quarter 1990 (Ottawa: Supply and Services Canada, 1990) ix.
7. Richard Deaton, The Political Economy of Pensions (Vancouver: University of British Columbia Press, 1989).
8. Ibid. 280.
9. Ibid.
10. Wood Gundy, Evaluation of Investment Performance Report December 31, 1979 (Toronto: Author, 1979) MA-3. Cited by Deaton on p. 281.
11. Richard Deaton, The Political Economy of Pensions 282.
12. Peter Drucker, The Unseen Revolution: How Pension Fund Socialism Came to America (New York: Harper & Row, 1976).
13. Cowan V. Scargill (1984) 2 All, E.R., 750.
14. Ibid. 750–751.
15. Malcolm Rowan, In Whose Interest: The Task Force on the Investment of Public Sector Pension Funds (Toronto: The Queen's Printer, 1987).
16. Patricia Lane, "Ethical Investment: Towards the Best Interest of Everyone," The Advocate March 1987.
17. Ibid. 177.
18. Edward Waitzer, "Pension Fund Trustees as Shareholders," Paper presented at the Conference on Strategies for Responsible Share Ownership, University of Toronto, December 7, 1990, 8.
19. Malcolm Rowan, In Whose Interest? Sections III and IV.
20. Homes Now (Toronto: Ministry of Housing, November 1988).
21. Caisse de dépôt et plaçement du Québec, Annual Report for 1989, 2.
22. Ibid. inside cover.
23. Ibid. 16.
24. Rowan, In Whose Interest? 271.
25. Solidarité (Newsletter of the Fonds de solidarité des travailleurs du Québec) 1.
26. Class A Shares: Seventh Edition (Montreal: Le Fonds de solidarité des travailleurs du Québec, 1990) 3.
27. Ibid. 3.
28. Interview with Jean-François LeBrun, Director of Communications, Quebec Solidarity Fund.
29. Solidarité, 1
30. Jan Ravensbergen, "The Conversion of Louis Laberge," Quebec Business November 1988, 41.
31. Personal Communication with Jean-François LeBrun.
32. Ibid.
33. Personal Communication with Toronto Office of Working Ventures.

34. Government of Ontario, *Ontario Investment and Worker Ownership Program* (Toronto: Ministry of Treasury and Economics, 1991).
35. See the *Report of the Ad Hoc Committee to Study Proposals for a Labour-Managed Social Investment Fund* (Toronto: Ontario Federation of Labour, 1989) and Judith Brown, "Ontario Labour Opposes Buyout Fund," *Worker Co-op* Winter 1990, 10.
36. Christian Allard, "Venture Socialist," *Report on Business Magazine* September 1992, 47–53.
37. Sherman Kreiner, "Unionized Worker Ownership," *Worker Co-op* Spring 1991, 26–28; and Canadian Co-operative Association, *Worker Buyouts and the Industrial Restructuring Challenge* (Ottawa: Author, 1991) 58–60.
38. Henry Milner, *Sweden: Social Democracy in Practice* (Oxford: Oxford Univ. Press, 1990) 130–137.
39. *Canadian Co-operatives,* ed. Les McCagg (Ottawa: Co-operative Secretariat, 1990), Section IV.
40. Raymond Arsenault, "Evangeline, P.E.I.: the Uncontested Co-op Capital," *Worker Co-op* Winter 1988, 7–10.
41. Leopold Beaulieu, "New Ground for Labour," *Worker Co-op* Spring 1990, 26–29.
42. Personal communications with Art Daniels, Manager of Mortgage Services at Co-op Trust, Saskatoon.
43. John Jordan, *Towards a Multi-Stakeholder Model in Co-operative Insurance* (Guelph: The Co-operators Group, 1990) 3.
44. Personal communication with John Jordan.
45. Personal communication with the Credit Union Central of Canada.
46. *VanCity Community* brochure (Vancouver: VanCity, 1990).
47. Adreas Fuglesang and Dale Chandler, *Participation as a Process: What We Can Learn from Graemeen Bank, Bangladesh* (Oslo: Norwegian Agency for Development and Co-operation, 1990).
48. *Submission to the Credit Union Central Vision Task Force* (Toronto: Universities and Colleges Credit Union, 1991) 30.
49. Personal communication with Joanne Ferguson.
50. In 1989, Désjardins organizations donated $15.9 to "community development and environmental projects," slightly less than they had donated in previous years — *Désjardins, 1990* (Levis-Lauzon: La Confédération des caisses populaires et d'économie Désjardins du Québec, 1990) 16.
51. Maureen Edgett, "New Brunswick Acadians Finance Co-operative Development," *Worker Co-op* Summer 1990, 12.
52. Personal communication with Erik Jokinen, Chief Executive Officer, Sudbury Regional Credit Union.
53. *Désjardins* 1990: 34–35.
54. See Eugene Ellman, *Profitable Ethical Investment* (Toronto: Lorimer, 1989).
55. These figures are cited by Ellman on p. 58.
56. *The Désjardins Environment Fund* (Montreal: Désjardins Trust, 1990) 1.
57. *A Co-operative Development Strategy for Canada* (Toronto: Canadian Co-operative Association, 1984) 47.
58. Claude Carbonneau, "Tax Policy Changes," *Worker Co-op* Summer 1989, 8.
59. Eugene Ellman, *Profitable Ethical Investment* 71.

60. Alberta Heritage Savings Trust Fund, *Annual Report 1989/90* (Edmonton: Heritage Fund Reports, 1990); Saskatchewan Heritage Fund, *Annual Report 1989/90* (Regina: Province of Saskatchewan, 1990).

61. Deaton, *The Political Economy of Pensions* 293.

62. Personal communication with Claude Carbonneau, Director of Communications of the Société de développement des coopératives.

63. "Fair and Indexed Pensions," Document 1, Annual Convention of the Ontario Federation of Labour, 1988, 5.

64. Cited by Deaton, *The Political Economy of Pensions* 335.

65. Richard Deaton, "Book Review of *Age, Capital and Democracy: Member Participation in Pension Scheme Management*" *Economic and Industrial Democracy* August 1990: 430–432.

66. *Fair and Indexed Pensions* Document 1, 5, and Canadian Labour Congress, *Proposed Amendments to the Canada Pension Plan* (Ottawa: Submission to the Standing Committee on National Health and Welfare, June 1986).

67. A similar proposal for handling Ontario's CPP funds is made by Malcolm Rowan, *In Whose Interest?* 281.

Chapter 9

1. The Canadian Red Cross, *Annual Report: 1990–91* 26–27.

2. Statistics Canada, *Health Reports Supplement* No. 20, Vol. 3(1) (Ottawa: Minister of Supply and Service, 1991) 28.

3. David Ross and Richard Shillington, *Economic Dimensions of Volunteer Work in Canada* (Ottawa: Secretary of State, 1990) 4.

4. Samuel Martin, *An Essential Grace* (Toronto: McClelland and Stewart, 1985) 31.

5. *Ibid.*

6. *Ibid.*

7. *Ibid.* 32.

8. *The Economics of Nonprofit Institutions*, ed. Susan Rose-Ackerman (New York: Oxford University Press, 1986). A collection of essays on why non-profits have come about in particular sectors of the economy.

9. This point is discussed by Burton Weisbrod, "Toward a Theory of the Voluntary Nonprofit Sector in a Three-Sector Economy," in *The Economics of Nonprofit Institutions* 30.

10. See Henry Hansmann, "The Role of the Nonprofit Enterprise," in *The Economics of Nonprofit Institutions* Ch. 3.

11. David Easley and Maureen O'Hara, "Optimal Nonprofit Firms," in *The Economics of Nonprofit Institutions* 91.

12. See Susan Rose-Ackerman, "Introduction," in *The Economics of Nonprofit Institutions* 11–12.

13. Kurt Wetzel and Daniel Gallagher, *Union-Management Labour Relations in Co-operatives* (Saskatoon: Centre for the Study of Co-operatives, 1985)5.

14. John Dewey, *Democracy and Education* (New York: Free Press, 1944) 99.

15. *Ibid.* 316.

16. *Ibid.* 316–17.

17. This point is emphasized in social reproduction theory, for example, Samuel Bowles and Herbert Gintis, *Schooling in Capitalist America* (New York: Basic Books, 1976).

18. Information on regional school programs sponsored by co-operatives is available from the Canadian Co-operative Association in Ottawa.

19. *Coopératives en milieu scholaire* (Fédération des coopératives québécoises en milieu scholaire 1990) 13.

20. *Statistiques financières 1986–90* (Quebec: Les Coopératives québécoises en milieu scholaire, 1990) 5.

21. Personal communication with the Ontario region representative of the North American Student Co-operative Organization.

22. Candice Selby, "Youth Action Co-operative Ltd. Enjoying a Successful Summer," *Worker Co-op* Fall 1985, 24; and Lars Apland, "Believe it or not: A Worker Co-operative in Junior Achievement," *Worker Co-op* Summer 1986, 25–26; "Worker Co-ops in Junior Achievement," *Worker Co-op* Fall 1988, 26.

23. Maureen Edgett, "Jamie McGloin Leaves his Mark," *Worker Co-op* Fall 1989, 32.

24. Raymond Arsenault, "Evangeline, Prince Edward Island: The Uncontested Co-op Capital," *Worker Co-op* Winter 1988, 7–9.

25. The Toronto Board of Education, "Report No. 3 of the Central Staffing Committee (Elementary)," December 17, 1990, Appendix I.

26. Daniel Brown, *Decentralization and School-Based Management* (London: Falmer, 1990).

27. Rita Daly, "Grassroots School Councils Cut Red Tape, High Costs," *Toronto Star* March 15, 1992: A10.

SELECTED BIBLIOGRAPHY

Angus, Douglas, and Pran Manga. *Co-op/Consumer Sponsored Healthcare Delivery Effectiveness*. Ottawa: Canadian Co-operative Association, 1990.

Arsenault, Georges. *The Island Acadians: 1720–1980*. Charlottetown: Ragweed, 1989.

Associations Canada, 1991.Toronto: Canadian Almanac and Directory Publishing Company, 1991.

Badgley, Robin, and Samuel Wolfe. *Doctors' Strike: Medical Care and Conflict in Saskatchewan*. New York: Atherton Press, 1967.

Beale, Elizabeth. *Regional Development in Atlantic Canada: An Overview and a Case Study of the Human Resource Development Association*. Ottawa: Economic Council of Canada, 1990.

Bozzoni, Luciano. "Local Community Service Centres (CLSCs) in Quebec: Description, Evaluation, Perspectives." *Journal of Public Health Policy*. 9.3 (1988): 346-375.

Bridault, Alain, and Ginette Lafrenière, "A Social History of Worker Co-operatives in Quebec." *Partners in Enterprise*. Ed. Jack Quarter and George Melnyk. Montreal: Black Rose, 1989. Chapter 8.

Brown, Daniel. *Decentralization and School-Based Management*. London: Falmer, 1990.

Cape Breton Assessment Team. *From Dependence to Enterprise*. Sydney, N.S.: Enterprise Cape Breton, 1991.

Carrol, William. *Corporate Power and Canadian Capitalism*. Vancouver: University of British Columbia Press, 1986.

Community Health Co-operative Federation of Saskatchewan. "Brief to the House of Commons Standing Committee on Health and Welfare, Social Affairs, Seniors and the Status of Women." March 1990.

Co-op Atlantic. *A Proposal for Renewal*. Moncton: Co-op Atlantic, 1991.

Co-operatives Secretariat. *Canadian Co-operatives: Resource File 1991*. Ottawa: Co-operatives Secretariat, 1991.

Crompton, Susan. "Who's Looking after the Kids?" *Perspectives on Labour and Income*. Summer, 1991: 68.

Dahl, Robert. *After the Revolution: Authority in a Good Society*. New Haven: Yale University Press, 1970.

Deaton, Richard. *The Political Economy of Pensions*. Vancouver: University of British Columbia Press, 1989.

Decter, Michael, and Jeffrey Kowall. *A Case Study of the Kitsaki Development Corporation, La Ronge Indian Band, La Ronge, Saskatchewan*. Ottawa: Economic Council of Canada, 1990.

Defourny, Jacques, and José Monzon, eds. *Économie Sociale*. Brussels: CIRIEC, 1992.

Dewey, John. *Democracy and Education*. New York: Free Press, 1944.

Doyle, Cassie, and David Hulchanski. "Housing in the '90s: Common Issues." Proceedings from the International Conference University of Illinois, Urbana-Champaign, October 13–15, 1990.

Duchesne, Doreen. *Giving Freely: Volunteers in Canada*. Ottawa: Statistics Canada, 1989.

Earle, John. *The Italian Co-operative Movement*. London: Unwin Hyman, 1986.

Economic Council of Canada. *From the Bottom Up: The Community Economic Development Approach*. Ottawa: Minister of Supply and Services Canada, 1990.

Economic Council of Newfoundland and Labrador. *Equity Capital and Economic Development in Newfoundland and Labrador*. Ottawa: Economic Council of Canada, 1990.

Ellerman, David. *The Socialization of Entrepreneurship*. Boston: Industrial Cooperative Association, 1982.

———. *The Democratic Worker-Owned Firm: A New Model for East and West*. Boston: Unwin Hyman, 1990.

Fallis, George and Alex Murray, eds. *Housing the Homeless and Poor*. Toronto: University of Toronto Press, 1990.

Filion, Pierre, and Trudi Bunting. *Affordability of Housing in Canada*. Ottawa: Statistics Canada, 1990.

Friendly, Martha. "Moving Towards Quality Childcare: Reflections on Childcare Policy in Canada." *Canadian Journal of Research in Early Childhood Education*. Spring 1991.

Fuglesang, Andreas, and Dale Chander. *Participation as a Process: What We Can Learn from the Grameen Bank, Bangladesh*. Oslo: Norad, 1986.

Hagerman, David, and Scott Evans. "Co-operatives, Feminism and the Childcare Agenda: The Case of the Ottawa Parent/Staff Co-operatives." Paper submitted to the Canadian Association for the Studies in Co-operation, May 1990.

Hanratty, John. *The New Dawn Story*. Sydney: Centre for Community Economic Development, 1981.

Hartl, Karla. "A-WAY Express: A Way to Empowerment through Competitive Employment." *Canadian Journal of Community Mental Health*. 1992: forthcoming.

Hirschman, Albert. *Exit, Voice and Loyalty*. Cambridge: Harvard University Press, 1970.

Howland, Marie. "Plant Closures: Are Local Conditions Responsible?" *Plant Closures and Community Recovery*. Ed. John Lynch. Washington: National Council for Urban Economic Development, 1990.

Hulchanski, David. "Canada." *International Handbook of Housing Policies and Practices*. Ed. Willem van Vliet. New York: Greenwood, 1990. 309–313.

Jordan, John. "The Multi-stakeholder Approach to Worker Ownership," *Partners in Enterprise*. Ed. Jack Quarter and George Melnyk. Montreal: Black Rose, 1989. Chapter 5.

Kealey, Greg, and Bryan Palmer. *Dreaming of What Might Be: The Knights of Labour in Ontario, 1880–1890*. Toronto: New Hogtown, 1987.

Kenyon, Ron. *To the Credit of the People*. Toronto: The Ontario Credit Union League, 1976.

Lane, Patricia. "Ethical Investment: Towards the Best Interest of Everyone." *The Advocate*. March 1987.

Larranaga, Jesus. "Neoco-operativism." *Worker Co-op*. Summer 1990: 30–32.

Mackinnon, Wayne, with Jon Pierce. *The West Prince Industrial Commission: a Case Study*. Ottawa: Economic Council of Canada, 1990.

Macleod, David. *Building Character in the American Boy: The Boy Scouts, YMCA, and their Forerunners, 1870–1920*. Madison: University of Wisconsin Press, 1983.

MacLeod, Greg. *New Age Business*. Ottawa: Canadian Council on Social Development, n.d.

MacPherson, Ian. *Each for All: A History of the Co-operative Movement in English Canada: 1900–45*. Toronto: MacMillan, 1989.

Marshall, Katherine. "Household Chores." *Canadian Social Trends*. Spring 1990: 18–19.

Martin, Judith. "From Bad to Worse: Daycare in Saskatchewan, 1982–1989." *Devine Rule in Saskatchewan: A Decade of Hope and Hardship*. Ed. Lesley Biggs and Mark Stobbe. Saskatoon: Fifth House, 1990. Chapter 11.

Martin, Samuel. *An Essential Grace*. Toronto: McClelland and Stewart, 1985.

McCready, Ken. *The Role of Co-operatives in Childcare*. Ottawa: Co-operative Secretariat, 1990.

McQuaig, Linda. *Behind Closed Doors*. Toronto: Penguin, 1987.

Melnyk, George. *The Search for Community*. Toronto: Black Rose, 1985.

Milofsky, Carl, ed. *Community Organizations: Studies in Resource Mobilization and Exchange*. New York: Oxford University Press, 1985.

Oakeshott, Robert. *The Case for Workers' Co-ops*. London: Routledge and Kegan Paul, 1978.

Oderkirk, Jillian. "Food Banks." *Canadian Social Trends*. Spring 1992: 6–14.

Phillips, Paul. *Regional Disparities*. Toronto: Lorimer, 1982.

Quarter, Jack, and Judith Brown. "Worker Buyouts in Canada: A Social Networking Analysis." *Economic and Industrial Democracy*. February 1992: 95–118.

Quarter, Jack, and Paul Wilkinson. "Recent Trends in Worker Ownership in Canada." *Economic and Industrial Democracy*. Vol. 11. 1990: 529–552.

Quarter, Jack, and George Melnyk, eds. *Partners in Enterprise*. Montreal: Black Rose, 1989.

Rachlis, Michael, and Carol Kushner. *Second Opinion: What's Wrong with Canada's Healthcare System and How to Fix it*. Toronto: Harper and Collins, 1989.

Richardson, Gail, and Elisabeth Marx. "A Welcome for Every Child." *Report of the Childcare Study Panel of the French-American Foundation*. 1989.

Rose, Albert. *Canadian Housing Policies 1935–1980*. Toronto: Butterworths, 1980.

Rose-Ackerman, Susan, ed. *The Economics of Nonprofit Institutions*. New York: Oxford University Press, 1986.

Ross, David, and Peter Usher. *From the Roots Up*. Toronto: Lorimer, 1986.

Ross, David and Richard Shillington. *Economic Dimensions of Volunteer Work in Canada*. Ottawa: Secretary of State, 1990.

———. *A Profile of the Canadian Volunteer*. Ottawa: National Voluntary Organizations, 1990.

Rowan, Malcolm. *In Whose Interest: The Task Force on the Investment of Public Sector Pension Funds*. Toronto: The Queen's Printer, 1987.

Scoggins, Tony. "The Chéticamp Experience." *Worker Co-op*. Summer 1991: 23–25.

Selby, Joan, and Alexandra Wilson, *Canada's Housing Co-operatives*. Ottawa: Co-operative Housing Federation of Canada, 1988.

Sinclair, Peter R. *The Great Northern Peninsula Development Corporation*. Ottawa: Economic Council of Canada, 1990.

Status of Women. *Report of the Task Force on Childcare*. Ottawa: Minister of Supply and Services, 1986.

Taylor, Malcolm. *Health Insurance and Canadian Public Policy: The Seven Decisions that Created the Canadian Health Insurance System*. Montreal: McGill–Queen's University Press, 1978.

Thomas, Henk, and Chris Logan. *Mondragon: An Economic Analysis*. London: Allen and Unwin, 1982.

Trainor, John. "Consumer-Survivor Businesses in Ontario." *Canadian Journal of Community Mental Health*. 1992: forthcoming.

Webb, Beatrice (Potter). *Co-operative Movement in Great Britain*. London: Swan Sonnenschein, 1904.

Webb, Sydney, and Beatrice Webb. *Problems of Modern Industry*. New York: Longmans, Green, 1920.

———. *The Consumers' Co-operative Movement*. London: Longmans, Green, 1921.

Wetzel, Kurt, and Daniel Gallagher. *Union-Management Labour Relations in Co-operatives*. Saskatoon: Centre for the Study of Co-operatives, 1985.

Whyte, William Foote, and Kathleen Whyte. *Making Mondragon*. Ithaca: ILR Press, 1988.

Wiener, Hans, and Robert Oakeshott. *Worker-Owners: Mondragon Revisited*. London: Anglo-German, 1987.

Wilkinson, Paul. "Themes and Issues in the Formation of Co-operatives in the Evangeline Region of Prince Edward Island." Doctoral dissertation currently in progress at the Ontario Institute for Studies in Education.

INDEX

Alberta Heritage Fund, 159
Alcoholics Anonymous, 81
Algoma Steel: employee buyout, 37-38
"Alternative investment," 158
Amnesty International, 56-57, 171
Apex organizations, 22, 23
  in the labour movement, 66
A Proposal for Renewal, 106-107
Artisan co-operative, 19
Arts councils, 60
Association for Community Living, 59
Auto insurance, non-profit, 36
A-WAY Express, 98

Barter, 46
BCA Holdings, 101-102
Better Business Bureaus, 72-73
Big Brothers, 58
Big Sisters, 58
Blanchet's principle, 151-152
Block Parents programs, 82
Blue Cross, 52
Board of directors, 10
Board of education, 9
Board of trade, 70
Böök, Sven Ake, 35
Boys and Girls Clubs, 53
Business Council on National Issues, 70
Business organizations, mutual non-profit, 69-72

Caisse de dépôt et placement du Québec, 149-150

Caisses populaires, 23-24, 155
Caja Laboral Popular, 103, 178
Calmeadow Foundation, 100
Canada Assistance Plan, 135
Canada Mortgage and Housing Corporation (CMHC), 119, 120
Canada/Quebec Pension Plan, 162
Canadian Alternative Investment Co-operative (CAIC), 158
Canadian Association of Community Health Clinics, 21
Canadian Association of Volunteer Bureaus and Centres, 60
Canadian Automobile Association, 52
Canadian Cancer Society, 59
Canadian Chamber of Commerce, 70
Canadian Civil Liberties Association, 85-86
Canadian Co-operative Association, 22, 158
Canadian Diabetes Association, 59-60
Canadian Environmental Network, 84
Canadian Ethnocultural Council, 75-76
Canadian Federation of Agriculture, 71
Canadian Federation of Independent Business, 70
Canadian Food Brokers Association, 71

Canadian Home Builders'
Association, 71-72
Canadian Labour Congress, 66, 110
Canadian Manufacturers'
Association, 71
Canadian Medical Association, 68
Canadian Union of Public
Employees, 66
Canadian Worker Co-operative
Federation, 28
Cape Breton: government
assistance to business in, 93-94, 95
Carroll, William, 144-145
CCF (NDP), 4-5
Chamber of commerce, 70
Charitable donations, 7, 47-48
Charitable foundations, 50-51
Charities, 42-44
Childcare, community-based,
133-143
    charitable services, 59
    childcare co-operatives, 22, 137
    current policies, 135-138
    models for a childcare system,
        138-142
    parent-controlled, non-profit
        model, 141-142, 143
    preschool co-ops, 141-142
    school-based, 139-141, 143
    Report of the Task Force on
        Child Care, 137-138
Closed membership non-profits,
10-11
CLSCs: role in childcare, 142
Commercial non-profits, 52
Community Bonds Program of
Saskatchewan, 101
Community development
corporations (CDCs), 95-99
Community economic
    development, 89-111
    community development
        corporations (CDCs), 95-99
    financing regional development,
        100-102

government strategies to
    reduce regional disparities,
    91-95
organized labour and, 107-111
regional inequality, 89-91
regionally based co-operative
    systems, 102-107
Community foundations, 50
Community information centres, 60
Competitive sports, 54
Confédération des syndicats
    nationaux (CSN), 28, 108-110, 111
Conseil canadien de la
    coopération, 22, 158
Conseil de la coopération de
    l'Ile-du-Prince Édouard, 105
Consumer co-operatives, 4
Consumer organizations, 72-74
Consumers' Association of
    Canada, 73
Consumers' Co-operative
    Refineries Ltd. (CCRL), 27
Co-op Atlantic, 21, 22, 106-107, 111
Co-operative commonwealth, 174
Co-operative Energy
    Corporation, 26-27
Co-operative Housing
    Federation of Canada, 21
Co-operative insurers, 26
Co-operatively held
    subsidiaries, 26-27, 39
Co-operatives:
    co-operation between, 16-17
    member-owned-and-operated,
        15-16
    models of organization, 17-38
    co-operatively held
        subsidiaries, 26-27, 39
    marketing co-operatives, 17-19, 38
    multi-stakeholder co-operatives,
        32-36, 40
    multi-stakeholder co-operatives in
        Crown corporations, 36
    second- and third-tier
        co-operatives, 22-26, 38-39

user-based co-operatives,
    19-22, 38
worker co-operatives, 27-32,
    39-40
worker-shareholder
    co-operatives, 37-38, 40
views in the 1930s, 4
Co-operators Data, 34-35
Co-operators Group, 32-35, 36, 156
Co-operators Insurance, 26
Corporate capital, control of,
    144-145
Corporate foundations, 50-51
Cowan vs. *Scargill*, 146-147
Credit Union Central of Canada, 24
Credit unions, 24, 155-156, 157, 173
Crocus Investment Fund,
    153-155, 163, 178
Crown corporations:
    differences from private-sector
        companies, 2
    multi-stakeholder co-operatives
        in, 36

Dahl, Robert, 8
Deaton, Richard, 145
Democracy, and the social
    economy, 9-10, 12, 179
Democratic socialism, 4
Department of Regional
    Economic Expansion (DREE), 92
Désjardins, Alphonse, 23
Dewey, John, 175
Dividends for patronage, 8, 11, 16
Doctors' strike in Saskatchewan,
    127

Écoles maternelles program, 140
Economic mutual non-profits, 86
Education: role in advancing the
    social economy, 175-178
Elizabeth Fry Society, 57-58
Employee stock ownership
    plans (ESOP), 37
Enterprise Cape Breton (ECB),
    93-94, 95

Environmental groups, 83-84
Equalization payments, 91, 92
Ethno-cultural organizations, 74-76
Evangeline Credit Union, 155, 176
Evangeline group of
    co-operatives, 103-105, 111, 176
Extended care, 61

Family foundations, 50
Farm-marketing co-operatives,
    17-18
Farm-supply co-operatives, 20
Federal Business Development
    Bank (FBDB), 100
Federated Co-operatives, 20, 22
Feminist organizations, 84
Financial co-operatives, 23-25
Financing non-profits, 46-55
    charitable foundations, 50-51
    government funding, 47
    role of finance in building a
        social economy, 178
    United Way, 48-49
    worker co-operatives, 29-30
First Peoples' Fund, 100
First-tier co-operative, 22
Fishing co-operatives, 19
Food and shelter, charitable
    services providing, 58-59
Food banks, 58, 171
Food Institute of Canada, 71
Free Trade Agreement, 6, 90

Genealogical associations, 79-80
Girl Guides, 53
Good, W.C., 4
Government ownership, views
    on, 4
Government-sector non-profits,
    60-61, 62
Grain Growers Grain Company, 18
Grameen Bank of Bangladesh, 100
Grange (Patrons of Husbandry), 17
Great Northern Peninsula
    Development Corporation
    (GNPDC), 98

Health advocacy, 59-60
Healthcare, 124-133
   community health clinics,
     126-128
   comprehensive health
    organizations (CHOs),
     130-132
   co-operatives, 21
   costs, 125-126
   local community service
    centres (CLSCs) in Quebec,
     128-130, 133
   in Saskatchewan, 125, 126-127
Heritage funds, as sources of
  investment capital, 159-160
Hospitals, 61
Housing:
   affordability problems, 112-115
   co-op housing, 21, 118-122
   government involvement in
    the housing market, 115-116
   labour's involvement in social
    housing, 110-111
   social housing, 116-118, 123
Human Resource Development
  Association (HRDA) of Halifax, 97
Human rights organizations, 85

Independence from government, 3-6
Index-linked mortgage, 120, 121,
  122
Informal economy, 6
Informal volunteerism, 45-46
International Co-operative
  Alliance, 16, 35
Interprovincial Co-operatives, 22
Investment capital, sources:
   heritage funds, 159-160
   labour-sponsored funds, 150-155
   pension funds, 145-150, 162-163
   social funds, 155-159
   strategies for change, 160-163

John Howard Society, 57-58
Jordan, John, 33-34
Junior Achievement, 53, 176

Kitsaki Development
  Corporation (KDC), 98-99
Kiwanis, 57
Knights of Labour, 29

Labour movement:
   in community economic
    development, 107-111
   labour federations as sources
    of investment capital, 150-155
   unions as mutual non-profits,
    65-67
Labour Sponsored Venture
  Capital Corporations (LSVCC), 38
Land trusts, 121, 122
Lane, Patricia, 147-148
Learned Societies, 79
Lions Clubs, 57
Local employment and trading
  systems (LETS), 46
Lottery revenues, foundations
  created from, 51

MacPherson, Ian, 4
Managerial associations, 69
Marketing co-operatives, 17-19, 38
Martin, Samuel, 47
Meals-on-Wheels, 58
Megarry rule, 146-147, 152, 163
Member-owned and -operated,
  15-16
Milieu scholaire program, 139-140
Minority cultures, and
  co-operative systems, 106-107
Mondragon model, 102-103, 178
Multi-stakeholder co-operatives,
  32-36, 40
   in Crown corporations, 36
Mutual Insurance, 25-26
Mutual non-profit organizations:
  economic, 65-74
   business organizations, 69-72
   consumer organizations, 72-74
   labour organizations, 65-67
   managerial associations, 69
   professional associations, 67-69

social, 74-86
   ethno-cultural organizations,
      74-76
   mutual self-help groups, 81-82
   mutual socio-political
      organizations, 83-86
   neighborhood groups, 82-83
   religious organizations, 76-78
   social clubs, 78-81

National Action Committee on
   the Status of Women (NAC), 84
Native Women's Association of
   Canada, 75
Neighborhood groups, 82-83
Neighborhood Watch, 83
New Dawn, 96-97, 99, 101-102, 111
Newfoundland Economic
   Council, 94-95
Non-profits in public service:
   financing, 46-55
   form and philosophy, 42-44
   government-sector non-profits,
      60-61, 62
   with user payments, 51-55
   volunteer-based non-profits,
      55-60
   volunteers in, 44-46

One-member/one-vote, 9, 12,
   63, 172
Ontario Coalition for Better
   Child Care, 142, 143
Ontario Coalition for Better
   Daycare, 138-139
Ontario Labour-Sponsored
   Investment Fund, 152
Open membership, 10
Organizations in the social
      economy, 2-3, 6
   democratic control by
      members, 9-10, 12, 172-174
Ownership rights, 8

Parents Preschool Co-operative
   International, 22

Patrons of Industry, 17
Peace movement, 84-85
Pension funds:
   as a source of investment
      capital, 145-150, 160, 161, 162-163
   in Quebec, 149-150
   ethical debate concerning the
      use of, 146-148
Performing arts, 54-55
Phillips, Paul, 90
Political parties, 83
Potter, Beatrice (Beatrice Webb),
   29-30
Private sector, 2
Professional associations, 67-69
Profit and loss, 7-8
Proxy voting, 25

Quebec: local community service
   centres (CLSCs) in, 128-130, 133

Rape crisis centres, 171
Recreational groups, 80-81
Red Cross, 56, 168
Regina Manifesto, 4
Regional development. See
   Community economic
   development
Registered retirement savings
   plans (RRSPs), self-directed, 163
Religious congregations, 173
Religious organizations, 76-78
Retirement savings plans:
   total reserves in 1987, 145
Rochdale Pioneers, 10, 17, 155
Royal Canadian Legion, 79

Salvation Army, 58
Saskatchewan: healthcare in,
   125, 126-127
Saskatchewan Heritage Fund,
   159-160
Scouts, 53-54
Second- and third-tier
   co-operatives, 22-26, 38-39
Shareholders, 7

Shares, 7, 8
Shriners, 57
Social assistance programs, 91-92
Social clubs, 78-81
Social dividends, 8, 11
Social economy:
    definition, 1
    economic impact of, 168-169
    finance, 178. *See also*
        Investment capital, sources
    organizations in, 2-3, 6, 9-10, 12,
        172-174
    reasons for, 169-172
    role of education in advancing,
        175-178
Social enterprises, 3
Social funds as a source of
    investment capital, 155-159
Social housing. *See* Housing
Social investment, 179
Social mutual non-profit
    organizations, 86
Social objectives, 2-3
Social ownership, 5
Social service. *See* Childcare;
    Healthcare
Société d'investissement
    Désjardins, 157
Solidarity Fund sponsored by
    Quebec Federation of Labour
    (FTQ), 150-152, 163
Sports Federation of Canada, 54
St. John Ambulance, 78
Stakeholder theory, 33
Student co-operatives, 176
Swedish Wage Earner Funds, 154

Taxes: financing of public
    services through, 47

Third-tier co-operative, 22
Toronto schools: staffing and
    program plan for, 177

Ukrainian-Canadian Congress, 75
Unemployment insurance, 91, 92
Unions. *See* Labour movement
United Church of Canada, 76-77
United Way, 48-49
User-based co-operatives, 19-22, 38

VanCity, 156
Victorian Order of Nurses, 126
Voluntary membership, 10
Volunteer-based non-profits in
    public service, 55-60
        domestic organizations, 57-58
Volunteers, 6-7, 44-46, 168-169
    economic impact of, 169

Waffle Manifesto, 5
Waitzer, Edward, 148
Webb, Sidney, 29-30
Winnipeg Declaration of 1956, 5
Women in the paid labour force,
    134, 135
Worker buyouts, 107-108
Worker co-operatives, 27-32, 39-40
    financing, 29-30
Worker-shareholder co-operatives,
    37-38,40
Working Opportunity Fund in
    British Columbia, 152-153
Working Ventures fund, 152

Young Men's Christian
    Associations (YMCA), 53
Youth programs, 52-54
YWCA, 53